*How to*
*Protect and Maintain Your Own Financial Fortress By Flying*

# UNDER THE RADAR

*Asset Protection, Income Tax Reduction & Wealth Preservation*
*for You and Me*

Protect against:
IRS
DOL
Attorneys
Life Changes
Risk Management
Other Creditors, Predators, and Bad Actors

By Mitchell L. Levin, MD, CWPP™, CAPP™
With Kyle A. Levin, JD

This publication is designed to provide accurate and authoritative information regarding the subject matter covered. It is presented with the understanding that neither the publisher nor the authors are engaged in rendering legal, financial, accounting, or other professional services through the issuance of this book.

"UNDER THE RADAR"

By:     Mitchell L. Levin, MD, CWPP™, CAPP™
        With Kyle A. Levin, JD

Investors Advocate, LLC.
800 N Magnolia Ave., #105
Orlando, FL 32803
ISBN 978-0-9907906-8-6

Cover Design: "B-2 Spirit" original photo by Staff Sgt. Bennie J. Davis III /US Air Force. ID 060530-F-5040D-22. Use of this US Air Force photo does not imply Air Force's endorsement of this book. Background sky image Copyright © 2015 Slonme/iStock.

# Other books by Dr. Mitchell Levin

*Power Principles for Success*

*Goal! The Financial Physician's Ultimate Survival Guide for the Professional Athlete*

*Shift Happens*

*Smart Choices for Serious Money*

*Cover Your Assets: How to Build, Protect and Maintain Your Own Financial Fortress*

# Table of Contents

# Introduction

Welcome to possibly the most succinct, clear, and organized overview of some extremely important yet overlooked issues facing the successful and affluent. This is definitely not an encyclopedic textbook. It definitely is for you. Why another book on this "arcane" topic?

Why *any* book about these issues?

Because the subjects discussed here are of vital importance for those of you who have substantial assets, and who may wish to protect and preserve them from predators, creditors, and bad actors. Or anyone who desires to be a good steward of their bounty.

Those who read this, probably wish to continue to make the good and to avoid the bad decisions-decisions that can have a profound impact on your future. Isn't this information that you expect from your attorney, accountant, or financial advisor? No, and this why: many of these professionals lack the time to research a topic which only affects a small proportion of their client base, people sometimes identified as the "middle class millionaire."

You are in the top 1-5% of their client base. In addition, the professional educational systems may not give these issues the attention they deserve. And it is an extremely dynamic, politically charged field with ever changing rules and regulations. Add into the mix, that such a thorough analysis of the available options requires substantial mathematical study, investigation, and testing.

Not to mention that some of the tools may actually *reduce their compensation* by diverting some assets to a different professional. And, finally, it is rare to find a provider who does this on a regular basis.

"Avoiding the losses is more powerful than picking the winners."

By this we do not mean to imply you can have an investment account that only goes up. We do mean that you can avoid unnecessary taxation, costs, fees, and risks. And those can be substantial. So, unless you are the "Ultra-Wealthy," your advisors are unlikely to have the resources to provide you with all of the needed tools supplied in this book. What about those attorneys, CPA's and financial planners who have never learned about some of the advanced strategies in this book?

Do not blame them. It is not in their "wheel house." It is the rare few who engage in the comprehensive, collaborative, advanced planning to coordinate current income tax liabilities with other potential and contingent liabilities. Many have wondered or worried about whether:

- Your personal and/or business assets are properly protected from predators and creditors;
- There are viable income tax reduction plans that will allow deductions between $25,000-$1,200,000 per year, in addition to a traditional 401 (k)/profit sharing plan;
- Your estate is properly set up to minimize, defer, or eliminate estate taxes and care for the family in the event of disability or death;
- Your estate is arranged to mitigate against the divorce of your children;
- You have made the correct choice regarding ownership entities, structures, and trustees;
- Your personal finances are invested correctly and whether there are ways to allay investment risk/volatility and reduce or defer capital gains on investments. Additionally, if there are actions that you could take to mitigate or eliminate capital gains taxes on the sale of appreciated real estate or stocks;

- Your financing is optimized to your advantage;
- Your intellectual property can pass to heirs;
- Your business is run in the most financially efficient manner.

Let me first state that there is no "perfect" way to build, protect, preserve, or transfer wealth; nor is there any one plan that is a good fit for everyone. This book will show you how to "Maximize Your Wealth with Maximum Security" using simple, verifiable math.

**How would you respond to the following few questions?**

1. Are tax-deferred retirement plans tax-hostile or tax favorable? Most will say that tax-deferred accounts are always tax-favorable. Our readers may be surprised to discover the real truth.
2. Are income tax rates most likely going to be the same in future years, and are you most likely going to be in the same income tax bracket? Most of us will acknowledge that income tax rates are at historic lows for modem times and that the chance of them going up significantly is high.
3. From a financial standpoint, is it a good idea to pay down the mortgage on your home? While the answer for most of our readers is no longer a secret, it could be that it is not necessarily the optimum financial way own your home. This book shows you why and how.
4. If you reduce your taxes by 11-17%, how much return, and how much risk, do you need?

There are risks we know, risks we know we don't know, and risks we don't know that we don't know.

**Taxation is a risk we know.**

Taxation is probably the biggest risk you face. For example, you may think that FDIC insured CD's are the safest form of investment. However, as counter-intuitive as it may be, and however contrary to what some financial media "pundits" have espoused, a simple fixed annuity may turn out to be far safer.

No one can stop or predict the date of your death. And, I wrote this book specifically to show you how to avoid, defer, eliminate or reduce your tax burden, through "bright line", legal, safe, and proven strategies.

First allow me to digress. John Maynard Keynes, who is venerated by some and abhorred by others, nevertheless was a clever and educated person. He said in the "long run, we are all dead." That is a truism. But how do we measure the long run? For us, I submit it is 20 years or more. Taxes and death are two sure things in life. In modern life, *the third sure thing is inflation.*

No one can stop inflation. Not enough inflation is a bad thing. Think deflation, and the depression. Too much may be a worse thing.

Inflation destroys wealth and income and results in perverse incentives and behaviors. The "right" amount of inflation seems to be in the 2-3% range. Historically, over the past several centuries, by all measures, in all countries examined, inflation has averaged 3-3.5%. That also has been the average rate of inflation over the past 50 years in the United States when my father purchased his first house.

How does the long run relate to inflation? As an example of inflation, my father recently purchased a Lexus. Not the top of the line model, either. In fact, it was the entry level ES 330. He paid twice as much for that car as he did for his first house. That is inflation's long-term erosion of your purchasing power.

That erosion is inevitable. We must plan for inflation and be prepared for it. It may be urban myth, but someone once calculated that if you took the $24 in *wampum* paid for Manhattan Island 400 years ago, and invested it at 1.5% over inflation, that investment would now equal the total value of all the real estate on the island.

Even if that is untrue, the point is clear. Inflation is another major threat to your assets. These pages may provide you some alternative weapons to combat this inflation threat. Could inflation be the world's eighth deadly sin? Well, inflation is the inverse of **compound interest.** Albert Einstein called compound interest the eighth wonder of the world.

**It is not how much you make; it is how much you keep.** If you wish to keep, protect, and control your fortune, this book can help you fulfill that goal. I am not advising you to be miserly.

On the contrary, sharing your bounty with loved ones, and charitable giving are some of the things I believe in, try to live by, and participate in. It is in our culture to be charitable. Imagine how much worse off we would be if the ultra-wealthy did not achieve their wealth, and then did not give it away. (And yet, we must exert ever more caution, as many charities have morphed into either a perversion of the original intent, or have another intent altogether.

Hospitals, libraries, museums, universities, and concert halls -- all were funded by philanthropists who created tremendous wealth. And then they gave it away. Some achieved their wealth by nefarious means to be sure. But without amassing that wealth, their impact would have been dramatically reduced.

Giving small amounts in frequent doses is helpful. Giving very large amounts is meaningful. But charitable giving is not the point. Rather, properly retaining what is rightfully yours, and obtaining and utilizing the smart tools available in this book, can provide you with the freedom to exercise your choices for your wealth.

What I *am* saying is that there are numerous and tremendously treacherous traps set by those who apparently may have designs to separate you from your wealth - the IRS, trial attorneys, government policy, unscrupulous bankers, unwitting advisors, feckless associates - waiting to take what is yours.

Beware of these traps. In these pages, you will learn how to combat some of these traps, how to protect yourself from them, and best of all, how to avoid them. It is our hope to bring you a process for prudence and prosperity. Then, if you choose, and if you have enough, you can be charitable as well.

Read this book and reap. You are the backbone of our society. It is exciting to help strengthen you. As always, we appreciate your feedback.

# Dedication and Acknowledgements

This book is dedicated to all those who strive to make great decisions; who work hard; who do the right thing. Like my parents and like my wife. With this book, we strive to make sure you are rewarded, and not punished, for those admirable traits. No one is perfect. We all make mistakes. We all will continue to make mistakes. Let them be new ones. Let them be small ones. Let us not repeat our errors. Use the combined knowledge of our professional expertise to help you avoid the big ones.

If you are not familiar with "Three Felonies a Day" by Harry Silverglate, you should be. In addition, I recognize the Wealth Preservation Institute, The Asset Protection Society, Money Trax, FPA, NAIFA, Roccy DeFrancesco, Don Blanton, Dan Worthington, Greg Crabtree, Nick Murray, Bill Kovacs, and Nelson Nash. Other sources include, and are not limited to: Jay Adkisson, Christopher Riser, Erik Banks, Bruce Udall, Nicholas Misenti, Gary Forster, and so many more. You may avail yourselves of their expertise too.

# Preface

This book is written specifically for the 1%. And many of you may not know that you are in the 1%. It only takes about $350,000 per year in earned income, or $1 million in assets. For many of you whose net worth is in the $2-20 million range, you may feel middle class. And you would be correct. When asking all economic ranges, what it takes to feel wealthy, the common response is more than $30 million. If you have less than $30 million, this book is for you. What is your critical capital mass?

## Critical Capital Mass (CCM)

The term Critical Capital Mass (hereinafter CCM) will have a different meaning for different people in different situations:

- To a schoolteacher, it might mean that he has enough money to pay all the bills and live a life comfortably.
- To a young professional, 38 years old or younger, CCM might mean that student loans have been paid in full, and now they are able to purchase the house they wanted.
- To an older small business owner over the age of 50, CCM could mean they are out of debt, have paid the children's education bills, and they will have enough to retire on.
- To most, it is sufficient passive income and the ability to do what you want, and to work because you want, not because you must.

The following is the definition of CCM for purposes of this book and should be your definition while reading this book and beyond: A client reaches CCM when he has *"accumulated enough money and assets and income to retire and live in a financially comfortable manner for life, and to leave something behind for others"*. Even though it sounds easy enough, most people will not reach CCM until later in their lives than they thought.

**So how much do you need to reach CCM?** Well, it depends. Here are some of those factors:

- Are you married?
- Are you divorced, or likely to be?
- Do you have children?
- Do you have grandchildren?
- Do you live within your means?
- Do you wish to leave wealth to your heirs?
- Do you want to give to charity?

Every answer will be different based on factors such as how much money does a client wish to leave after their death, or what lifestyle a client wishes to live in retirement. The amount of money a client will need also hinges on when a person wants to retire. The younger you want to retire, the longer you plan, and the more money you need to accumulate.

**How can you reach CCM?** In our opinion, there are only two ways to reach CCM. Those ways are through: 1) Good Luck, or 2) Good Planning. And, we believe you can break those down into sub-categories of trying to reach CCM: A) Non-Tax Favorable Manner; or B) Tax Favorable Manner. How do most people attempt to reach CCM?

Typically it is through 1-A above. See if this example is familiar to you. Dr. Smith, who makes $400,000 a year, has a stockbroker at a Big Brokerage House whom he tries to give $100,000 a year (usually it winds up only a fraction of that amount, as lifestyle takes over) in an effort to build a large stock portfolio for retirement. Dr. Smith also has an online trading account where his goal is to beat market returns and get rich as quickly as he can.

Aside from his brokerage account, his online account, and his new five-bedroom, 5,000-square foot house, Dr. Smith does not have any other investments. He is the typical physician investor. Most stockbrokers never beat indexes. Even though the broker does not do all that great of a job for Dr. Smith, he still manages to make a nice living for himself

Dr. Smith paid capital gains taxes and dividend taxes on the money invested with his broker, which cut down his *real* rate of return. Dr. Smith, when day trading, incurs short-term capital gains, which also reduced his rate of return. There are also the opportunity costs of the trading expenses, the associated losses, and the taxes paid on the gains that need to be considered. And these costs carry forward for the rest of his life.

**Investing:** Most clients think the only way to create a sizable nest egg for retirement is to max out their 40 I (k)/profit sharing plans and invest their after tax take home pay. While this is not an automatically wrong approach, the client would be better off if he could figure out a way to get more money invested in a tax-favorable manner.

This book gives examples of plans that will allow you to defer up to around $400,000 with only a 5% fee as well as plans that are more tax favorable than the $100,000 example outlined above.

You will learn about the most under-utilized, and misunderstood method of deducting up to $1.2 million from your business into an asset protected, exempt from estate tax, corporation that you own and control, where the money grows tax-deferred, and comes out at long term capital gains rates. This portion of the book is really to get you thinking about CCM and how to get there.

**Principal protection:** Achieving CCM is easier if clients do not have to concern themselves with down years in the stock market, and can take advantage of only positive compounding—tax-free. So many clients lost millions of dollars when the stock market incurred massive losses on several occasions in the recent past.

Clients who protect their investments are much more likely to reach CCM than those who don't. Many of the topics in this book involve investment strategies that allow an investor to benefit from growth in the market while protecting the client when the market goes down.

Hedging against losses costs. Because this book illustrates for clients how to put money aside in a tax-favorable manner, the need to take excessive risk in order to get higher returns is eliminated. Because more money is invested, receiving returns of 3-5% works well to help a client reach CCM.

**Asset protection:** A higher net-worth client cannot reach CCM unless he is completely asset-protected. How awful it would be for a client who saved all his life to be hit with a $20,000,000 lawsuit that eliminated a significant portion of that person's wealth.

We believe that reaching CCM without being asset-protected is only half the battle. Without a proper asset protection plan, you are at risk of having CCM snatched from under you.

**Tools used to reach CCM:** There are many tools that you can utilize to reach CCM. Some of our favorites are: Equity Harvesting, a 401(k) Profit Sharing Plan, a 412(I) Defined Benefit Plan, a Section 79 Plan, a Leveraged Bonus Plan, a Freeze Partnerships, Private Capital Reserve Strategies, and Captive Insurance Companies.

**Flexibility in planning:** Some of the tools are flexible, others not so much. My opinion as a Certified Wealth Preservation Planner, and Certified Asset Protection Planner is that, the more flexible the plan, the better. The best wealth-building plan would be one that is tax favorable and can be varied at the end of the year.

**What happens when you reach CCM?** This is a great question. The short answer is that you may do what you want without worrying about running out of money in retirement. If you want to retire immediately, that is entirely possible. If it is your desire to continue working, that is possible too.

Once you reach CCM, you want a varied investment mix so that a stock market crash will not force you back to work. Usually when you reach CCM, you shift modes and examine your estate plan so as to minimize estate taxes and maximize wealth transfer.

**Charitable giving:** Some clients are seriously involved in charity, and we recommend that they look to set up a charitable gifting program a few years before retirement. We believe that more clients would give to charity if they knew of the concept of Simplified Planned Giving (SPG).

You will be leaving something because you cannot take it with you. You only have three places to leave your money: Children, charity, and government. How much do you wish to leave to each?

SPG is client focused, and is great for creating immediate tax deductions and guaranteeing a future stream of income. Clients who give to charity typically want their children and, potentially grandchildren, involved. We discuss a unique way to use charitable giving that maximizes the tax savings while enabling a client's heirs to direct the flow of the charitable donation. Even if you are not charitably inclined, you may use some of these mechanisms to help you achieve your goals.

**Again, how do you reach Critical Capital Mass?** The first step to CCM is to properly understand the tools you can use to reach it. A great first step was purchasing this book. So please, enjoy the book; and when you are done reading it, you will be ready to sit down with a qualified advisor to map out your road to Critical Capital Mass.

# Chapter 1

# Asset Protection Planning

The number one concern facing clients with wealth recently were the runaway, out of control, personal injury attorneys who seem to be suing anyone and everyone they can. Slip and fall; errors and omissions; medical malpractice; business litigation; employee claims; class actions. Personal injury lawsuits can be a liability for any wealthy person, they are a much greater problem for "professionals," and those in high-risk businesses.

Now, it seems perhaps the primary risk many businesses, property owners, executives, and any one with substantial assets face could be regulatory risk. This may be in the form of the Internal Revenue Service, or the Department of Labor, or the FTC, the FCC, the FEC, or BLM, the EPA, or any variety of local, state, and federal agencies. We will touch on business structure later to help isolate these risks from spilling over into all aspects of your financial life.

A professional, as used in this book, is limited to physicians and surgeons, attorneys, CPAs, insurance agents, financial planners, stockbrokers, hedge fund managers, mortgage brokers, architects and engineers. Professionals have unique asset protection problems due to the fact that they often cannot hide behind a "corporation" to limit their personal liability for work done for clients or on patients.

Therefore, even if a professional is working on behalf of a corporation, the professional can be sued personally, and all the professional's personal assets could be subject to the creditor. Physicians, by far, have a higher probability of being sued, nearly 100% for a surgeon, sometime during their career.

In fact, in many states, medical malpractice insurance is becoming so expensive that physicians are being forced to lower their coverage from $1,000,000 down to as little as $100,000; and in some states, physicians are going without any malpractice coverage. Alternatively, many insurance companies are dropping physicians from their policies due to poor claims' experience; and those physicians sometimes are forced to go "bare" because they cannot find an insurance company to insure them, even in the secondary market.

**The History of Asset Protection:** We believe that asset protection planning began in the early Renaissance in England. The feudal system imposed onerous financial burdens on owners of real estate, entitling the lord to payments of "relief" by the owner for the occurrence of passage of property to heirs, the marriage of a daughter, or holding of a "tenant" for ransom.

To avoid paying relief, property owners transferred ownership to a "trustee", who was bound to direct proceeds to a "beneficiary". The asset was placed in "trust" for the benefit of the original owner's children. This was an 11th century maneuver to avoid the financial burdens of legal ownership, displacing creditor rights. (The "creditor" is the one who collects from you after giving you, the "debtor" credit for the debt owed).

Trusts defeated the collection of taxes; prevented the government from taking assets; defeated claims of tenants against landlords; and avoided public disclosure and costs associated with transferring the assets from one generation to the next.

Trusts became so popular by the early 1400s, the time of Henry V, that they became the predominant form of ownership. They were so effective that they provided legal means allowing criminals and debtors to avoid forfeiture. Thus, was created the forerunner of our current Fraudulent Transfer Act.

## Section 1: *Why Should You Plan to Protect Your Assets?*

We are all at risk; and from so many fronts. When I speak on the topic of asset protection and when we get to the slide that asks professionals, specifically physicians, why exactly do they need asset protection, we typically receive several incredulous looks from the audience. The reason is that asking certain physicians why they need asset protection seems self-explanatory.

When the question is, "Should a physician be asset protected?" most physicians will see this as a rhetorical question. Other professionals might not see the question as a rhetorical one; you should, because a lawsuit against any professional will put your personal and business assets at risk.

**Regulatory Risk:** This is growing rapidly. You may have already heard about the left-leaning, environmentalist, whale-watching tour operator who was arrested under the Endangered Species Act for whistling at a whale to gain its attention for the guests aboard her boat. Or the commercial fisherman who was arrested under the Sarbanes-Oxley Act (which was designed for CFOs who signed their publicly traded companies' financial reporting documents to certify accuracy) for, allegedly, throwing away 3 fish—under the pretense that he was "destroying evidence." And of course you recall the Duke lacrosse team, among many others. Harry Silverglate wrote "Three Felonies a Day" on the premise that the average American citizen may be un-wittingly violating federal laws.

Silverglate clearly documents how the average American citizen may be in violation of the more than 100,000 Federal laws, rules, and regulations that are on the books. Nobody knows for sure how many there are. Many may even be in contradiction to others. The prosecutorial abuse of the Duke LaCrosse team may be the most memorable.

Have you heard of the West Coast timber company that was found in violation and fined $55,000,000 for a forest fire? It turns out the Feds allege a part fell from the company's truck, hit a rock, sparks flew and the fire raged. However, there was no evidence according to the Federal judge. He awarded $30,000,000 in reparations. Too late. They are out $25,000,000 plus legal fees to defend. "Where do we go to reclaim our reputation?" We are all at increasing risk.

So what do surgeons really worry about? If you are a surgeon, anesthesiologist or radiologist, the likelihood of you being sued sometime in your career is almost 100%. Why you ask? Because with surgery, there is always room for error, thereby, always leaving a door open for a potential lawsuit, even if that lawsuit may be entirely meritless.

**Frivolous lawsuits:** Larry Smarr of the Physician Insurers Association of America testified in Congress at hearings on medical malpractice caps that over 70% of all claims made against physicians are **without merit.**

Attorneys are practiced at using the legal system to benefit themselves and their clients. Any decent personal injury attorney is aware of the fact that if a case gets past summary disposition, the insurance company representing the physician will more than likely settle the case.

**Non-specialized attorneys:** Many people do not think highly of attorneys. Yet no one likes an attorney until you need one. While many people dislike attorneys, other people do believe that attorneys, in general, are intelligent people.

The truth is that there are attorneys who are very smart, and there are attorneys who are not. Many medical malpractice lawsuits are filed by attorneys who lack the expertise to determine the cases' merits.

A good personal injury attorney is one who takes on cases where there was a legitimate mistake made by the physician and where there were significant damages. If those types of attorneys were the only attorneys taking cases, the amount of medical malpractice cases would drop significantly.

**How is it that an attorney can file a medical malpractice case without knowing anything about medical malpractice?** The following is an example of a case that should never have been filed. A client consults an attorney after seeing a billboard stating that the attorney handles family law, and personal injury claims.

The client informs the attorney that he went to a surgeon for a hip problem. The doctor performs surgery on the hip, there may have been a mistake because now the client is unable to walk properly. The attorney is enticed and attracted to a potentially huge settlement after listening to the clients' story. The client signs a contingency-fee contract stating that, only in the event of a recovery, does the attorney receive 40% of the recovery.

The attorney does minimal due diligence and finds an expert witness to testify that the treating physician breached the standard of care. He then files suit, naming the physician, his office, and the hospital's surgery center where the surgery was performed. It ends up that the physician was not in the wrong. The case ends up dismissed, but only after the insurance company shelled out 40,000 dollars to defend the claim.

Or how about this one? The patient comes in, with a pre-existing limp, for a routine cataract surgery. The surgery goes very well. A few weeks later the patient feels "something" in the eye. The eye is dry; not enough tears manufactured. This is un-related to the surgery, but was un-covered by the surgery. The patient was so intent upon the decreased vision from the cataract, that he ignored the irritating symptoms prior to the surgery. He finds an attorney to take the case. Why? Because the patient failed to sue the doctor that "caused" the limp. Now he wants the cataract surgeon's insurance to pay for that malady. Meanwhile, the dry eye symptom is easily solved with no further surgery. How do I know? That cataract surgeon was this author. Fortunately, I was able to talk the patient out of the lawsuit. What if I were not that fortunate?

**How could the above scenarios happen?** In the American legal system, almost anyone may file a lawsuit with only the most flagrantly frivolous lawsuits denied to proceed.

This is quite different than the British legal system where the loser of the lawsuit pays the court costs of the other party. The differences between the two systems are easy to explain. In America, we did not want to make it hard for impoverished parties to file a lawsuit.

If the loser of a suit had to pay court costs, impoverished parties would not be able to file suit because it would further push them into poverty.

**So, how could the prior scenario happen in American legal system?** It is called the "lottery syndrome." The novice lawyer, who does not have a lot of experience with medical malpractice suits, sees the client as his meal ticket. That attorney believes that a golden ticket medical malpractice case is going to drop into his lap, and that case is going to allow them to buy the big house he wanted and the fancy car.

The problem is that most of the medical malpractice cases filed by non-medical malpractice lawyers, is that those cases are usually without merit, and should never have been filed in the first place. That is little consolation to a physician dropped by their insurance carrier for having to many claims, even if those claims were without merit.

Please do not confuse our "tort" legal system with truth and beauty. It is only about the *allowed* and documented evidence presented, and the credibility (or "spin") applied to convince a judge or jury of your guilt or innocence. Hence, if a plaintiff attorney can "paper you" enough, you may just roll over and settle. The cost of doing business.

**The big mess-up:** While in prior pages we illustrated why claims are filed, most of the time medical malpractice cases settle or come back with a jury verdict where nothing is paid to a patient/plaintiff. If that were the case, then why would a good physician need asset protection? To avoid having personal assets taken by the patient who was injured because of a mistake when treating or operating on the patient.

A 1994 Jury Verdict Research survey stated that the median award for compensatory damages in medical malpractice lawsuits was $362,500. By the year 2000, it was $1 million, and in 2010 it was $1.6 million - amounts that seem to only go up. As we all know, if you mess up in a malpractice case, usually you mess up big and, therefore, that once-in-a-lifetime mess-up in 2015 (the time of this particular edition) could be a $35,000,000 verdict.

- A New York plastic surgeon lost a $60 million verdict recently in a botched case.
- $49 million was awarded in Illinois for brain damage in a car accident.
- $2.86 million for spilled hot coffee was awarded in New Mexico

Yes verdicts of that size have happened. And the hits keep coming, for many businesses and professions.

That means a good portion of the verdicts were in excess of $1,000,000. If a physician gets the $35,000,000 verdict against him and only has $1,000,000 or even $10,000,000 worth of coverage, that is when there is a great need for asset protection.

**Deep pockets:** Many professionals are good targets to sue because they are perceived by the plaintiff's attorney to have "deep pockets" or a lot of money. Personal injury attorneys almost always sue everyone remotely associated with the physician, and certainly the party they believe has the most funds. There are cases where a physician clearly committed malpractice, but because her did not have insurance, the hospital was sued instead and ended up having to pay for the doctor's negligence. It did not even matter that the hospital was blameless.

Why? It is because the hospital had a lot of money and there was a sympathetic judge and jury! Local judges come up for *election* frequently, and need to keep voters happy. A local judge who wants to curry favor with the local populace is unlikely to let a badly hurt patient go uncompensated; and even though the hospital is only 1% responsible, because they have the money to pay it, the hospital will be the one footing the bill.

## Why Any Client with Wealth Need to be Asset Protected

As stated earlier, all "professionals" have personal liability and, therefore, can be sued individually for acting in their course of employment, putting all of a professional's personal assets at risk. What if you are not a "professional" with personal liability? Should lawsuits by personal injury attorneys still concern you? Unfortunately the answer is still yes, and the following pages will demonstrate the negligence lawsuits that the wealthy still need to worry about.

## The Good News

In the bad old days, before tort law, before the age of enlightenment, if you committed or were accused of an act of damage, your castle was burned, the women were ravaged, the peasants were enslaved, the crops burned, and the tangible goods were confiscated. Now, we only face attorneys. And now we have asset protection planning and asset protection tools available to help.

## Targeting the "rich"

Surveys show that wealthy clients have growing concerns and yet underestimate the danger of multi-million-dollar verdicts. And so many are over paying for under-insuring. Being wealthy actually attracts lawsuits.

The widespread doctrine of "joint and severable" liability means that if there is more than one defendant, the attorney will usually concentrate on the person with the highest net worth, rather than the one who is most at fault.

We collaborate with appropriate property and casualty insurance agencies to help our clients have the liability insurance you need. This is critical, and often over-looked. For a white paper on this, please contact the author.

## Homeowner Liability

Most wealthy people with asset protection worries own their own home. Homes pose particular liability problems that many clients are not aware of; if they were, they would immediately implement an asset protection plan. Examples:

1. Many homeowners will have a few parties a year at their home. If one of your guests leaves your home after drinking all night, and ends up in fatal car crash that ends the life of four people, who do you think will be sued for negligence?

You are the likely party to be sued. Most people think that a one million dollar umbrella policy will be enough; but, if your negligence causes a serious injury or death, a one-million-dollar umbrella policy is unlikely to fully protect you. If there is more than a one million dollar verdict, the plaintiff is going to go right after your hard earned assets.

2. Most homeowners believe that their homes are in good repair, many times that is not the case. Many homeowners will put off necessary repairs for months or even years. As a homeowner you have a duty to keep the house in good repair when you have guests over. There is an even higher standard if you run a business out of your home. If you have a damaged floor or any other defect that could cause your guest injury, then you could possibly be found liable, and put all your assets at risk.

## Teenage Children

The following illustration is one that we tell when giving asset protection seminars. It always brings a smile to anyone in the audience who has children because they can all relate, but the liability is no laughing matter and one that you need to protect yourself against. Example: If you have teenage children, there is a good chance that you will go on a trip and choose to leave your children at home. What do you think that the children are going to do. Have friends over or have a party.

Perhaps you tell your teenage child that you will be leaving town for the weekend to go to a resort. What happens that day at school? Your teenager goes around the school telling everybody that the party tonight is at his house. He also says "don't worry about bringing alcohol because my parents have more than enough to drink. 5:00 PM rolls around and you take off. Who is walking in the back door? A whole mess of teenagers looking to have a good time. Eventually it is time for everyone to go home, and the house full of now inebriated teenagers pile into their cars and drive off into the night.

What happened next? A car, with three teenagers speeds down the road, hits a guardrail, and flips over. While most car crashes of this severity would result in death, in this instance that is not what happens. All of them sustain debilitating injuries that will necessitate years of recovery, and one of the teenagers becomes a quadriplegic.

Lets assume a different set of facts. Assume that the same three teenagers were speeding down the road, but now assume that instead of hitting the guardrail and flipping over, the teenagers instead hit the local surgeon who was on his way home from a late dinner.

The surgeon earned over a $1,000,000 a year, and now is completely unable to perform his duties as a surgeon. So, who do you think is liable in this situation? The teenage driver who is uninsured, and whose parents have no significant assets? What about the homeowner, who, although unaware, still had the party thrown at their house?

If you guessed the homeowner, then you would be correct. The homeowner is the most attractive target to the plaintiff's lawyer, and they will come after all the homeowner's assets because they are the ones with the deepest pockets. If you think you are protected because you purchased a $1,000,000 umbrella liability policy on your home, how protected do you think you would be if a jury handed down an eight million dollar verdict?

**Automobiles, Boats, Planes, Snowmobiles, (and other "Toys")**

If you own an automobile, boat, Jet Ski, Plane, snowmobile, or other toys, then you could be found liable if someone were to use these toys negligently. Examples:

1. Drunk Driving - Everyone knows that it is wrong to drink and drive, but it is also true that everyone seems to know a person who has done this before. How many of us have gone out to dinner for the evening and had a few glasses of wine. Every year it seems that they lower the legal limit for alcohol, and it becomes more precarious to drive home after a few glasses of wine.

Clients with wealth always say "this would never happen to me.", but we believe that they should not be so flippant. If you were to have an accident and you were impaired you would most likely face a personal lawsuit, and your assets would be at risk. Even if you were not impaired and it was determined that you only drove negligently, you would still likely be personally sued, and your assets would be placed at risk.

This would not be such a problem for a person who does not own his or her own home and does not have many assets that would be attractive to a plaintiff's lawyer. Negligent actions are a problem for the wealthy; and if you have purchased this book, we assume that there is a certain amount of wealth you would like to protect.

2. Teenage Driver - If your teenager is driving an automobile, boat, Jet Ski, or snowmobile that you own, in a negligent manner and happens to harm someone else, you are more than likely going to be the one getting sued. You will also face the same problems as in the above examples regarding a shortfall of proper asset protection.

A very wealthy family had a teenage child, a boat and a big problem. The problem was that the child took his friend out tubing, and ended up hitting the friend with the boat, instantly killing him. The parent had commercial liability coverage up to $1,000,000, but it was obvious that the suit was going to be for multi-millions. Ultimately what happened was that the parents had to pay two million dollars of their own money to settle the lawsuit? Had they gone to trial, it is very likely that the verdict would have been much higher.

**Vacation Rentals**

Diversifying one's portfolio into real estate is very popular today. This is especially true in times when the stock market is providing less than stellar returns. While vacation rentals may or may not be great investments, they can still create liability issues for their owners. As stated earlier, if the property is commercial, there is an increased duty to keep the property in good repair.

Problems will vary depending on which part of the country you live in. If you live in an area of the country where it snows, an increased duty to keep the property in good repair may mean that you have to make sure that snow and ice does not accumulate on your property, which could lead to someone slipping and falling. ,

If you are a resident of California and an earthquake has occurred in the vicinity of your rental property, then the underlying stability of the home could result in a state of deterioration that could cause injury to your tenant. Most people will have any investment properties that they own in their own name; and if an injury were to occur on the property, then the lawsuit would most likely be against the property owner, and all of their assets would be at risk.

Summary of Examples: The previous examples should remind readers that the possibility of being sued is all to real, and that without an adequate asset protection plan, your assets could be at risk. You can continue to believe that it won't happen to you, or you can choose to implement the asset protection strategies discussed in the upcoming material.

***Why isn't normal negligence a problem for everyone and not just "professionals?"*** It is, except most of the "normal" public does not have the wealth necessary to satisfy a million-dollar jury verdict. Many indigent people who can barely afford to buy an automobile will not be able to afford insurance.

They are not worried about the million-dollar verdict because they have nothing to lose. Many professionals, on the other hand, sometimes have millions of dollars in assets to protect. Anyone can be sued for negligence, but only those clients with assets have to worry about asset protection.

A quick note on why insurance to cover negligence is not always adequate. Underinsured - As discussed, you could get a jury verdict for negligence that is above your insurance coverage, which is typically the $1,000,000 umbrella. Exclusions: You could be sued for something that is not covered by your insurance policy.

A good example is intentional torts, where you were found to do something intentional, and many insurance carriers will not cover you for intentional torts. Another example is a criminal act. Most insurance carriers will not cover you for acts that are deemed to be criminal in nature.

Insurance company goes bankrupt - As medical malpractice insurance companies struggle to stay profitable, you could be one of the unfortunate few who gets insured with a company that goes out of business.

**Divorce Protection:** Besides protecting your assets from typical creditors, you might want to protect them in the event of a divorce as well. Not that we advocate trying to hide assets from divorce (that is usually not even possible in most states), but there are some cases in which some spouses are gold-diggers, and some children of wealth creators make poor choices when it comes to spouses. One ex-college-girlfriend, had her trust fund run through by her first husband.

**Long- term Care Expense:** Besides death, the one-thing clients need to protect themselves against most are expenses associated with the need for long-term care. Mostly because we tend to under-estimate our life expectancies—by a long shot. We are not alone. The largest insurance companies have made this same error, and as recently as September 2014 the society of actuaries increased life expectancies, for the average American, by two additional years. This is a huge topic right now as more and more people are going into assisted living centers, and yet it is an expense that most clients just refuse to pay for and plan for.

**Estate Taxes:** You might not normally think of avoiding estate taxes as asset protection; but when saving your heirs possibly millions of dollars in estate taxes, you are asset protecting your wealth from the government. You can read about Family Limited Partnerships (FLP) or Family Limited Liability Companies (FLLC) in the Estate Planning section of the book to learn about one tool that will help you lower your taxable estate.

**What Assets Should You Protect?** Most of the time, when a client writes down ALL of his assets on a piece of paper, he is surprised at how much he has that needs to be protected. If you own any of the following, you are a good candidate for asset protection:

- Family Home or Condominium
- Rental Property
- Non-Rental Property
- IRA
- Stocks or Mutual Funds
- Life Insurance
- Bank Account or CD's
- Planes, Boats, Automobiles, or Motorcycles
- Other business entity
- Any other collectible items that have value
- Accounts Receivables
- Intellectual Property
- Future Inheritance for Family

Most medical, law, or accounting practices are worth very little to a personal injury attorney trying to satisfy a judgment for malpractice.

Most of the value in a practice is in the good will, which comes from the professionals who work there. Typically, the ONLY major asset of a professional practice that is not protected and has any worth at all is the office's accounts receivables.

For a medical, law, or accounting practice to be completely asset protected, the A/R in the practice should be protected. Due to space issues, the concept of A/R financing/leveraging to protect A/R from creditors will not be discussed. If this is a concern for you, please contact the author for more information.

## Risk Matrix

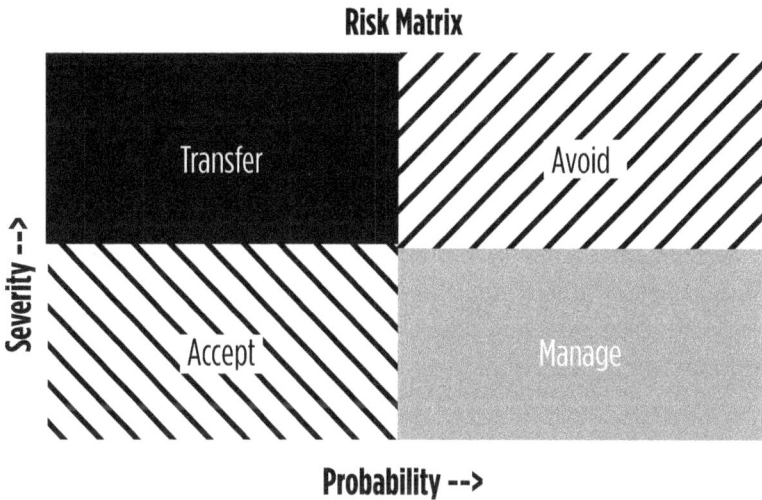

**Conclusion of Why You Need Asset Protection:** For many professionals, there are very few things in life that are more important than protecting assets. Most professionals work hard and long hours to accumulate wealth; and with one malpractice claim or general negligence claim, the majority of a professional's wealth can be taken from him/her by a creditor. While most non-professionals don't typically think asset protection is a major problem, it is for anyone with wealth.

Hopefully, this book will be an eye opener for those non-professional readers with wealth, and will motivate them to be proactive when thinking about protecting their wealth. A good asset protection plan can be implemented for $2,500-$10,000, and to do so would be some of the best -spent money a client can have.

**Section 2:** *Asset Protection Planning*

THIS IS IMPORTANT—DO NOT SKIP!

Asset protection, in general, is about <u>putting barriers in front of creditors to make it difficult or impossible for them to get your personal and business assets</u>. Asset protection is NOT about hiding or concealing assets or about committing fraud to conceal assets from creditors. Good asset protection discourages lawsuits to the point where a client can bluntly state to a personal injury attorney that he has millions of dollars in legally "protected" assets; and, if sued, the attorney will not be able to reach any of those assets.

Concealing assets may constitute fraud and is illegal. Attorneys who advocate plans where you hide assets are not helping their clients, but instead are subjecting them to further litigation in a fraudulent concealment proceeding.

**Good Asset Protection Can Help Prevent Lawsuits.** The more personal assets of a client that are not protected, the more likely a personal injury attorney can satisfy a judgment; and, therefore, the personal injury attorney is more willing to go after a client who's not asset protected than one who is. Imagine the following two scenarios:

1. A neurosurgeon makes a mistake in the operating room, thereby causing a substantial injury to a patient. The surgeon's bedside manner is not very good; and when the patient runs into a personal injury attorney, the attorney talks the patient into signing up with him to look into a potential medical malpractice claim.

The attorney files the needed paperwork to start the discovery process and finds, after minimal discovery, that the cardiologist has

$1,000,000/$3,000,000 in malpractice coverage and several million dollars in personal assets, which include a brokerage account of $1 million and personally-owned real estate worth $2 million.

After some time, the patient, due to the negligence of the surgeon, has several more surgeries to correct the problem. Now the patient is totally disabled for life and has $1,000,000 worth of medical bills. After discovery revealed the assets of the physician, the personal injury attorney files a suit and asks for $5,000,000.

2. Same scenario with the damages of scenario number one except this time, when the personal injury attorney does his discovery, he finds out that, while the physician has $3,000,000 of personal assets, those assets are fully protected and are not going to be available in a malpractice suit.

Because the medical bills are $1,000,000 and the malpractice coverage limits for the surgeon are $1,000,000 per claim, the personal injury attorney decided not to spend the $85,000-plus in expenses to get the case to trial. The $1,000,000 policy coverage will have all been spent first on medical bills, with nothing left to split between the patient and attorney. He tells the patient that while it is clear malpractice took place, the case is not financially viable. Therefore, the attorney does not take the case. The only difference in the two scenarios is in the second one, the physician's $3 million worth of personal assets were totally asset protected from lawsuits.

**Asset Protection Cannot Guarantee You Will Be Lawsuit Free.** While the previous scenarios seem to indicate that good asset protection may prevent a lawsuit, well, that is not the case. Good asset protection will discourage lawsuits, but any attorney, or any client acting without an attorney, can sue whether you are technically asset protected or not.

The goal with asset protection is to protect your assets **before** a lawsuit, and keep the assets after the lawsuit is over. In the coming pages, you will be given the tools to asset protect yourself so that after a lawsuit is over and the collection process is through, the assets you started with on a personal level are still owned by you.

**Legal Asset Protection:** Correctly set up, asset protection plans are ones that use existing laws and are 100% legal in the eyes of the U.S. Government. It might sound obvious to the reader that an asset protection plan needs to be legal, but as you will find if you search the country for information on asset protection planning, some of the solutions are what we would call a bit edgy, or based not in law but in the absence of law.

**Section 3:** *Fraudulent Transfers*

Fraudulent transfer laws will prevent you from removing assets from your estate after you know of potential claims against you for damages for malpractice or normal negligence. The only surefire way to prevent transfers of assets from being overturned by a court is to make the transfers before any liability occurs. That includes those you know or knew about—or should have -- in the eyes of the legal system.

Even if a creditor cannot prove actual fraud, you still need to worry about constructive fraud when making transfers of assets after a claim for damages has occurred. Bottom line - protect your assets now by using experts in the field who will help you shield all your major assets from lawsuits whenever they arise.

**Section 4:** *Existing Laws Automatically Help Protect Some of Your Assets*

**Homestead Exemption**

They say a man's home is his castle, but is that really the case? Most states have some form of exemption against creditors for personal residences. Each state varies in the application of the exemption, and you should check with your advisor to determine what the applicable exemption is in your state.

The public policy concern to protect the family created the homestead exemption. The theory is fairly simple-the legislators wanted to protect some portion of the family residence so families have a safe haven.

- **Interest protected** - The homestead exemption is a statutory right to protect "homestead property." This is typically the real estate owned by a person as his personal residence. Again, each state varies on their definition so be sure to check with your local advisor to make sure the piece of property you are concerned about is covered. Interestingly, 21 states now specifically include mobile/manufactured homes. Some states do not require that a client be occupying the home, or have any intent to occupy the home before they utilize the homestead exemption.

- **Homestead exemption value** - The homestead exemption varies widely by state. States such as Rhode Island, Delaware, New Jersey, Pennsylvania, and the District of Columbia do not have homestead exemptions. Texas and Florida, and a few others, have unlimited homestead exemptions; however there are some limits under the new bankruptcy laws.

Some states have a different amount for married couples, some base the amount by the number of dependent children an individual or couple has; other states raise the exemption if someone has high medical debts, and some states will increase the amount in case of bankruptcy. An average number for states that do not have an unlimited exemption, and those that have no exemption, is between $5,000 and $50,000.

- **Debt exclusions** - Certain debts in all states are excluded from being covered by the homestead exemption. Almost all states exempt out consensual liens, mechanic liens, and property taxes from being covered by the homestead exemption. Many states are now adding debts for child support and spousal support to the list of exemptions.

The IRS is also a creditor that you will not be able to avoid using the homestead exemption. So, if you owe back taxes that you are unable to pay, the IRS can take your home notwithstanding the state-allotted homestead exemption. Please see <u>Section 5: Equity Harvesting or Debt Shields</u> for more information on this topic.

- **Procedural issues** - The homestead exemption is useless if the property can be sold off before the exemption is utilized. In many cases, the homestead exemption is automatic. Some states allow for a waiver of the homestead exemption. This will almost always require the spouse's consent if you are married.

While a useful tool, in certain states, the homestead exemption will not always prevent the sale of your home. The rules for how homestead property is sold, even when the homestead exemption is applied, vary by state. Sometimes a house can literally be sold for any price above the homestead exemption. This means that a house could be sold for substantially less than its fair market value. The amount of the exemption would be paid to the homeowner, but the remaining amount would be used to pay the creditors.

- **Practical example of how the homestead exemption would work if sued:** Assume a patient sues Dr. Smith and a jury verdict comes back for $1,000,000 over the amount he is covered by his malpractice insurance. Dr. Smith is single and has a home worth $1,000,000 with $500,000 in equity.

If Dr. Smith lived in a state with an **unlimited** homestead exemption, the patient would not be able to force a sale of the $1,000,000 home. If Dr. Smith lived in a state with NO homestead exemption, it is possible that the patient could force a sale of the $1,000,000 home. If Dr. Smith lived in a state with a $50,000 homestead exemption, it is possible that the patient could force a sale of the $1,000,000 home to satisfy the judgment. In this example, the patient would receive all the proceeds of the sale that are over the $50,000 exemption. That first $50,000 would go to Dr. Smith.

## Life Insurance and Annuities

All assets are not created equal. Importantly, the cash value in life insurance and the principal in or the income from annuities in many states are, specifically protected from creditors. Like many laws, the laws protecting life insurance and annuities are rooted in public policy. The legislators in some states believe a life insurance and/or annuity benefit is essential for citizens and/or their families to maintain at least a minimum level of financial well-being and, most importantly, from becoming wards of the state.

The state's interest to avoid paying for the indigent is tempered by a creditor's right to collect a legal debt; but as you can understand from the government's point of view, it is always better for someone to support themselves than for the government to dig deep into their pockets to support even more needy citizens.

**Life insurance:** Due to the public policy arguments surrounding life insurance contracts, the bankruptcy laws have specifically addressed giving protection to life policies even if individual states have not. We are not going to get into all the protections afforded to life insurance by the bankruptcy laws, but we would like to point out that the federal government has specifically addressed the issue.

• **State laws** - Like the homestead exemption, state laws vary widely when it comes to protecting life insurance. Some states, Florida and Texas, give an unlimited exemption to life insurance policies that have cash value in them, and some states give none. South Carolina, for example, provides a limited protection for cash value in the amount of $4,000. The death benefit in almost all jurisdictions is exempt from creditors who would be left to sue the estate of the deceased debtor. Hawaii specifically exempts the death benefit and the cash surrender value of policies, provided that the policy is payable to a spouse of the insured, or to a child, parent, or other dependents of the insured.

- **Estate taxes** - In this section of the book, we are discussing asset protection as it usually pertains to protecting assets from creditors, like a patient who sues for malpractice. Beside a potential creditor who would come from a negligence suit, the biggest way to lose a significant portion of your life insurance proceeds is to pay the government 50% of the death benefit for estate taxes.

While you have an unlimited ability to have death benefits paid to your spouse, any other death benefits paid to other people have a significant chance of being taxed at the 50% bracket to pay for estate taxes. We discuss this topic in more detail including how to avoid having your life insurance proceeds taken by the government for estate taxes in the Estate Planning section.

**Conclusion on Life Insurance:** Know whether or not your state exempts some, all, or none of the cash surrender value in your life policy, and if the state exempts the death benefit. Be aware that many "asset protection experts" in the marketplace are really life insurance agents looking to sell a massive amount of life insurance as protected investments for clients who are funded on a post-tax basis.

We have nothing against the concept of purchasing life insurance to protect one's assets; we recognize and utilize life insurance frequently. However, there are a number of alternative ways to protect assets, in a tax favorable manner, to explore in addition to pumping dollars into a life policy on a post-tax basis.

**Annuities:** Annuities are treated similarly to life insurance by each state when it comes to being treated as a protected asset. The main difference is that annuities are designed to payout a stream of income at some point, whereas a lump sum death benefit is paid with a life insurance policy. Some states will exempt all the cash built up in an annuity and the annuity stream, and some states will not protect either.

Then there are the hybrid states that protect all of one and not the other, or some of each. Florida, not surprisingly, exempts the cash in an annuity and the stream of income from any annuity. Pennsylvania generally permits the exemption of only $100 per month of the proceeds from an annuity, and North Carolina doesn't exempt any proceeds that come from an annuity.

**Be careful.** The state and federal exemption laws as they pertain to annuities follow the same public policy reasoning to provide for families in the long term similar to ERISA plans. Variable annuities have become much more in vogue, not so much to provide for families later but simply as a way to have money grow tax-deferred.

### Section 5: *Qualified Retirement Plans (ERISA Department of Labor Governed Plans)*

The biggest single asset of many clients over the age of 50 is the money in their retirement plan or IRA. That money also happens to be the most liquid money in their entire portfolio; and, therefore, if not protected from creditors, that "qualified" money would be the first asset a creditor would go after to satisfy a judgment.

In 1990, the United States Supreme Court made clear that a creditor **could not reach** "ERISA qualified" plan assets. In 1992, the issue of whether an ERISA qualified plan was subject to bankruptcy was raised; and the answer from the Supreme Court was, "No."

**What is an ERISA qualified plan?** Unfortunately, there is no definition of an ERISA qualified plan in the IRS code or under the <u>Employment Retirement Income Security Act</u> (ERISA). The Supreme Court did fashion its own definition and the factors to be considered are:

1. The plan must be subject to ERISA;
2. The plan must be qualified under Section 40 I of the Internal Revenue Code;
3. The plan must contain the anti-alienation provisions which are required under both the IRC and ERISA
4. IRAs though treated in similar fashion for tax purposes, are NOT

covered under ERISA or the Department of Labor, and in some states have some limited asset protections.

Instead of explaining in detail what the above requirements mean, we instead will list the plans that you know are ERISA qualified. In general, however, the plan must cover employees and cannot discriminate in favor of highly compensated employees.

1. 401(k) Plan
2. Profit Sharing Plan
3. Money Purchase Plan
4. New Comparability Plans
5. Defined Benefit Plan
6. 412(I) Defined Benefit Plan

Be sure to check with your pension plan provider to verify your plan is in compliance with ERISA laws. If your plan happens to fall out of compliance for whatever reason, then it will be left up to the courts and possibly the IRS to determine if your plan qualifies for exemption from creditors.

**Non-ERISA Plans and IRAs**

Simplified Employee Pension plans (SEPs) and Keogh plans are not specifically protected by federal law. The determination of whether SEP and Keogh plans are protected will be left up to each state to determine. If you have a SEP or Keogh plan that includes multiple employees and is funded in a non-discriminatory manner similar to ERISA governed plans, you will have a good argument for why those plans should be protected.

An IRA is not considered an ERISA qualified plan; and, therefore, the assets in an IRA have no federal protection from creditors. Individual states, however, can and have protected IRAs in full or in part. In states where IRAs are not specifically protected, it is up to the state courts to determine if, in a particular case, the IRA asset, in full or in part, is protected.

**Section 6:** *Asset Protection Solutions (that are not always effective)*

There are different forms of Co-ownership, and most clients, and some attorneys and CPAs, believe that through the use of co-ownership a client can adequately protect his assets. Technically co-ownership has the ability to protect your assets. There are a number of issues that come along with co-ownership that make its use not appropriate for many clients.

**Types of Co-ownership**

There are three main types of co-ownership:

1. **Joint Tenancy (JT)** - Definition of Joint Tenancy: "A single estate in property, real or personal, owned by two or more persons, under one instrument or act of the parties, with an equal right in all to share in the enjoyment during their lives. On the death of a joint tenant, the property descends to the survivor or survivors and at length to the last survivor," Barron's Dictionary of Legal Terms.

The rights of the owners of a piece of property owned as Joint Tenants are the same. Those rights are:

- The right to use or control the whole property;
- Each owner has the right to transfer the interest in the property without the knowledge or input of the other co-owners. Each co-owner's interest is owned individually and, thus it can be sold, gifted, encumbered, or transferred without the other owners' involvement or input or knowledge or permission. When a Joint Tenancy interest subsequently is transferred, the new owner also may acquire control over the whole asset; and,
- A survival right- when a joint tenant dies, the share of the deceased tenant automatically becomes that of the other co-owners. In other words, a joint tenant cannot transfer his interest at death. This sub-type often is known as Joint Tenants with Rights of Survivorship (JTROS) and often must be specified, though in some states, it is automatically applied to married couples.

The probate issues seem helpful; so why don't we like Joint Tenancy for asset protection?

- Joint Tenancy can be severed. If one of the joint tenants were to sell or transfer his interest in the property, the Joint Tenancy would become a tenancy in common. Since there are no regulations on preventing such behavior, one joint owner would be able to transfer his interest without the other owner's permission, or even their knowledge. This, in many cases, will defeat the original purpose of the Joint Tenancy.
- Since each co-owner is an owner of a Joint Tenancy asset, it may be subject to each owner's creditors. So, if one joint owner lost a lawsuit for any reason, it would be possible for the plaintiff to seize that joint owner's interest in the property. Thus, any co-owner of a Joint Tenancy can place the other owner(s) position at risk of creditors' liens and/or seizure.
- Joint Tenancy is a real gamble for the owners. The co-owner who lives the longest gains possession of the asset. Often that may not have been the true intent of the co-owners,. Many times, the co-owners in a joint tenancy situation are not even aware of the potential problems that could arise. This may happen when a parent is trying to avoid probate and estate taxes on a piece of property and is trying equally divide the property among the children.

**Summary on Joint Tenancy:** If you are going to utilize Joint Tenancy, make sure that you are aware of the issues involved. For the majority of clients, Joint Tenancy is not a great option for asset protection and estate planning. Jointly owned assets are not asset protected; and unless a highly specific set of occurrences happens, chances are good that the joint asset will *not* pass on to your heirs as planned.

2. **Tenants in Common (TIC)** - Definition: "An interest held by two or more persons, each having a 'possessory' right, usually deriving from a title in the same piece of land. Though co-tenants may have unequal shares in the property, they are each entitled to equal use and possession. Thus, **each is said to have an undivided interest**

**in the property.** An estate held as tenancy in common can be partitioned, sold, **or encumbered**," according to Barron's Dictionary of Legal Terms.

Rights of an owner in property held as Tenants in Common:

• Each owner of property held as Tenants in Common owns an undivided interest in the property. For example, four people, all with separate families, own a vacation home as one owner.
• Ownership interests of a tenant in common are transferable. If a tenant in common died, his interest in the property would pass to his heirs along with his other assets.

**Summary of Tenants in Common:** There are many potential downsides for a tenants in common, but the bottom line is that Tenants in Common is not an effective tool to protect your assets, and using tenants in common could cause you more of a headache than you would imagine.

3. **Tenants by the Entireties (TBE)** - Definition of Tenants by the Entireties: "Ownership of property, real or personal, tangible or intangible, by a husband and wife together. Neither husband nor wife is allowed to alienate any part of the property to be held without (the) consent of the other.

The survivor of the marriage is entitled to the whole property. A divorce severs the tenancies by the entirety and usually creates a tenancy in common." Barron's Dictionary of Legal Terms

Characteristics of Tenants by the Entireties:

• Only applicable to married couples, who are considered one entity or "person".
• The property right, therefore, is not "divisible or alienable". That is, the property cannot be divided into parts, or taken from one co-owner to an outside agent or creditor.

- The property is wholly owned jointly as opposed to two individuals with divisible interests that can be transferred or encumbered.
- One co-owner's liability does not place the other co-owner or the asset at risk of lien or seizure.
- Property is subject to joint creditors such as the IRS.
- Automatic rights of survivorship.
- It now is automatically assumed in joint ownership by spouses in Florida.

Side note (Community Property (CP) States): Nine states treat the property of married couples differently from the other states. These states are called "Community Property" states. The community property states are: Arizona, California, Idaho, Louisiana, Nevada, Nebraska, New Mexico, Texas, Washington and Wisconsin.

If you are married and live in a community property state, these property ownership rules apply:

- Each spouse's interest in the community property is subject to the claims of the other spouse's creditors.
- If you acquired property before you were married, this property belongs to you alone even after you are married.
- Any property you accumulate during your marriage is considered to be community property. You and your spouse own an equal, one-half interest in this property.
- If you receive personal gifts or inheritance after you are married, that property continues to be owned separately by you.

Remember: Beneficiaries are the persons or organizations you mention in your will. Heirs are the people the law says will get your estate. We will not go into any major details about the differences between community property states and non-community property states. If you happen to live in a community property state, contact an attorney who is familiar with your state's laws before you set up an estate plan.

**Pros of Tenants by the Entirety**:

Asset Protection - If one spouse is sued, creditors are unable to seize the asset since it is the property of both spouses.

Estate planning - The assets owned as Tenants by the Entirety pass to the surviving spouse and do not go through the probate process.

**Cons of Tenants by the Entirety:**

Asset protection - Tenants by the Entirety does not protect property from *joint creditors of the spouses.*

Divorce Protection - If your state allows assets other than your primary residence to be owned as Tenants by the Entirety, in a divorce or at death, your spouse will likely get 50 percent of that asset. It would be immaterial that the asset was inherited by one spouse or whether the asset was meant to be passed down to the children.

For more on TBE and home ownership structure, go to section 10 of this chapter.

**Summary of Tenants by the Entirety:** There are many positives of owning the family home as Tenants by the Entirety and that is the main reason when implementing an asset protection plan we typically do not recommend putting the marital home in a limited liability company. A better way to protect the marital home could be through the use of a debt shield, which will be discussed in detail.

**Co-Ownership Conclusion:** Never ever own property just in your name. We did not really address this issue in any major way in the preceding pages. However, the worst of all worlds for a client is to own property just in your name. If you get sued, the property is absolutely at risk. When you can avoid it, also do not own property as JT only.

TIC is used most often in 1031 tax free exchanges of real property to defer capital gains taxation, and for several unrelated investors to together own a piece of real property for investment reasons. There are risks inherent in this form of ownership as well. The entire property is subject to your creditors and that of the other joint owners. When you can avoid it, do not use Tenants in Common. Your creditors can seize the share of property that is in your name, and it is possible for the court to order the property sold in order to satisfy the debt of one of the co-owners.

If you must, and your estate is quite simple, and your state recognizes and allows, utilize the TBE. In some cases it is required, such as married couples owning a home in certain states. Using Tenants by the Entireties is a good idea for the marital home. In doing so, you protect the marital home from each individual spouse's creditors. Because the divorce rate is about 50 percent and many "professionals" have an above-average divorce rate, we do not suggest titling too many other personal assets as Tenants by the Entirety.

### Section 7: *Corporate Entities*

If joint ownership arrangements are not that advantageous, then who or what should "own" your assets? Most clients think that great asset protection comes through the use of "corporations." What most clients do not realize is that there are different entities and types of corporations and limited liability companies; and depending on which entity you chose, your asset protection and tax consequences could be different.

### Partnership

From an asset protection standpoint, a partnership is the *absolute worst entity* you could possibly be involved with. With a partnership, you have the same personal liability of a sole proprietorship with the additional burden of having a partner who can inflict even more liability. Definition: A partnership exists when two or more people run a business together that is not a "corporation."

## Sole Proprietorships

Second to partnerships, sole proprietorships are the worst way to run a business. Owning and operating a business without any other structure defaults to a sole proprietorship. While there is no requirement to register a business in any other legal entity, this affords virtually no separation between the owner and the business. They are treated as one and the same, and there is no asset protection. Very bad idea.

Why is this bad? If a sole proprietor commits negligence while operating the business that results in injury to someone, the sole proprietor could be held personally liable for any and all injuries to that third person, and their assets would be at risk. If the business puts out a product and the product were defective and caused injury to someone, the sole proprietor could be held personally liable for that injury.

## Corporations (not Limited Liability Companies or Professional Companies): General information about formation and structure

- Corporations are a legal entity formed under state laws.
- Corporations are owned by its shareholders.
- Shareholders elect a board of directors, which is responsible for overall management, and hires corporate officers to run daily operations of the corporation. A corporation can have as few as one shareholder who can elect himself to the board and can run the daily operations of the corporation.

**Limited liability:** Businesses often choose to become corporations because it allows them to avoid personal liability for the actions of the corporation. This includes limited liability of the corporate shareholders as well as individual liability of the employees of the company who are acting within the scope of employment.

The main exception to the corporate limited liability is in the area of personal services. Those personal service liabilities include work done for or on behalf of clients by Physicians, Attorneys, CPAs, Accountants, Insurance Agents, Stockbrokers, Financial Planners, Mortgage Brokers, Architects and Engineers. For example, if a physician treats or operates on a patient, he cannot hide behind the corporate veil that would normally shield owners and employees working in the normal course of business from liability.

If a patient sues for malpractice, the physician is named individually. A "professional" does have limited liability from negligent acts of his employees, but not for individual advice given to clients from the professional himself. There is no distinction in how liability is treated in an S- or C-Corp or LLC or Professional Association (in the state of Florida) or Professional Corporation (P.A. or P.C.). All of these will provide limited liability to owners and shareholders.

**Piercing the corporate veil** is every corporation owner's worst nightmare. A court may choose to discount the corporate structure and the asset protection that goes along with it in the following cases:

1. A party is tricked or misled into dealing with the corporation rather than the individual.
2. The corporation is set without a legitimate business purpose or set up never to make a profit or always to be insolvent, or it is too thinly capitalized.
3. Statutory corporate formalities are not followed.
4. Personal and corporate interests are commingled so that the corporation has no true separate identity.
5. The Corporation or its officers engages in illegal or fraudulent activities.

Piercing the corporate veil is not that big of a deal in professional companies due to the fact that most lawsuits will come out of personal liability for professional services where a professional cannot hide behind the corporate defense shield anyway. The other main reason businesses are a corporation is to avoid personal liability for debts of the corporation. "Respecting the entity" is critical for your success.

## Who can incur debts on behalf of the corporation?

- Officers
- Managers (with authority)
- Employees (with authority)

If your corporation incurs significant debt and the corporation goes out of business, the remaining debts WILL NOT become personal debts of the officers, shareholders, or employees.

## Types of Creditors

- Inside creditor - This is a creditor who has its exclusive remedy as one against the assets of the corporation. Example: A person incurs injures on the property owned by a corporation. They have exclusively, claim to the assets and income of the corporation.
- Outside creditor - This is a creditor who can go not only after a corporation's assets, but also after your individual personal assets. Example: A surgery is performed incorrectly and the patient sues. The patient goes after the physician individually and not the corporation.

Just because the physician works within a corporation does not mean his personal assets are protected. The corporate assets are at risk to the extent the corporation did something wrong to cause injury to the patient, AND to the extent the claimant can get at assets of the corporation that are owned individually by the professional providing the services.

**Rule of thumb:** Inside creditors can get whatever a corporation owns, and outside creditors can get at a client's personal assets, which include ownership interests in corporations.

## Director and Officer ("D&O") Liability

The type of corporation in which you are an officer or director will determine your degree of liability. As is the case with many professionals, more and more suits are being filed against directors and officers of corporations. Most of those revolve around publicly traded companies where suits are being brought either by shareholders or by the federal government.

Professional offices by their nature are privately owned by the professionals providing the services, and any lawsuit would likely come from one of the co-owner professionals. Since that type of lawsuit is tough to file, we are not going to spend time on it in this book.

**Trustee/Fiduciary Duties**

One of the most overlooked and important liability an owner in a small-to-medium business is that of the 401(k)/pension plan. Most businesses with qualified plans have the owners as the trustees. As trustees, owners have an impossible duty imposed upon them by the Federal Government through the Department of Labor (DOL). [For more on this increasingly important and dangerous risk, please see my colleague's latest book: *"RESCUED! How to Escape or Avoid 401(k) Plan Traps for the Business Owner"* by Andrew Dickens. Contact him at **ADickens@MySummitWealth.com** ]

**The DOL Requires Pension Plan Sponsors to: "... Prudently select & monitor plan investment options ...:"** The duty is for pension plans that allow for self-directed investments by the employees. Self-directed means your plan has multiple investment options, like mutual funds, and the employees pick their own funds. For added protection, we recommend you know and follow the Uniform Prudent Investor Act (UPIA) **http://www.uniformlaws.org/shared/docs/prudent%20 investor/upia_final_94.pdf** and implement these guidelines in your company's investment choices. One good investment that complies is the True Market Modelsä. [For more information go to **www. TrueMarketModels.com.**]

**DOL duty is impossible to comply with:** In our opinion, it is impossible for an owner/trustee to comply with the DOL's requirement to prudently select and monitor the investment options given to the employees in the plan. In order to technically comply, every trustee would effectively become a financial adviser who would be forced to monitor the market returns and associated risks and expenses, just so they could say that in good faith they researched and selected prudent investments.

**Non-delegatable:** The duty by the DOL described above is also non-delegatable. That means you cannot pay someone a fee to take the liability for you. Pension providers might help give you investment information so you can review it to comply with your duty, but the duty itself cannot be outsourced or delegated.

**Pooled account:** If your company has a pooled account, where all the money of the owners and the employees is combined in one account that is managed by someone, the duty is a bit different. The duty for a pooled account is to ensure that the plan's money is invested prudently.

**The First Union case** is from a bank (before they merged with Wachovia, which then went bust in 2008, and merged into Well Fargo) in Florida. The employees of the bank sued the bank and the individual trustee for violating their fiduciary duties as they pertained to the bank's pension plan. The investments did not do nearly as well as the averages over a set period of time. The suit ended up settling out of court for $26,000,000, and the lawyers pocketed $8,000,000 out of the deal.

**The First Union Case is a Cautionary Tale.** Now that we have told you there is no way to comply with your duties as a trustee with any pension plan, what do you do? First things first - unless you have disgruntled employees and you have done a terrible job with the company's pension plan, the likelihood of your company getting sued and you getting sued INDIVIDUALLY as the trustee, is extremely remote. P.S. First Union thus became Wachovia, which thus became Wells Fargo.

**Conclusion on Trustee Liability:** Be aware that you have corporate and personal liability when it comes to your business's qualified pension plan. If you are a trustee, that liability is personal and cannot be delegated. If you are worried about this type of liability, we would suggest that you seriously look to make sure your pension plan is set up as technically sound as possible from an investment standpoint.

## Limited Liability Companies (LLCs), Family Limited Liability Companies (FLLCs) and Family Limited Partnerships (FLPs)

LLCs, FLLCs and FLPs are "the" tools to use when it comes to asset protection. The following material will give you examples as to why an LLC, FLLC, or FLP is used by the best asset protection experts around the country when advising clients. We will not be explaining how to technically set up an LLC.

LLCs are not recognized by the IRS, but by the states. The IRS requires you to make an election as to whether you wish your LLC to be taxed as an S- or a C- corporation or as a partnership.

Setting up an LLC is very simple and can be done by getting on the Internet and finding the appropriate form on your state government's website. However, each LLC should have an operating agreement and should be funded, so you may prefer to have an attorney help set up your LLC.

*Be careful here.* LLCs in Florida (particularly after the Olmstead decision of October 2011) and many other states are not asset protected unless they are "multi-member" and "manager-managed." Be certain, again, you respect the entity. Your LLC should have more than one member (your spouse may be eligible). The manager can be you or your spouse or anyone else, so designated in the Operating Agreement.

**Major Difference between an LLC and an S- or C Corporation - The Charging Order: What exactly is a Charging Order?** A charging order is the single remedy for a creditor who is attempting to seize the assets of debtor when those assets are in a limited partnership or an LLC.

A charging order **DOES NOT** grant the creditor the right to sell the asset of the LLC or to force distributions of income. In order to illustrate how a charging order works, we will use an example: Patient, Mrs. Plaintiff, sues and obtains a judgment against Dr. Smith for $3,000,000. Dr. Smith has $1,000,000 worth of medical malpractice insurance coverage and the rest of his assets are owned by an LLC. Dr. Smith is a 9 percent member of the LLC.

Mrs. Plaintiff asks the court for satisfaction of the claim, and requests the court to force Dr. Smith turn over the assets in his LLC to her. The court tells Mrs. Plaintiff that the only remedy the court can give her is a "charging order." What does the charging order get Mrs. Plaintiff in the above example? The right to the distributions received by the member, Dr. Smith, to the extent such distributions are made. If none are declared and disbursed, Mrs. Plaintiff must wait. Mrs. Plaintiff is not permitted to "step into the shoes" of the LLC member, and receives no voting rights, either.

**Where to Incorporate**

Most of the time you are going to file your LLC in your home state, where the corporation will be headquartered or where the assets will be located, unless there is a tax reason to incorporate in another state, or if your state has a "weak" charging order statute. Ninety percent of the time a client who creates an LLC for asset protection will not need to use a DE, AZ, NM, MO, AK or NV LLC.

If you use a "foreign" state domicile to incorporate, a state where the company does *not* operate substantial amounts of its business, you must file a declaration of "foreign corporation" with your home state. Most of the time this will subject your corporation to the state tax laws, fees, and regulations of your home state.

If, however, you form a company that creates significant director, officer, and shareholder liability, or a company that you anticipate will generate a significant amount of income, using a Nevada or Delaware corporation might be your best bet.

**Conclusion:** Unless you have a specific reason to incorporate in another state, a state that borders your own, or the state in which the assets are located, we suggest that you do not. It would only add to the costs of your asset protection plan.

**Advanced Business Structuring Bonus:** When properly structuring your business, why not consider going even further than one LLC or FLP or "S" or "C" corporation?

What do I mean? Your business is really several different entities within the scope of your "business." You have equipment (EquipCo), operations (OpCo), marketing (MarkCo), financing (FinCo), management (ManCo), and more. Each has costs, liabilities, and employees. If you arrange your business through a "holding company" (or HoldCo) it can "own" other entities to protect you and even give you greater tax advantages.

True this is more complicated. True this has a cost. But the benefits can often far outweigh the disadvantages. We have structured many of these, with legal and tax help.

Here is just one example. Business owner (or surgeon) whose business gross revenue is $12 million with a profit of $1.5 million, creates these other entities. HoldCo is owned by your Family Limited Partnership, for example. Your equipment is asset protected. You may place debt shields through leases, and UCCs. Your MarkCo may provide services to other business. And you get to improve your current income tax situation.

Result: By spending $89,000, you could have saved in taxes alone over $360,000 – net, *after* spending that money to asset-protect yourself. And you have more clarity on the "profit" centers of your business. For help on this, contact the author, who would be happy to discuss this with you.

**Section 8:** *Trusts as Asset Protection Tools*

As general principle, using a domestic trust if revocable, provides questionable, if any asset protection. And many irrevocable domestic asset protection trusts ("DAPTs") have not yet been fully tested in the courts. Caution is key here.

**Types of Trusts:**

**Revocable** - a trust that is set up where typically the client is the "grantor" as well as the "control" person, and often may be a beneficiary, and is amendable and revocable at any time.

**Irrevocable** - A grantor sets up an irrevocable trust like a revocable trust except the grantor can

NEVER get the assets back that were used to fund the trust. Nor may the grantor be a beneficiary, usually either directly or indirectly. Though the grantor may remain in control. There are ways to draft irrevocable trusts so family members have control of the assets; but technically speaking, the grantor is not supposed to have any control over who gets what assets from the trust.

**Inter vivo** - simply one that is set up and used during a grantor's lifetime.

**Testamentary** - one that is set up at the death of a client, or is created by will and takes effect upon the death of a client.

**What Asset Protection?**

Revocable trusts provide NO asset protection. While revocable trusts are used sometimes for estate planning purposes, they provide a client with no current asset protection. Because a grantor client has the power to take assets out of the trust, a court of law can demand just that at the insistence of a creditor.

Irrevocable trusts provide total asset protection when done correctly. Because the grantor client irrevocably funded assets to an irrevocable trust, those assets are no longer owned by the grantor and can never revert back to the grantor; thus, there is nothing a court of law can do to make the grantor take back those assets to satisfy a judgment.

**Trustee Selection**—this is a good time to discuss trustee selection. Especially for irrevocable trusts, where the beneficiary is not the trustee, take extra caution, and please do not be cheap.

You may feel it is a great honor to offer or to be selected as a trustee. And while it may be, it is also a hornet's nest of potential problems. The beneficiaries often do not agree among themselves, nor with the trustee and his administration, investments, distributions, and so on. There is a whole industry of professional or "corporate" trustees—for a reason. And they are not prohibitively expensive.

A friend of mine was chief trust officer of one of the nation's largest multi-family offices, and now is legal advisor to one of the nation's largest trust companies. He goes around the country describing the issues trustees face. Though on the face, this may seem self-serving for him, there are myriad trust companies to choose from. And it is clearly in the best interests of the grantor and beneficiaries.

The cost for a trustee generally is around 0.5% per year, and this is negotiable downwards depending on the asset size. The trustees are responsible for asset manager selection (I encourage you to write the trust to require, and to hire trust companies that honor "directed" not "delegated" asset managers—as this helps avoid conflicts of interests and cross selling from associated entities), investment policy statements, tax returns, audits, distributions, respecting the grantor's discretion, and protecting beneficiaries from themselves or outside forces. These professionals may be changed at the discretion of the beneficiaries or the "trust protector" depending on how the document reads.

**Section 9:** *Offshore Asset Protection Strategies*

We do not intend to make you an expert in offshore planning. We will be giving you the basics of offshore and enough information for you to determine if offshore planning is something you need to explore further.

**Why Offshore?** We think the better question to start with is: **why not go offshore?** Do not consider going offshore just because you heard through the grapevine that offshore asset protection is the most effective way to protect your assets. Further, you should definitely not go offshore if you think you will save on U.S. federal income tax. You will not.

If an advisor tells you to move your assets offshore in order to save on taxes, you should run. While there are ways to have assets in certain investments that are tax favorable offshore, simply moving your $1,000,000 brokerage account to an offshore asset protection trust is not going to save you annual income taxes on dividends earned from your brokerage account. And your tax compliance costs may increase as the reporting becomes increasingly complicated.

In truth, most of the people who need asset protection can accomplish your goals domestically through the use of LLCs. Offshore is usually more expensive and more complex. While at the end of the day you might get more assets protected with offshore planning, the real question you need to ask yourself is: Does offshore planning make sense in your particular situation?

**What are the main offshore tools?**

• **Offshore Limited Liability Companies (LLCs)**

Several offshore jurisdictions implemented LLC legislation similar to that of existing LLC legislation in U.S. Jurisdictions. Nevis, the Cayman Islands, Turks and Caicos, Anguilla, the Bahamas , and the Isle of Man all have existing LLC legislation. We will not be going into detail about specific country's laws, but know that in Nevis the LLC laws are comparable to the laws in the United States, and some people even consider them superior. So we believe that Nevis's laws are more applicable when implementing an asset protection plan.

The Nevis LLC is great because, similar to U.S. LLCs, the only remedy for a creditor is a **charging order,** *and* has the added benefit of being located offshore -- in order for the creditor to be granted the charging order, they also would have to file an additional suit in Nevis, and incur additional expense and risk.

Asset protection, combined with **litigation deterrence** make the use of an offshore LLC the simplest and one of the best offshore planning tools. Because we have not dedicated pages of this book to offshore LLCs, do not take it as a sign we do not prefer that option for asset protection. Our preference for offshore asset protection many times is through the use of an LLC.

**Offshore Trusts** go by different names: Foreign Asset Protection Trusts (FAPT), offshore trusts, or asset protection trusts, are similar in some respects to traditional trusts in the U.S. Offshore trusts have all the same flexibility of design as domestic trusts when it comes to adding provisions to the trust such as a discretionary provision where the trust is not required to make distributions.

Offshore trusts are supposed to protect your assets because: US Courts do not have jurisdiction in a foreign country and are unable to seize assets in a foreign offshore trust. U.S. Courts typically do not use **Contempt of Court** - where the court would send you to jail until you brought back your assets from the offshore trust - when assets are properly transferred to offshore trusts.

We say typically because there have been cases where clients have gone to jail for long periods of time for contempt because they refused to bring back assets from an offshore trust to satisfy a judgment. Offshore asset protection havens are your friends. Most of the offshore asset protection havens have drafted their local laws (in conjunction with

American attorneys) to be as friendly as possible to U.S. citizens looking to shield assets from lawsuits.

Offshore trusts require trust protectors and sometimes other trust administrators. While it is another layer of protection, there is also a risk that the protector may not act in accordance with the "wishes" of the grantor or the beneficiary, depending on the foreign legal interpretation of the trust documents. And they represent another layer of expense. Not only that, but also the foreign domicile is loath to have the trust terminate or become worthless, because that reduces the foreign government's revenues.

**Conclusion on Offshore Trusts:** Offshore trusts under today's laws are a viable option for asset protection. Some commentators say offshore trusts are the best way to protect your personal assets and some say the concept is dead because of the potential for a court to order a contempt citation, thereby sending a client to jail if they do not bring money back from the offshore trust.

It is our belief that if an offshore trust is set up in a timely manner, well in advance of litigation where creditors will be after your assets, and if you do not retain too much control over the assets in the trust, and if the documents are properly written, offshore trusts will work very nicely to not only protect your assets but deter any litigation attempts to even go after your offshore assets.

• **Closely Held or Captive Insurance Companies (CICs)**

In addition to the traditional offshore LLC or offshore trust there is the option of the CIC. Many small to medium size business owners choose to use CICs for estate planning and income tax reduction, planning, but since CICs are located offshore they are a great way to protect assets as well.

Go to Chapter 3, Section 10 for much more detail.

**Conclusion on Offshore Planning:** Offshore planning for asset protection is a great way for a high net-worth client to protect their assets from creditors. The question you have to ask yourself from a practical standpoint is: "Is offshore planning and its expense worth it?" For most clients, there is no need to go offshore when domestic LLCs will do the job just fine.

**Section 10:** *Asset Protecting the Marital Home/Personal Residence*

Unfortunately, there is not an easy solution as far as how to properly protect a client's personal residence. We will discuss the problem in more detail below. Most client's personal residences are their greatest asset in terms of dollars. That makes it one of the most important assets to protect from creditors. The options are usually the default JTROS; one must push the title company and the mortgage company to list ownership as TBE, if that owners structure is allowed in your state.

**Tenants by the Entireties (TBE)**

States like Florida allow married couples to own property titled as "Tenants by the Entireties" (TBE). In fact, in Florida, it now is the presumed ownership structure of spouses. Each spouse has an undividable right to use the whole property, even though; individually they only own 50%. A creditor is unable to force the sale of either spouse's interest to settle a debt, because doing so would affect the other spouse's claim to the "whole" property. So, if you are lucky enough to live in a state where married couples can own property as TE, you can sleep easy knowing that your marital residence is protected.

**Problems with TBE:**

1. Very few states actually allow property to be held as TBE. Also TBE will not protect the marital home from **joint creditors** of both spouses. Example: Dr. and Mrs. Smith hold Christmas party at their residence **and** invite all of the staff from Dr. Smith's office.

After dinner, till about midnight, several of the staff members proceed to drink multiple cocktails, followed by a round of shots that Dr. Smith provided from his bar. Dr. Smith's personal nurse consumed eight drinks that night, before announcing that she was going to drive home.

Dr. Smith knows that the nurse is impaired, but decides to let her drive anyway. He rationalizes the decision by saying she only lives a few miles away. On the way home, the nurse crosses the median and swerves into oncoming traffic, which results in an accident that kills a car carrying four passengers. The nurse is also killed in the accident.

The four passengers are all cardiologists coming home from their Christmas party, and each one of them has an income in excess of $750,000. In this case, who do you think will bear the brunt of liability? The nurse's estate will be sued. Her auto insurance company will likely not try and fight any suit, and simply hand over whatever amount of her coverage.

Dr. Smith AND his wife will also be sued by the doctor's families and the nurse's estate. The reason is that Dr. Smith gave liquor to an obviously intoxicated person. You may have heard of the term "dram shop" case. A dram shop case is when a bar serves alcohol to a visibly intoxicated patron and then is found liable when that patron injures a third party.

In our example Dr. and Mr. Smith are sued just like a bar would be sued who had let an impaired patron drive home. The Smith's home is owned as Tenants by the Entireties, doesn't that provide some protection for Dr. and Mrs. Smith? Unfortunately not.

Why? Because the Smith's own the house where the party was held. The negligent act of allowing the nurse to drive home impaired took place at the home, and they will both be sued, putting their jointly owned assets at risk. A house owned as TBE is owned jointly and is at risk of being seized in a lawsuit.

1. What about unmarried clients? If they are not married, then Tenants by the Entireties would not be available to them. This could be a potential

problem for an unmarried individual who has significant equity in his residence. What about divorce? The minute the divorce is final, the house is no longer titled as Tenants by the Entireties. Therefore, when a client gets divorced and owns a house, the house is at risk to creditors.

## Other Solutions: *Qualified Personal Residence Trust (QPRT)*

You know that someone is not an asset protection planner when their first suggestion to asset protect a residence is through a QPRT. We believe that a QPRT is inappropriate for most clients. Having said that, a QPRT is a great way for a client who does not have a homestead exemption or live in a TBE state can protect his personal residence from liability.

A QPRT is an irrevocable trust, which is our least favorite type of trust. A QPRT gifts the personal residence to the children in an irrevocable manner.

## Fans point out the QPRT Benefits:

- Gifting to heirs at low tax effect
- Grantor gets to remain in property, rent free
- Specified term, usually limited to a maximum of 20 years
- Grantor surviving the term enable complete transfer of the asset
- Grantor still maintains property and associated taxes and expenses

The term holder should continue to make the mortgage payments. Caution: since a mortgage includes principal and interest, the principal may be deemed a gift for estate tax purposes incurring additional reporting and taxation.

This would add to the complexity of the calculations for the trust. Let's look at an example of a QPRT. You and your spouse are both 65 years old. You do not live in Florida or Texas, and are therefore unable to avail yourself of the homestead exemption.

You also do not live in a TBE state. You are a surgeon and fear that a malpractice suit may put your house at risk of being seized by a creditor. The house is valued at $400,000 with no debt, and you decide to gift it to a QRPT. If we assume the term of occupancy is four years, the present day value of the gift to the QPRT should be approximately $210,000.

It is possible for you to use some of your estate tax credit to pass the house to the QPRT gift-tax free. To determine the value of the estate tax owed, it is the difference between the mortgage and the reversion. It is good that all appreciation in the property is not estate taxed.

Once the fixed term ends, you have options. Your house is retained in trust for your spouse's lifetime, residence is available to enjoy before it is ultimately distributed to the children upon the spouse's death. Or you have the option of entering into a lease with your children that would allow you to live in the residence for as long as you choose.

If you choose this option, you must pay fair value rent in order to make sure the house is not subject to estate tax. If you survive the fixed term of the QPRT, the value of the residence would not be considered part of the estate for estate tax purposes.

Even if you do not survive the fixed term, the estate tax consequences will be no worse than if you had never created the QPRT. From an estate tax point of view, there is no potential downside to a QPRT. A QPRT is a relatively efficient way to remove a residence's value from one's estate at a greatly reduced gift tax cost.

**Critics emphasize QPRT Downsides:**

1. If the client passes away prior to the end of the term, the asset will be includible in the client's estate.
2. If the client outlives the term of years, he will be losing control of his property, and could face eviction if he were to have a fight with the beneficiaries of the QPRT.
3. If the client has established that he will live in the property past the

term of years, the client must pay rent to the ultimate beneficiaries of the trust at the Fair Market Rate.

4. Moreover, the renter may not deduct the rent payments.

5. And, finally, the beneficiaries' rent income must be reported as taxable.

**Conclusion on the QPRT:** While QPRTs sometimes work as an asset protection tool, younger clients should be wary, due to the difficulty in selecting the appropriate term of years on a property that will likely be sold before it is able to be transferred to the heirs. If the client lives through the term of years of the QPRT, he runs the risk of being evicted from his own residence by the beneficiaries, or having to pay non-deductible rent payments which will be taxable to the beneficiaries.

The QRPT is not a great asset protection tool. However, the value of the QPRT is that it is not a bad estate-planning tool for clients over the age of 60 who want to gift away a large asset at a significant discount. If the client lives through the term of years of the QPRT, the asset will pass income- and estate-tax free to the beneficiaries. This holds true even if the asset significantly appreciates in value.

### LLCs and FLPs

Many attorneys and CPAs may recommend that clients transfer their personal residence to an LLC or FLP for asset protection purposes. Why use an LLC or FLP for asset protection purposes? In simple terms, a properly designed LLC or FLP offers a charging order to shield the personal residence from creditors.

However, we believe that they overly-recommend this option. Depending on which state you reside in, there could be four potentially significant downsides to putting a personal residence in an LLC or FLP.

1. It is possible the client may lose the capital gains tax exemption upon selling the residence. Each spouse has a $250,000 capital gains

tax exemption on the sale of the personal residence. In order to utilize this exemption, the spouse must make the house his primary residence and own it personally for two years out of five.

Therefore, if a client chooses to transfer his personal residence to an LLC or FLP, then needs to sell it quickly, if the client had not lived in the residence for at least the last two years out of five, the client would lose the capital gains exemption. If the client did not want to lose the exemption, it would be possible for him to put the back into his name, live in the home for two years, and then sell the home.

1. The client will lose the home mortgage deduction if the property is owned by an LLC or FLP. This is a huge blow for most clients who have a mortgage. One of the biggest itemized deductions for clients is the home mortgage deduction, and most clients would rather have the deduction rather than asset protect the personal residence in this manner.

2. It is quite likely that your homeowners' insurance may be cancelled and you may be subject to the much more expensive commercial line of property and casualty insurance.

3. In some states, like Florida, if the marital residence is not owned individually, the client would lose the ability to claim it as the "homestead." The consequence in Florida for not being able to claim the home as the homestead is loss of limiting the increase to less than 3% per year in property taxes.

For example, if a client had a $500,000 house and claimed it as his homestead, the property taxes may be $9,000. These taxes are limited in increases to 3% per year. If the client's personal residence was instead owned by an LLC, thereby not giving the client the ability to claim it as his homestead, the taxes could climb dramatically. The City of Orlando recently announced an 18% increase in non-homestead commercial property tax for 2015. You would not be happy had you given up your homestead exemption for not much more asset protections.

Most clients will not want to pay extra property taxes just so they can protect the value of their personal residence. Especially when there are free and automatic protections available. Like with any asset protection strategy, the decision for a client to implement the plan is usually based on the fear of losing the asset, and the cost and headache of protecting it. In medical parlance, it is the risk-benefit ratio we must evaluate. Does the cost of the action warrant the action's benefit?

**Conclusion on LLCs and FLPs:** Unless a client has a specific and highly unusual need, we do not recommend placing your personal primary residence into LLCs or FLPs as an asset protection tool.

**Debt Shields (Equity Harvesting)** have been around for some time and in the last few years since the Great Financial Meltdown of 2008 have been under-utilized. Prior to that time it was over-utilized, even if it was unwitting. While debt shields and equity harvesting sound fancy or exotic, the terms simply stand for taking out a large amount of debt on an important asset that would otherwise not have debt. *For More on This Subject, Please See CHAPTER 4: Section 5: Equity Harvesting or Debt Shields*

The idea behind a debt shield is very basic; if an asset has an unattractive amount of debt, a creditor will not want it. If a creditor does want it, he will have to stand behind the first creditor holding the loan against the valuable asset.

And as an important aside, is it really debt if you can pay it off immediately from another asset-protected source? We could make a great case it is not. That being in debt and having debt are different. If you buy a sports car or yacht or jet with money you do not have, but must pay for it out of future earnings, that is being a debtor. Your balance sheet is negative.

If you create debt and can pay it off without relying on future income, then you are not a debtor. True you must watch the costs of the debt and earnings of the cash that provide the "collateral capacity" of that debt. And you must watch the tax implications, too. So if you have $1 million in the "bank" somewhere that is asset-protected, and you also have $1 million of debt on another, especially an appreciating asset, then you are not a net debtor. Your balance sheet is neutral. You are a wealth creator. More on this in the chapter on Private Capital Reserve Strategy.

**How does equity harvesting work?** You borrow money on an asset that has equity. For your primary residence, there is rule 143, the "acquisition indebtedness rule." This limits you to deduct mortgage interest on $1 million for a new purchase, or a re-finance of an existing mortgage plus any improvements made to the property plus $100,000. The rest of the interest is not deductible from your income taxes.

For a "commercial" building there are no limits. These could include a beach side or ski-house, or any other *business* or rental property. So, be careful how you structure the ownership and usages.

**How Can You Use This In Your Business?** Here is in an example. You own a business that does $3 million in revenue, and $350,000 in annual profits, after you take out $200,000 income to support your lifestyle. You have retained $700,000 in cash, after tax in your business account. This is at risk to creditors, and has significant opportunity cost.

**The solution:** Take out the cash. Place it into an asset protected, liquid, tax-deferred, conservative account. When you need the money to fund your operations, you *lend it to your business*. Then, you file a "U.C.C." that secures your loan. You are now a secured creditor in first position, should there be a future judgment against your business. The business owes you the money and then pays you back with interest, when and as you have determined.

**Even better:** Don't ever lend it to your business. Rather, take out a loan against your account value, and charge your business a higher loan rate. Now your account continues to grow unfettered. And you have the best of all worlds. Liquidity. Asset protection. Deductible expenses. This is discussed in greater detail in the section on Private Capital Reserve Strategy.

**Where is the money repositioned?** We believe it could be financial malpractice for an advisor to recommend that you "invest" those proceeds. Too much risk. However, placing large amounts, over a 7-year period, into a low expense, high cash-building life insurance policy where the death benefit is at the minimum rate allowed so the client can take "tax free" loans *against* the life policy may be one appropriate alternative. The money is asset protected, untaxed, can never go down in value, and can grow *triply compounded*: compounding on the principal; compounding on the interest; compounding on the tax not paid

**How financially viable is Equity Harvesting?** So financially viable that the IRS acted to *limit* the use of this tool by restricting the interest deduction on primary residential housing. As a general statement, if the cash value life insurance policies perform as they have for the last 40+ years, and if interest rates remain anywhere near what they have for the last 40 years, then the answer is that Equity Harvesting will work well for a client financially.

**Added benefit:** Also, keep in mind that if a client uses equity harvesting to asset protect the marital home, he will most likely be able to get rid of any other life insurance policy for which he is paying. Why? Because with the equity harvesting concept, the client is buying a life policy with a sizable death benefit; and, therefore, in most cases the client will not need to purchase additional life insurance. When you calculate the economics of equity harvesting factor in the money the client will save by not having to purchase additional life insurance products.

**The downside:** There is one major downside that could stick in your craw. You must not only pay interest to get your money, you also must *qualify* for the loan. And as of this writing, the major qualification is your "earned income," and not your net worth or asset base. So, if you are wealthy and retired, and wish to place a debt shield on, and borrow $1 million from your $5 million beach house (that you diligently paid off years ago), you may not qualify, even if you have another $7 million invested in marketable securities.

**Conclusion on Debt Shields:** There is no perfect way to asset protect a personal residence. By using Equity Harvesting, the safeguarding the house by making it unlikely a creditor would make a claim against the equity value of the house, and making it likely that the concept will be a good investment for the client, assuming the advisor utilizes a life policy that is specifically designed for equity harvesting.

## Summary of Asset Protection Planning

Every professional, or high net worth non-professional client should have an asset protection plan. In the U.S. today, lawsuits are a dime a dozen; and professionals specifically have the added burden of working in an industry where they can be sued individually.

If you have a: Personal residence, Business, Vacation home/condo, Brokerage account, CDs/cash in a bank account over $75,000, Vacant investment property, Rental property, Plane, Boat, Wave Runner, or a Snowmobile, IRA, Significant accounts receivables, then you need asset protection. Most of the time, you can use domestic LLCs to own all of the above-stated assets, except the IRA. Example: Assuming a client had all the assets above, what could an asset protection plan look like?

- Personal residence - The client should consider a debt shield to protect the home and to build wealth in a tax-favorable manner.
- Vacation home/condo - would be in domestic LLC #1.
- Brokerage account, CDs/cash in bank account over $75,000 - LLC #2.
- Vacant investment property - LLC #3 due to the extra liability with vacant rental property.
- Rental property - LLC #4 due to the fact that it is rented. This property would not go into LLC #2 because if a liability arose from

the vacant property, the creditor could go after any assets in the LLC, which would include the rental property.
- Plane, boat, Wave Runner or snowmobile - LLC #5 due to the fact the individual liability with each is significant, and you do not want to subject any other asset to that liability by sticking it into the same LLC.
- IRA - should be rolled into a Profit Sharing Plan at work or into a newly created Profit Sharing Plan in one of the four new LLCs.
- Business – often, if it is large enough, we recommend separating your business into several subsidiary LLC entities: equipment company; finance company; marketing company; operating company; consulting company; etc.

**Cost of the prior plan?**

Each domestic LLC should cost $1,500-$3,500 for the first one, and then $1,500 for subsequent LLCs. It costs nothing to roll the IRA into a business' current Profit Sharing Plan and very little to set up a new Profit Sharing Plan in one of the newly created LLCs. Total costs should be less than $19,000 for this example.

Lastly, in this example, it is likely that the client would want to use an FLLC for estate planning purposes to discount the value of the client's overall estate and to start a gifting program to the children. An FLP will work just the same as an LLC for asset protection purposes.

In the preceding pages we have given you a fairly detailed summary of asset protection. While you can purchase a book just on asset protection, the topics discussed in this book will be sufficient to help most people formulate a complete asset protection plan, and to be able to intelligently discuss the options with your attorney and accountant.

Implementation is a key component of putting together an asset protection plan. And so it is important to work with an advisor who will understand the topics discussed in this chapter and will collaborate with your tax accountant and your attorney, and has what it takes to follow through until implementation is complete.

Unfunded, or un-implemented asset protection plans cannot work. Likewise, if you fail to "respect the entity" and commingle assets, or liabilities, or uses, and cash flows, you may be sabotaging your own asset protection plan.

Feel free to contact the author. The author will be able to determine in short order whether you are properly protected and, if not, what needs to be done to ensure that your assets are protected, your estate plan is in order, and that your overall plan is done in as cost efficient and tax favorable a manner as possible.

# Chapter 2
# Estate Planning

Estate planning is *not estate tax planning*, especially now, in 2105, that the thresholds exceed +/- $11 million. Recall, however, the high frequency of changes to the tax rates and thresholds that apply to estate taxation. When we give seminars for clients, they are advertised as Asset Protection and Income and Estate Tax Reduction *Planning* seminars. In the normal seminar, we also cover several estate planning mistakes we see over and over with our clients. Many clients believe their estate plans are set up correctly, even if that is not the actual case.

Many believe that they have competent CPA's and attorneys. While it is true that many CPAs and attorneys know how to put together a complete estate plan, rarely do they ever actually accomplish this goal. Following are statistics we've gathered from our seminars that should hold true to the readers of this book.

These estate planning tools, which will be explained on the following page, are just the basic tools needed in almost every estate plan of a client with any amount of wealth. Of the people we speak with before becoming a client:

- Half will **NOT** have a simple will. (Usually those are the younger client. Without a will, you will be allowing the state where you live to dictate who gets your assets at the time of your death.)
- Almost all will **NOT** have Durable Powers. (Durable Powers gives instructions in the event a client becomes incapacitated or

where a decision needs to be made about discontinuing the use of life sustaining procedures).
- More than half will **NOT** have standard marital trusts (also called A&B trusts).
- Almost all will **NOT** have a Family Limited Liability Company or Family Limited Partnership. (FLLCs are used to discount the value of an estate).
- Most will **NOT** have an Irrevocable Life Insurance Trust (ILIT). (An ILIT will pass a death benefit from a life policy income- and estate tax free to the heirs/beneficiary).

Without these tools, you could be costing your heirs millions of dollars that will go to the government via taxes or to the probate system via fees. Trusts help avoid the probate process. Probate can cost between 4-10% of the entire estate, takes a long time, and breaks whatever privacy we have left. While you will be dead and will not have to worry about it, your children, or other heirs, will curse the fact that you did not find time to set up a proper estate plan.

**Section 1: *Wills***

A will is the cornerstone of any estate plan. One should start with a will and then adds different estate planning documents as the client gets married, has children, and increases the size of the estate. There is nothing all that groundbreaking that we can tell you about a will; so we will not devote much time to it, but there are a few items that you should be aware of.

**If** you die without a will you will be considered to have died intestate. This means that your estate will be divided up per your state's statute on intestacy. Each state has a procedure that decides who gets what and in what percentages if you die intestate.

**If** you were married when you died, some states would give the entire estate to the spouse; however, this is not always the case. You should check your state laws concerning their distribution of assets in intestacy, but the more prudent solution would be to go out and get a will.

**How much should a will cost?** A will should be fairly inexpensive. A will for you and your spouse should cost between $350 and $950. Attorneys don't have to work that hard to create a will; however, the professional liability with the document created lasts until the client passes, which more than justifies the fee.

**How frequently should you amend a will?** You should amend your will any time you get married, get divorced, have children, increase the size of your estate, if the tax laws change, or if one of your children predeceases you. You should also amend your will if you do not have A&B Marital Living Trusts and want to change the dispersion of your assets when you die. It is also a good idea to review your will every five years.

**Why not just handwrite a will?** A handwritten will is known as a holographic will. Many states do not recognize holographic wills as a binding legal document. If you want to create your own will without an attorney, that is fine, but you will want to maker sure that your state recognizes holographic wills. If you do decide to go this route, make sure that you have properly followed your state's statutes when creating the will.

**Can I omit my spouse from my will?** Most states will not allow you to omit your spouse from your will, and so we suggest that you look at your state statutes before undertaking any action. It's important to note that if you do get a divorce, you should immediately change your will so your estranged spouse does not receive any of your estate.

Some high profile divorces that involve a large amount of assets will continue for more than a year. If you were to die in this interim period, without having changed the will, your ex spouse may be able to take from the will as if they were still married to you, since the divorce was not finalized.

If this happens, your estranged spouse could, quite possibly, receive the bulk of your estate. We imagine most of our clients would turn over in their grave if they could see their estranged spouse spending all of their money.

**Conclusion:** If you want to prevent the state from dictating who gets your belongings when you die, then you definitely should have a will. Wills are extremely easy and inexpensive to put in place, and so we strongly suggest that everyone get a will as soon as possible.

**Section 2:** *Durable Powers of Attorney*

It is expected that during the course of our lives we may become incapacitated and unable to act whether because of a physical infirmity or mental incapacity or in the case where you are otherwise indisposed (think Turkish prison, or kidnapping, or lost in a jungle, or taking your sailing trip around the world and lost on a desert island, or...). When unforeseen events such as this happen, it is important to have a Durable Power of Attorney (DPA) in place.

A DPA is a document that allows someone you designate in advance as "attorney in fact," who acts on your behalf if you have been incapacitated or you are otherwise unavailable. It is a document necessary to allow your designated agent to handle financial matters.

When most people hear the words, "Power of Attorney" they believe that they might be giving away some power that will enable them to be taken advantage of. In reality, a *DURABLE POWER OF ATTORNEY* could actually save you and your estate, both money and time.

**How would such a document save you time and money?** For example assume you are employed and in good health. Unfortunately you suffer an accident resulting in incapacity. If you do not have a Durable Power of Attorney naming someone to act in business matters i.e., paying bills, operating your checkbook, paying taxes, signing business papers, then your family will generally have to go to court to determine that you are incapable of acting on your own and that someone is needed to handle your affair. This is needlessly complicated, and could have otherwise been included in the Durable Power document.

The court proceeding will usually require a hearing and testimony concerning the extent of the disability before the spouse is able to act for the incapacitated person. The hearing procedure, typically referred to as a guardianship proceeding, is time consuming, expensive and will usually require the services of one or more attorneys.

If you had a pre-signed DPA in advance of the incapacity, you would be able to forego the hearings and court orders that could elect someone you do not want.

**What types of Durable Powers are out there and what should you look for when you have one drafted?** In the above example a Durable Power can be drafted so that the appointed person is able to act for you concerning those accounts.

This could be very important for a couple that is retired and is primarily living off the income from the client's IRA. Without a DPA, the money from the IRA may be inaccessible without going to court to determine who is able to act on behalf of the incapacitated spouse.

Some DPAs have **"springing** powers" which only become effective once the party is incapacitated, and will typically end once it is established that the party is no longer incapacitated. Springing Powers of Attorney are generally activated when one or two physicians state the nature and extent of the disability to verify that it is appropriate for the DPA to be used. The physicians will also determine when the incapacity has ended, and facilitate the end of the Durable Power, which would put the client back in charge of their own affairs.

Other powers are effective immediately upon signing and allow the designated attorney-in-fact to act on behalf of the incapacitated person right away. It is important for you to check your state laws to determine what is permissible in that state in regards to Durable Power of Attorney.

**Delegating medical treatment options:** In some states, like Florida, a Durable Power of Attorney can also be used to appoint an individual called a Health Care Surrogate (HCS). The HCS is empowered to make health-care decisions on behalf of any adult of sound mind that authorizes an HCS.

This patient advocate form would commonly include language typical of the "living will" in which the grantor states his opinion and quality of life. In many cases, the patient advocacy matter would now be included in the Durable Power. A separate document called a "Patient Advocate" form would determine what treatment, or lack thereof would be given to a person who has appointed another to handle their affairs should they become incapacitated.

The Living Will, which is used in some states, is similar to the Patient Advocate form, which appoints someone close to the nominee to make decisions concerning medical treatment.

**Why is a Patient Advocate Designation or Living Will important and why should you have one?** Many Americans will pass away in a Hospital or other care facility. It is typically the duty of the staff in these facilities, to preserve the patients life.

If you are incapacitated, you will not be making your own decisions, and it is quite possible that you do not want the hospital to make decisions on your behalf. Health Care Directives enable you to give directives in advance and ensure some legal respect for them if you are ever incapacitated and unable to give instructions yourself.

**What is a Living Will?** A Living Will, also known as a Health Care Directive in some states, spells out a person's directive about what treatment should be provided, should they become unable to communicate those wishes. The directive creates a contract with the physician providing treatment.

Once a directive is properly signed and witnessed, the physician is under a duty to either honor its instructions or to transfer the patient to the care of another physician who will follow them. Health Care Directives have other uses than instructing physicians to withhold life-prolonging treatments.

Some people want any and all medical treatments should they become incapacitated, The Patient Advocate Form or Health Care Directive is where you can specify what treatment options that you want. You must be 18 years old in most states to sign such a directive.; state laws throughout the country require that the person making a Health Care Directive must be able to understand what the meaning of the document, as well as what is said and how the document will function.

If you are already disabled, you may direct another person to sign the document for you. A properly drafted, signed, and recorded Medical Directive, Living Will, Patient Advocate Form, and DPA gives you the effective control over your health care decisions through your delegates, rather than leaving it up to the physicians or hospital personnel or the courts to decide what sort of treatment you will receive.

There can be issues when family members disagree about what medical treatments the disabled person should receive. It is very possible that in circumstances such as these, the court will decide the treatment of the incapacitated person, even though the judge may have no familiarity with the treatment you are to receive, or your wishes.

Court battles are expensive, and can drain the resources on an incapacitated person, who would have not wanted his family to battle over what type of treatment he was to receive. The execution of a Living Will, Patient Advocate Form, Medical Directive, and/or other appropriate Durable Power would have saved a lot of money time and aggravation.

A Health Care Directive will take effect when you are no longer able to communicate your own directives for your medical care. If this were to happen, your Medical Directive would be given to the medical personnel taking care of you; and the Medical Directive, spelling out the type of care you want, would then be followed.

**Conclusion:** Durable Powers and Health Care Surrogate Forms should be incorporated into every estate plan so as to specify specific medical treatment or the general management of an incapacitated person's affairs. Because there are large costs associated with the litigation required to determine who will act for an incapacitated person, not having Durable Powers and Health Care Surrogate forms in your estate plan would be a tremendous mistake.

### Section 3: *A&B, Marital or Living Trusts*

Besides a will, A&B/Marital/Living Trusts (hereinafter A&B Trusts) are the most commonly utilized estate planning tool. If you are married, we recommend their use in almost every estate plan. Most of our clients expect to live for at least another 20 years, but future circumstances are always unforeseen.

In 2015, the estate tax exemption is about $5,500,000 per spouse with "portability". Our best explanation: when the second spouse dies, then about $11 million is estate-tax exempt. That tax rate is now 45% on the balance of the taxable estate. For the "middle class millionaire," this tax has less importance than it used to (see the section on Income Tax Planning, as it becomes more meaningful).

**What if the couple had A&B Trusts when the first spouse died?**
Three and one-half million dollars would have poured into the A Trust for the benefit of the surviving spouse until death, and $500,000 would have gone to the surviving spouse without estate taxes. If the second spouse were to pass the very next day, the remaining $500,000 would pour through the B Trust to avoid probate; and $500,000 of the remaining $3.5 million exemption would be used.

The estate taxes due at the second spouse's death would be zero, but be careful with this fact pattern. You might not want $3.5 million going to the A Trust. Instead, the surviving spouse might rather have more of that money in her control where she does not have to ask a trustee for the money.

**What should a Will and standard A&B Trusts cost?** In a recent poll of Florida attorneys who specialize in estates and trusts, you probably can expect the following:

| Size of the estate | Cost in USD |
|---|---|
| Up to $3 million | 4,500 |
| $3 to 5 million | 5,500 |
| $5 to 10 million | 9,000 |
| $10 to 25 million | 10,000 |
| Over $25 million | 50,000 |

Unless your estate is over 25 million dollars, you should be able to get an entire estate plan for less than $25,000. If your estate is less than five million dollars, you should be able to get an entire estate plan done for around $8,000.

These fees do not include a lot of specific asset protection planning or advanced planning with Family Limited Partnerships. When it comes to estate planning, attorneys will very rarely come up with something entirely new. If you have read this book carefully, you will know as much as your attorney about the basics of estate planning.

You may be asking yourself why estate plans cost so much when the same shell documents are used over and over. It is because of estate plan's lingering liability. The malpractice liability for estate planning attorneys lasts until the client passes away. For some clients, this could be a rather long time.

**Revocable:** A&B Trusts are revocable trusts. Many attorneys will set up an A&B Trusts and never put anything into the trusts. We estimate that 90% of the A&B Trusts are funded incorrectly. Our suggestion is that you fund them when you implement them.

**Conclusion:** EVERYONE who has assets should have a A&B Marital/Living/Revocable Trust. If you are not married you can have a single trust, which will help to avoid probate and maximize the estate tax exemptions. It is just that simple.

### Section 4: *Life Insurance (different types and the ones that are right for you)*

How well do you like life insurance? Typically, the answer is not very much. That may be due to lack of understanding. Often, it is sold and not bought. Often it is misapplied. Often the wrong entity owns it. Often the wrong policy is sold. Often it is improperly funded.

Proper life insurance use, however, is critically important and really cost effective for a variety of different purposes, such as wealth accumulation and future income and income tax planning being the primary, while legacy planning and estate tax planning is secondary.

Life insurance benefits are always dependent upon the claims-paying abilities of the "carrier" or the issuing company. It is important to use highly rated companies.

See the article I wrote entitled "Truth about Life Insurance" at **http://www.myassetprotectiongroup.com/#!white-papers/c12kr.** Here you will learn basics many agents forgot or never learned or never shared with you. We simplify this product so you understand what it is, how it works, and how to make it work best for you.

INSURANCE IS A VERY SIMPLE PRODUCT. Yet many people don't understand how it works and make it complicated. Let's keep it simple.

There are only two things that go into insurance; 1) the premium and; 2) the interest on the premium. And only two things come out of insurance; 1) the death benefit and; 2) the expenses associated with it. Insurance companies must make a profit and we know that they are not going to sell insurance and lose money.

At some point in time the amount of money that goes into insurance, must equal or exceed the amount of money that comes out of insurance -- otherwise the carriers would go broke and wouldn't be able to pay the death benefit claims or their expenses. Many have long recognized that insurance carriers are very successful.

We know that there is a dollar for dollar available "reserve" such that if every person currently insured were to die today, every single policy would be able to be paid out. Insurance carriers are very well managed. So, ask yourself, "How can insurance carriers sell you $1 million in insurance for pennies on the dollar?"

And before you answer that let's talk about the banks. Today, banks are offering mortgages at rates of about 4.5% for a 30 year fixed mortgage, and 3.5% for a fifteen year fixed mortgage. Which mortgage do you think is better for the bank? Now think about this carefully. Most people would say the 30-year mortgage, because the bank is getting more interest. However, if that were the case, why would they offer an incentive with a lower interest rate for the 15-year mortgage? It doesn't make sense, does it? The reason they do this is because the 15-year mortgage is better for the banks.

Why is that? Because the banks used something called the velocity of money multiplier. If the bank has $1 of deposits, the bank is able to make $10 of loan. And for every $1 of loan that gets paid back they get to lend out another several dollars. So, the more rapidly the money gets paid back, the more rapidly the banks can loan it back out again and make a profit.

THE VELOCITY OF MONEY MULTIPLIER FOR BANKS TODAY IS SOMEWHERE AROUND 10. It changes as the regulators change the requirements. Remember that number and the velocity of money multiplier.

So, now that you know that, let's ask the question about insurance carriers. If the insurance carrier is able to sell you a $1 million life insurance policy for let's say $2,000 a year, or sell you that very same life insurance policy for let's say $50,000 a year, depending on your age and health, which one do you think is better for the insurance carrier?

Think carefully. Remember when we talked about the things that go into life insurance and the things that come out? Well, let's look at that on a graph. The death benefit is generally going to be flat, and it would be high going from left to right on the page. The premium paid for the life insurance policy, plus interest over time will go from the bottom left of the graph to the top right of the graph until it matches and meets up with the death benefit and expense line.

AT THAT POINT IN TIME, THE LIFE INSURANCE IS SAID TO ENDOW. However, you can reach that with that $50,000 a year premium for say seven years, or you can make a $2,000 premium payment for 20 years, and then the line is almost flat from lower left to lower right.

In order to get up to that upper line you'll have to put in a whole bunch of cash that nobody warned you about.

INSURANCE CARRIERS BASE THEIR PRODUCT ON THE LAW OF LARGE NUMBERS. An entire city was built on the law of large numbers and it's called Las Vegas, and here's how it works simplified. Regardless of how much you spend, or how much money you bring with you to Las Vegas, the house knows they're going to make 4%. They know that some people win, but most people will lose and they will make 4%. Their job is to keep you at the table as long as possible so that your winnings turn into losses.

However, they also know that of the thousands of people who spend thousands of dollars, their take will be 4%. Insurance carriers also know this. They know of a cohort of 10 million people, by using the law of large numbers, exactly how many people will die at a given age. They don't know who, but they know how many.

Let's break this down into slightly smaller numbers. Let's just say there are 100 people in a cohort, and everybody wants $1,000 worth of life insurance. If that's the case, and we know that in the first year, one person is going to die of the 100 people.

IN THE SECOND YEAR, two people will die of the 100 people.

IN THE THIRD YEAR, three people will die, and so forth until you get down to the tenth year, at which point, 10 additional people will die.

SO, IN THE FIRST YEAR, if one person will die and we don't know who, but everybody's willing to get $1,000 worth of life insurance, how much will those 100 people have to pay in order for the insurance company to have enough money to cover that $1,000 worth of life insurance for the death benefit of the one person who will die?

Well, that's pretty simple. You take the $1,000, divide it by the 100 people and that equals $10. Everyone pays $10 and therefore, there is $1,000 available for the death benefit for that one person who dies. Look at what happens in the second year, when we know that two people will die, therefore, the insurance carriers are going to have to pay out death benefits totaling $2,000.

How much in premiums will carriers have to charge those people in the second year? Well, many of you might say $20, but that would not be the case, because one person died in the first year, leaving only 99 people to pay premiums. Carriers would have to charge 99 people a premium of $20.21 each.

IN THE SECOND YEAR, 99 people paying $20.21 would put into the insurance a total of $2,000. Therefore, two people die and the carriers pay out the $2,000—terrific.

SAME THING IN THE THIRD YEAR; 97 people are left, because three people have died. We know that three new people will die. We'll have to write $3,000 worth of death benefit claims.

IN THE FOURTH YEAR, four people pass away. We are left with 93, we might have to charge everybody $43, and so on and so on, until we get down to year 10, in which case we know that 10 people will die, maybe 20 or so people have already died. That only leaves 80 people to pay premiums equal to the death benefits. We know we're going to have to spend $10,000 divided by 80. That number might be $125 per person.

Now, when you sell that life insurance to the 100 people you're not telling them that insurance is going to go up every single year. On the contrary, you're telling them that they can pay a level premium every year for 10 years. What will that level premium have to be? Well, it might have to be something on the order of say $95 a year.

Now, think about that. I have to pay $95 a year. Let's call it $100 for round easy arithmetic. I write $100 a year premium for 10 years. I've written $1,000. A hundred people have then written $100,000. Yet the insurance carriers have only had to write death benefit claims for, approximately 25 or so people.

The difference between what they write in claims and what they to collect in premiums is called the reserve. And there is something else the insurance carriers know based on the Law of Large Numbers. They know exactly how many people will drop out and quit paying their premiums and they know about what point in time those people will discontinue paying their premiums.

Consider that they know by the fifth year, five people will drop out and won't make payments.

By the tenth year, another 10 people or so may have dropped out and will not pay premiums, so they're really not collecting $100,000, maybe they're only collecting $85,000. Still, they only had to pay approximately $25,000 in death benefit claims.

That leaves them a $60,000 reserve. Ask yourself this question. Would you rather the insurance company owned that $60,000 reserve, or would you rather own a piece of that $60,000 reserve?

Nobody has ever answered that question incorrectly. Of course, you would rather own that reserve.

HOW DO YOU GET TO DO THAT? Well, there is a way to do that, and that's to develop something approaching a maximally efficient contract. That's when you put in that $50,000 for the $1 million premium for seven years versus $2,000 for 20 years or $10,000 for 40 years or whatever that number may turn out to be. In fact, for every illustration that we have seen of over 80 different policies that have come to us from somewhere else, 100% of them were underfunded. This means that their lines were never going to match. They were always on the lower line.

THE INCENTIVES IN THE INDUSTRY ARE MISALIGNED AGAINST THE CLIENT. Their profits are in the inventory turnover business of selling more, and the commissions don't change very much if the premiums go up a lot. That is because the insurance commission is typically based on the cost of the insurance. Commissions are not that large. It's nominal on the amount that goes toward the reserve. That is your cash value build up.

The carriers are incentivized to lower the price so that they know that,

1. You are going to drop out or not die, or
2. They get to keep the reserve.

However, if you write a large premium between four and 11 years, depending on your age and your health, and how it's constructed, every dollar that you put into the premium, you should be able to take back out within four to 11 years.

## IT'S A GUARANTEED RETURN OF PREMIUM ON LIFE INSURANCE.

Very few people know about this, very few people will tell you about this, and the reason is because it's harder for carriers or agents to sell it. Now, why would I want to put in $50,000 besides getting my premium out?

## WELL, THAT'S ONE MAJOR THING, BUT HOW ABOUT THIS?

There is something in the tax code. You have all heard about a 401k, which is a tax deferred vehicle. Let's never call it tax deferred any longer, let's call it tax postponed. You take a payroll deduction to put money into an account. The government tells you when you can put it in, how much you can put in, and what you can put it in. And then the government tells you that you don't have to pay tax on it now. They tell you when you have to take it out, how much you have to take out, and oh, by the way, when we figure out how much we need, we'll let you know what the tax rate is. That is a 401k or 403b, a tax-deferred vehicle.

Everyone knows about the taxable vehicle. That's where you put money into a taxable account, and if you have taxable gains, it might be tax deferred as well, but at some point in time you're going to have to pay tax on it.

But, how many of you know of a 7702 plan? IT'S IN THE TAX CODE. IT IS 7702.

A 401k is in the tax code under Section 401; 412 is in Section 412; 437 is in Section 437; and 7702 is in Section 7702 of the tax code. Sometimes it's better to pay tax on the seed rather than on the harvest. Many of you would agree with that—you understand that intuitively.

The benefits are:

• You can put in any amount
• It grows tax deferred
• You can it access tax free (In most states it is asset protected)
• It has guaranteed loan provisions
• You have easy and quick access to your capital
• Competitive rate of return
• Guaranteed completion plan, which means that if you die your beneficiaries will get some money

That death benefit can be free, because you can have a maximally efficient contract that will pay you 3%, 4%, or even 5% or 5.25%. And if you're in the upper tax brackets, you can do the arithmetic and even get a 9% rate of return, taxable.

So, how much would you like to put in your 7702?

For many of us the answer is, as much as we can. The way to get access to the reserves is the same way that you're going to receive your premium's guaranteed return rather than have it going to the carriers.

## USE A MAXIMALLY EFFICIENT CONTRACT.

### Benefits of the 7702

• Tax deferred growth,
• Tax free distributions
• Competitive rate of return
• High contributions with virtually no limits
• Collateralization opportunities
• Safe harbor

- No loss provisions
- Guaranteed access to your money,
- Unstructured payments
- Liquidity
- Full access
- Control.

**MEC? What is that?** A "MEC" is a Modified Endowment Contract. That is government jargon for a high cash value life insurance policy that has NO 7702 Tax benefits. Why? Because the IRS limits the amount of cash you can put into a life insurance policy. There is only so much cash value for a related death benefit. What does that tell us? That cash value was so good, the IRS needed to limit our usage.

A MEC works like this: the death benefit remains income tax-free to the beneficiaries. The cash you put into the policy may be taxed at ordinary income tax rates—just like the money in your 401(k). For most clients, we try to avoid a MEC. For some clients, a MEC is the best way to go. Every situation is different. There is no right way or wrong way. Just understand when to use which tool.

We have used a MEC in the following situation: an elderly client has $500,000 in CDs earning 2% that she wishes to leave in its entirety to beneficiaries. She has no need of the money. Life expectancy is 10 years. So the CDs might earn $10,000 per year, or $100,000 over the 10 years, taxable at a 40% rate. Net proceeds to beneficiaries, $560,000. Instead, you purchase a MEC with the $500,000 with a guaranteed income tax-free death benefit of $730,000. This MEC may be better, yes?

**Term Life Insurance**

Most people are aware of term life, and most of the breadwinners in a family household will have had term life insurance at one point or another in their lives. Term life is the least expensive type of life insurance policy you can purchase. That is because it is least likely to be needed.

Unlike the other life insurance policies we will discuss, later term life has no cash value; and if you do not die, neither you nor your beneficiaries will get any benefit. You get a receipt. For a 40-year-old to get $1,000,000 worth of term coverage for 20 years, it might cost as little as $850 a year. Term insurance is the best way to get high coverage for a finite period of time. What are the options to improve your value for the cost?

**Types of term life:** *Non-Premium Guaranteed Term*

**Non-guaranteed term** simply means, as you get older, the company will charge you more every year for the insurance. The pros of non-premium guaranteed term is simply that every year you will get the lowest possible term cost, but you have no guarantee what that will be in any given year.

The most common is **Level Term**. Almost any company will sell 5-, 10-, 15-, 20- and 30-year term policies. Level term means that the premium will be level for a particular death benefit. After the term expires, you will generally have the right to purchase insurance from the company, but the rates may have fluctuated.

**Convertible Term:** Many insurance companies will allow you to convert your term policy to a whole, universal, or variable policy without having to go through the underwriting process. One of the main reasons that you would want to purchase a convertible term policy is that as you get older, you get closer to *your age of un-insurability*. The additional costs associated with convertible term are nominal. We recommend convertible term for most clients. With convertible term, you do not have to go through the underwriting process again in order to switch into a permanent insurance policy.

The main problem with all term insurance is that at some point the contract expires, assuming you survived the contract period, and you may no longer be insurable if you want to extend. Another important problem is if you do not convert to permanent, and you do not die during the term of the contract, all your premium payments vanish into the carrier's pocket. Which leads us to...

## ...Return of Premium Term Life Insurance (ROPT)

***Purchase almost "Free" Term Life Insurance with a Return of Premium Rider:*** Most clients under the age of 60 have purchased term life insurance at some point in their life. Typically our clients purchase 10- to 30-year-level term insurance, where the premium is set for up to 30 years. They do this because it is an inexpensive way to fund a death benefit without increasing costs for a determined time period.

Even though most of our clients purchase level term life insurance, at the same time they also hate the concept of term life because they believe that they will not die during the time period that there policy is in effect. And they would be correct, or else the carriers could not stay in business. If you do not expire during the policy, the premium at the end of the period was a total waste; although the policyholder was able to rest easy knowing they were covered during the policy period.

Insurance companies think that term life is great. Statistically speaking, 93% of all clients who buy term insurance do not pass away while their policy is in effect. That means that if you have a term life insurance policy, there is a 93 percent chance that you will see no return on your investment. That is what you want. You want to survive.

A few of insurance companies have developed Return of Premium Term Life Insurance (ROPT). The basis of ROPT is easy to understand. You premiums are higher than the typical term life policy, but if you do not die while the policy is in effect, you get the premium payments returned to you.

While you will get your premium back, you have effectively given an interest free loan to the insurance company. Not great. Not bad.

Most 40-year-old insurance customers would normally buy 20-30 year level term to take care of the family needs through life insurance until discovering the ROPT option:

30 Year Term premium  -  $2,500/year

Total cost for 30 years  -  $75,000

ROPT annual premium - $4000/year

ROPT total Cost          - $120,000

Differential Cost        - $45,000 over 30 years or $1,500 per year

The amount of premium paid per year was $1,500 *more* with the ROPT. Most people typically choose the less expensive insurance product and choose to invest the amount they saved in the stock market. So let's analyze that position.

If you invested the difference in premium, the $1,500 per year, into a taxable brokerage account each year for the 30-year period; you would have in that account approximately $125,000 before tax, assuming a 6% annual investment return. You, alternatively, with the ROPT will receive a guaranteed return of premium of $120,000 income tax free.

The difference between the amount in your brokerage account, $125,000 and ROPT, $120,000 is $5000 – over 30 years or about $167 per year. So effectively the insurance only "costs" $167 per year with ROPT.

Importantly, there is ample evidence you might not invest all that "extra" $1500 per year. You might just spend it somewhere else. Your investments would have to earn 6% pre-tax in order to have more money than you would receive with ROPT. In addition, there is NO guarantee that your money invested will earn 6%.

**Conclusion on ROPT:** If you would rather not "waste" your term life insurance premiums (due to the fact that it is highly unlikely that the policy will ever pay out because you have a 93% chance of living beyond the term), then you should consider ROPT. With ROPT, you are getting virtually **free death benefit** because you will receive all the money you paid in premiums back via the Return of Premium Rider. This will free you from the feeling of waste we all get when purchasing a term life insurance policy.

We all feel that the money could have been better spent; that is assuming we ended up being in the 93% category of people who did not die during the term period.

**Other thoughts on term life:** You can purchase all sorts of different term riders like increasing and decreasing term. You might want *increasing* term because you believe that as you age the size of your estate will grow, and you want a policy that will increase its death benefit correspondingly.

Others choose *decreasing* term because they believe that as their estate grows larger, their need for insurance will decrease because they have accumulated enough assets for their heirs to live on without the need for a higher death benefit. There are also those who would rather buy ROPT because they know that that all the premiums they pay during the life of the policy will come back to them via the Return of Premium Rider.

**Our Recommendations:** We recommend 10-30 year level term for those clients who need high life insurance coverage to take care of the family in a manner to which they have become accustomed, when main provider and less than 60 years old. We suggest term insurance of at least two million dollars so that if a younger client dies, there will be no need for the spouse to return to work, and there will be enough money to send the children to college. In that particular case, the family could spend $100,000 per year or so for 20 years. Is that enough?

Term life insurance is good for younger clients because it is inexpensive. If you are going to be paying term life premiums for 10-30 years we strongly recommend you consider purchasing ROPT-if the numbers make sense. Changing interest rates and changing mortality tables can change the example above. With ROPT you essentially receive free term life insurance unless you pass away during the time the policy is in effect. This fact should substantially dull the pain when you are paying your term life premiums.

## Whole Life Insurance Policies

Whole life provides both a death benefit and an accumulating cash value. By definition, it has a **fixed premium** and a level **death benefit** to age 121. Although there is a high internal up front "load" with whole life, the **premiums do not increase** with age. This helps to average the client's cost over the life of the policy. Whole life is perhaps the primary way to enjoy the 7702 benefits.

The cash value increases with time until it equals the death benefit at age 100. There is a trade off between cash value build up and death benefit available. When most client look at a whole life they ask why there is very little cash surrender value for the first several years of the policy. One of the main reasons is that they are often improperly constructed. Sometimes in order to increase your death benefit. Sometimes to increase the agent's commission.

The premium costs for the client remain the same over the life of the policy.

**So where do whole life premiums go?** Premiums pay insurance costs (true administration costs, the "reserve", and other costs of doing business including commissions, profits, and death benefit claims), and cause cash value to accrue in a separate account, through "dividends". This cash value is typically and partially invested in the bond market.

The dividends on the cash value come only partially from the bonds' returns. In addition the profits of the company are pro-rated to your account in a participating mutual company (more on this is beyond the scope of this book). And finally, the "abandoned" premiums of terminated policies, term life policies, and policies that never had death benefit claims, is also pro-rated to your benefit. The net result of these three components is how these companies get an internal rate of return (IRR) of 4-5.5%--tax-free.

Dividends are not guaranteed. They depend on company profits, and low claims. The guaranty portion of the cash value occurs even if the carrier *never* pays a dividend. Dividends may be suspended if the carrier goes out of business, or if a major catastrophe requires massive death benefit claims payments.

The build up of your dividends is the cash value. You will be able to borrow against the cash value. Please, be aware that premiums are due in your whole life policy every single year the policy is in force. That is for your whole life. These lifelong premiums may be covered by the cash value, if it is sufficient. That is how you may only be required to pay for a certain period of time.

If, at some point, you are unable to pay your premium, the policy will pay the insurance expenses from built up cash value, if there is any available. Eventually, however, the policy will "surrender" itself (expire worthless, or "lapse" in industry jargon) if you do not ask the insurance company to lower the death benefit or if the policy runs out of cash to pay the premiums. We should note that not every insurance company will be willing to lower the death benefit.

**Why would anyone want to use whole life?** Whole life, one form of permanent life insurance, is great for estate planning purposes. There are few moving parts. Your premium costs are guaranteed for life. Your death benefit is guaranteed for life. Your dividends are not guaranteed. But, almost. If there is catastrophic event, there may not be a dividend.

However, the carriers we like have not missed a dividend payment for over 170 years! Through the Civil War, Lincoln, multiple depressions, the Panic of 1907, World War One, 30% of Philadelphia dying of the flu, the Great Depression, World War Two, the Cold War, Kennedy, Vietnam, Nixon, Watergate, stagflation, Carter, and more…

In the rare event the company goes bust, there is re-insurance, the reserve, and the ongoing internal expenses that another company is likely to take over. Even if your insurance company goes bankrupt, as long as you pay your premiums, you will have that death benefit. And, unless there is an enormous catastrophe, as long as your carrier survives, you should get the dividend.

In addition, if you like **tax-free compounded guaranteed growth** and can front load the policy premiums (within 7 years is the optimal, though 10 or 15 years can work too), you may be able to enjoy over 5% (currently) internal rates of return over time. Did I mention tax-free? And you should be able to access that money at any time for any reason. Tax-free.

The above way is the most efficient way to own a policy. However, if you do not have the cash flow to make the premium payments, your whole life policy is not much of a valuable resource for *your* life. You will have a guaranteed death benefit as long as you pay the premium, but the death benefit may not be as high as with term. And do not look to the policy as a major liquid asset of your estate unless you create and properly fund that efficient policy. Therefore, for young policy owners, we often will use a combination of term and whole to optimize the position.

**Miscellaneous:** As with term policies, whole life policies may have a number of variations. Clients who are unable to afford whole life today, but believe that they will have the assets to purchase in the future can purchase a policy that has low initial premiums that go up usually after the third year. This gives you some time to build your assets up.

Limited pay policies, or guaranteed life, are great for the client who wishes to avoid paying premiums till their death.

## Universal Life Insurance

Universal Life (UL) is best described as a continuous, non-cancellable term insurance. The costs and the premiums are flexible. They can go up. However, that very same flexibility is your friend if you do not have the cash flow to pay the premiums for a few years. UL is the most flexible type of life insurance. It does not require you to pay that a premium into the policy every year if you have enough cash value to maintain the costs for a period of time. Of course, the flexibility entails some risks on you part, too, including a potential decrease in the death benefit.

Premiums can be paid in a lump sum, annually, or somewhere in between the two. Typically interest on the cash value is guaranteed, but the actual amount will fluctuate. The policy will remain in force as long as there is enough cash value to maintain the monthly costs. The main characteristics of Universal Life is that it is interest sensitive and allows for adjustable premium payments and often an adjustable death benefit.

Universal Life comes in a variety of flavors: plain, Guaranteed UL, Survivorship Guaranteed UL, and Equity Indexed UL. Plain was described above. We find very little use for plain UL.

Guaranteed UL acts as "permanent" term. You pay relatively low premiums for your entire life up to a certain age, such as 95 or 108, in return for a guaranteed death benefit. There is little cash value, and certainly not enough to provide benefits to you during your life. This is strictly to benefit those you leave behind. The premium, the costs, the death benefits are fixed and not flexible. This acts more like low cash value whole, except that whole provides coverage now to age 121. We like these for legacy building in certain cases.

Survivorship GUL covers both spouses. The premiums are lower than for the man alone because of the longer life expectancy for both. For example,

$20,000 per year premium on a couple aged 60 buys about $2.4 million in guaranteed, income-tax free death benefit through age 108.

**Family Legacy Retirement Fund:** Imagine, you have a $2.4 million retirement portfolio. You want to live on the returns *and the principal* to maintain your lifestyle. You now may live on 5, 6, 7% or more of your nest egg knowing full well that you will leave something to your children. After 10 years of you paying your premiums, your children, are now well established in their careers and they are able to save at least $10,000 each in their 401(k). Instead they divert that savings into your SGUL that is for their benefit, replacing your premium payments with their savings. If you both live to life expectancy, your children receive $2.4 million, income tax-free and guaranteed. This amounts to a rate of return of approximately 8.6%! On a taxable basis, they would have had to earn almost 15% in their 401(k). And you would have received a $20,000 "raise" in your income once they take over the premium payments. Both GUL and SGUL may be used here.

### Equity Indexed Universal Life Insurance (EIUL) Policy

An EIUL has an annual minimum return guarantee every year plus it allows for cash value gains if the stock market performs well. The policies cash value can only increase with the markets. When the markets decline, your cash value does not decline. Rather, it stays at the previous high level, which is a nice feature to have because the equity/stock markets are volatile.

**How are investment returns calculated in an EIUL policy?** The majority of EIUL policies are "indexed" to the Standard & Poor's 500 stock Index. The insurance companies DO NOT invest your premiums into the stock index. 95% of the premium is used to purchase income-producing Bonds. That income covers the internal expense of the policy. The remainder buys a "long" option on the market index. If the market goes up, you get some of that gain. If the market is flat or goes down, you lose nothing. The major attraction is your principal protection. Your account can only go up, never down.

How can this be? They odds are that the markets go up over 20% on average 1 out of 4 years, down 20% 1 out of 4 years, and up or down less than 10% half the time. The carrier usually has a "cap" on the upside. They do this to cover the down years. The cap may be 12% in some cases. If the S&P goes up 36% as it did in 2013, you get 12%.

And they permit your account to go up based on a certain percentage of the markets up years (in many cases 140%). This is called the "participation rate". If the market goes up less than the cap, you can get up to 140% of the gain, up to the cap. So if the market goes up 8%, you get 11.2%. Your account is adjusted upwards, usually on an annual basis. In down years your account value stays flat.

**Pros and Cons of the "new" EIUL policy:**

What is the catch? No catch. There are limits to your upside. You do not enjoy stock market dividends, which historically account for over 25-40% of the gains in an investment account. And due to the caps, you forego the major upside. Therefore, on a tax-deferred basis you can reasonably expect about 6% compounded growth inside the policy.

One caveat: if the stock markets experience several down or flat years in a row, the carriers have the rights to reduce your death benefit, or to increase the policy costs to cover the expenses, and your policy may not behave as hoped.

Cons:

1. If the market averages over the 8.3% it has historically returned with dividends, on a geometric, compounded rate, for the time you own your life insurance policy, which would be likely, you would have fared better had you invested in a "brokerage account" and purchased term insurance—buy term and invest the difference.

2. If the market averages return less than 5% over the time you have your life insurance policy, you would have fared better had you purchased a whole life policy.

Pros:

1. You have minimum guaranteed return every year.
2. The policy gets you the upsides of the stock market up to a specified percentage.
3. Flexibility. As opposed to whole life policies, the policy has the flexibility of a UL with its premium. This allows the owner to choose when he wants to pay the premium each year, and in what amount.

**A closer look at the S&P 500 stock index:** Without specific numbers, it is difficult for many to grasp how well they would have done in an EIUL policy to grow wealth.

Below are the returns for 30 years, starting in 1985 through 2015. These are "average" returns. That is arithmetic, not geometric. Geometric returns are what you would experience on a compounded basis. So expect about 2-3% less than the average, to account for the compounding without the associated expenses to own such an account. Taxes are not computed. See my article, adapted from Kevin Fink, "Math is Not Money." [http://creativespending.com/math-is-not-money-how-to-invest-your-money/] Before continuing, we should point out how EIUL polices actually credit the growth. Most of them use an "annual point-to-point" method.

That means the money in your cash value life insurance policy is valued when the cash account begins and is valued again exactly 12 months later. If the account was funded on January 1 in your policy, the S&P 500 will be valued on that date. Then 12 months later the account will be valued again; and the gains, if any, are "locked in".

Actual Returns of the S&P 500: The initial value of the S&P 500 in 1985 was 176.21. Light grey are negative returns, or years with losses. EIUL's by and large did not exist for this entire time. They are relatively new since the 1990s.

| Year | Ending Value | Index Growth | Year | Ending Value | Index Growth |
|------|-------------|--------------|------|-------------|--------------|
| 1985 | 189.82 | 5.43% | 2000 | 1320.28 | -10.13% |
| 1986 | 242.17 | 27.57% | 2001 | 1148.08 | -13.04% |
| 1987 | 247.08 | 2.02% | 2002 | 879.82 | -23.36% |
| 1988 | 272.72 | 10.37% | 2003 | 1111.92 | 26.38% |
| 1989 | 353.40 | 29.58% | 2004 | 1211.92 | 8.99% |
| 1990 | 330.22 | -6.55% | 2005 | 1248.29 | 3.00% |
| 1991 | 417.09 | 26.30% | 2006 | 1418.30 | 13.61% |
| 1992 | 435.71 | 4.46% | 2007 | 1468.38 | 3.53% |
| 1993 | 466.45 | 7.05% | 2008 | 903.25 | -38.49% |
| 1994 | 459.27 | -1.53% | 2009 | 1115.10 | 23.45% |
| 1995 | 615.93 | 34.11% | 2010 | 1257.64 | 12.78% |
| 1996 | 740.74 | 20.26% | 2011 | 1257.60 | 0.00% |
| 1997 | 970.43 | 31.00% | 2012 | 1426.19 | 13.41% |
| 1998 | 1229.23 | 26.66% | 2013 | 1848.36 | 29.60% |
| 1999 | 1469.25 | 19.52% | 2014 | 2058.90 | 11.39% |

The question then becomes, what would you have earned in your EIUL policy over this period of time and how would that change based on the caps on the returns in the life policy. What if the cap on the product is 12% and the policy credited 140% of the S&P 500 returns every year? You would have earned 6.21 % compounded.

The average mutual fund **investor** earned only 2.7%, while the market average compound return was 8.3% with dividends, according to DALBAR research, of Boston. That represents a whopping 5% "g-a-p". We call that the "*DALBAR Gap*". Most investors have a real propensity for *buying high and selling low*. When you use *any* high cash value, low death benefit permanent life insurance policy with guarantees, you may have safeguarded yourself from going backward.

**Conclusion on EIUL policies:** If you would like the *possibility* of earning upwards of a 5-7% return on the cash value in your life insurance policy and would like to hedge against a falling stock market with a 1-3% minimum guarantee, then you could consider an EIUL. We believe, this is a "niche" product of value in certain circumstances, though it is not for everyone

**Variable Universal Life Insurance**

These policies permit your cash value to be indirectly invested, through "separate accounts", typically into mutual funds with limited distribution specifically designed for these types of policies. Thus, the investment costs are usually very high.

Higher income clients typically had been sold variable life because the policy acts as an after-tax investment alternative wrapped inside life insurance. However, recent years caused many of these policies to "lapse" or implode. What happened? The variability included *losses* in the investments inside the policy, while the expenses persisted or increased.

**Where does your premium go?** Variable life is simple to understand. When you pay your premium, a percentage pays for the insurance costs; the rest of the money is invested. The insurance costs increase with age.

If you had a variable policy from 1999-2002, or from 2007-2011, then you know why these can blow up. Many forget that when you get over 75 years old, the costs of insurance in a variable policy increase -- sometimes dramatically. Further, the illustrations given to the client often assume a level rate of return, usually 8% each year of the policy.

That is not realistic, and if you throw in negative returns early on in the policy, or if the average return in the policy is a more reasonable 5-6% return, the entire illustration that you received when you were sold the policy may throw your entire financial plan off track.

**No Guarantees:** There is no guarantee on the cost of the policy, nor on the investment returns in the majority of variable policies. That means, if you have a negative year or several years, the cash value in your policy takes a nosedive with the stock market. You might think that is not a big deal due to the fact that over the long haul the policy will still average your assumed rate of return of 8-9%.

What you may not have calculated is the expenses in your policy increasing every year, regardless of whether you have insufficient cash value in your policy to pay premiums due to persistent market problems. The insurance company, on schedule, still takes out its chunk of your money for life insurance premiums. So you pay to transfer the risk of dying, but take back much of that risk with the cash value. Square peg-round hole.

**Big problem:** Many clients were sold variable policies with 12% illustrations in the 1990s, where they were told that they would only have to pay premiums for ten or so years. Many of those clients were told that the cash build up would be tremendous and that not only would the client not have to pay premiums, but they would also be able to take tremendous income tax-free loans from their life policies when in retirement.

Now agents may be in the uncomfortable position of telling their clients that they will have to pay premiums for an additional 10 years or more, and that their life company will not even let them run life insurance illustrations that exceed 8%.

**Our recommendation:** With the equity indexed universal life policy, we see no good application for anyone to own a variable policy. What if you currently have a variable policy? What can you do and what should you do? Our suggestion is simple. Unless you have massive surrender charges, we suggest *exchanging your variable policy* for an indexed universal life or traditional whole life policy. This can be done tax-free. It is called a 1035 exchange. Call us to find out if you are an eligible candidate.

**Private Placement Life Insurance:** This is a subset of variable universal life. The truly well off, may have their funds invested by a designated fund manager rather than the limited selection provided by the carrier. The benefits are the tax advantages, and the flexibility of the investment choices. It is the tax-advantaged investment that is most attractive. This must be offset by the cost of the insurance—that is NOT fixed. Thus, the major risk is that the costs may go up if the investments do not perform well. More later.

Private Placement Life Insurance: Private Placement Life Insurance is a subset of variable universal life, and may prove to be a valuable tool to those who are well off. For more information on this interesting topic, please see ***Chapter 4, Section 8: Private Placement Life Insurance.***

**High Cash Value-Low Death Benefit Permanent Life Insurance As "Safe Investment Alternative":** The National Association of Insurance Commissioners does not like calling insurance premiums an investment or any other euphemism. The NAIC prefers we call it what it is. How you utilize the cash value is to maximum benefit is different with each type of policy. You may enjoy the cash value for major capital purchases through the Private Capital Reserve Strategy, and you may enjoy it for retirement income.

## Life insurance policy loans (also known as "Tax-Free" Retirement Income)

When you build a non-MEC high cash value, low death benefit life policy, you should expect a reasonable rate of return that benefits you through first removing your "basis" or the amount of premium you put in after tax, so it comes to you tax-free, and then through policy loans that can be taken *against* the policy income tax-free. In order to understand why life insurance can be such a powerful and tax favorable wealth building tool, you first should understand how policy loans work.

You will pay NO income tax if you borrow cash value against a life insurance policy, assuming the policy stays in place until your death and was not purchased with deductible dollars. This is sometimes confusing for the insured. Often you will hear advisors talk about receiving "tax-free" income from a life insurance policy.

That's not technically accurate, as you now know. You do not receive "income" from your life insurance policy; instead you receive the cash via loans. Generally, loans are treated as debts, not taxable distributions. This can give you virtually unlimited access to your cash value on a tax-advantaged basis.

Also, <u>these loans need not be repaid</u>. After a sizable amount of cash value has built up in a policy, it can be borrowed systematically to help supplement your retirement income. In most cases, you will never pay one cent of income tax on the gain. The main circumstance you will need to guard against is taking too much cash out of your policy through loans.

If you do that, you will run the risk of the policy not having enough cash left in it to pay the premiums for you until death. Typically, cash value policies are funded over a specific period of time, 5-7-10-20 years. If the policy is "over funded" at the "minimum" death benefit, significant cash should grow in your policy.

After your premium payment period, there is still an annual cost of insurance that is owed in the life policy. This cost is paid for from the cash value of the policy. When an insured borrows cash from a life insurance policy, the policy must stay in place until death to avoid the taxation of a MEC.

**More on life insurance policy loans:**

If you have $2,000,000 worth of cash surrender value (CSV) in a life insurance policy, you could request from the insurance company, a "tax-free" loan from the policy. Assume that the loan is for $100,000. The insurance company will charge interest to the policy on the borrowed money.

If the loan rate is 4% on the borrowed funds, then the insured's policy will be charged 4% interest on the loan. Currently, many whole life companies credit 6%. This means your policy is unlikely to "max out".

If you borrow too much cash from the policy, and the cash value regresses for too long, it is possible that the policy will lapse. That is why many of the higher quality carriers have a free "rider" that prevents you from ever failing the MEC rules. Check to see yours does. If not, please contact me to see how we may help.

**Example:**

You have a lifestyle that requires $500,000 per year. You wish to enjoy this at retirement with the lowest possible tax consequence. You are 45 now and wish to retire in 15 years. Your current income permits you to save $600,000 after tax. Your current investments amount to $8 million. You purchase a 7-year pay life policy with a $550,000 per year premium. Age 60 you take out of that policy first the basis then through loans *$450,000 per year for at least the next 25 years—completely income tax-free.*

Your investment account brings in the remaining amount at long-term capital gains rates of only 15%. Not 20%, because your taxable **income**

**is below the threshold that increases the tax rate**. No 3.8% Medicare surcharge because you are below the threshold. No Social Security payments are taxed because you are below the threshold.

**Our Recommendation:** Unless you just don't want to take advantage of the tax code to your benefit, nor want the access to the tax-free cash value in your life policy, we recommend a term or universal policy for your life insurance to provide only a death benefit.

If you want to access and optimize your cash position, and have the cash flow to create the most efficient contract to take advantage of the tax provisions, permanent high cash value life insurance will usually be significantly less expensive than the traditional method of purchasing term life policies—the way it benefits the carrier and the agents at your expense. **You cannot have proper planning in many cases without proper life insurance products that are properly funded.**

**Use a "fiduciary" for your insurance:** It is a good idea to work with an *independent agent* who works with many different life insurance companies. This will give you access to several different policies, and enable you to contrast and compare the policies before you choose the best one. And preferably one who is also a Series 65 registered investment adviser representative, who will be held to the highest "fiduciary" standard of *only advising you to buy what is in your best interest,* not what is just "suitable".

Many agents, due to binding exclusive contracts, are only able to work with one insurance company. These agents are known as "captive agents" (*not* to be confused with Captive Insurance Companies!). Independent agents are able to offer more than one company.

We confidently state that a significant portion of the life insurance in force has been incorrectly placed, improperly constructed, and inadequately funded.

By this, we mean the client was sold an inappropriate policy for their needs, too much or too little death benefit, and, worst of all, we can demonstrate to the client that you may have paid far too much for your current policy.

People continue to live longer lives, and, taking into account inflation, insurance costs are the lowest they have ever been. If you have not looked at your life insurance policy recently, we suggest that you have it re-examined by an independent insurance agent that you trust. If you did not purchase your policy from a company that specializes in life insurance, there is a good chance that you are over paying your premiums.

If you would like a free analysis of your life insurance policy to determine if you have a policy that is appropriate for your needs, and to make sure you are paying the lowest possible premium, please feel free to contact the author for a FREE analysis.

## Section 5: *Irrevocable Life Insurance Trusts (ILIT)*

This brings us to the question of ownership of your life insurance policy. ILITs are a much-underutilized tool in the estate-planning arena. Few clients will have an ILIT, mostly because few clients believe they will have a taxable estate. That could be a mistake. ILITS are irrevocable. That makes them less attractive for many. However, they could prove highly valuable for asset protection, value protection, and tax protection.

Many estates are not sufficiently liquid. There could be a closely held business. There could be real estate. Or art. Or any number of other non-liquid assets. Thus the beneficiaries needing liquidity upon the death of the estate grantor may be forced into a fire sale for certain assets.

*Caution:* ILITs often make it impossible for you, the "grantor" to gain access to any cash value. True there are Spousal Limited Access Trust ("SLAT") provisions, which may permit your spouse to get at the cash. These contain their own set of risks. So we mostly recommend using term or GUL/SGUL in these.

**How much should I have?** Do you have enough? For clients overall, the majority have too little life insurance. When you are young you need life insurance to protect your family just in case you die young. And there may be the need for the taxable estate to cover estate taxes. But too many overlook the need for *liquidity* for the estates in between.

For the young client: Do you have enough life insurance so that if you die in the near future, what you want to happen will happen—guaranteed? So that your spouse does not have to go back to work? Have you guaranteed that what you want to happen to your family if you die, actually will happen?

Unfortunately most do not have enough or the correct life insurance to guaranty their wishes. While you may have little concern, your loved ones you leave behind may care greatly. Most clients intend to take care of their families as if they had not died.

That is usually not possible with less than $2,000,000 worth of insurance. And you cannot get rich on life insurance. You must have enough income or assets to warrant the death benefit. Most carriers will not write more than 20 times annual salary. So if you earn $200,000 the maximum life insurance you may be eligible for is $4 million.

So what is the right amount of insurance for you? We believe you should have as much permanent life insurance as the carrier will allow, and that you can afford to pay over a 7-10 year period. If you cannot afford that much cash flow, we would supplement the death benefit with Convertible Term. This avoids the later potential health issues that could make you uninsurable. Properly constructed, life insurance is a "want" product, not the "need" product too often sold.

For older clients, you too may be underinsured. Many high-net-worth clients over the age of 50 may have (future) estate tax or liquidity problems. (Or you may be under-estimating the future health care costs the affluent are likely to face. That extra death benefit may come in handy to help preserve your estate.)

You can either 1) gift assets away; 2) have your heirs pay 50% estate taxes on the assets above $11,000,000 in your estate, assuming you were married and properly used your A&B Marital Trusts and "portability" to minimize estate taxes; or 3) you can purchase life insurance to pay for that liquidity and those estate taxes. If your estate will exceed $11,000,000, we can readily justify $3 million of death benefit for estate planning tax mitigation.

More close to home for many "middle class millionaires" over the age of 50 whose estate is between $2-20 million, the concern is to be certain you will not run out of money to maintain your lifestyle before you run out of life. Life insurance often gives you "permission" to increase withdrawals for retirement income from other accounts, knowing you will leave something behind through the policy.

Another concern could be the potential for long-term care costs and health care cost escalation. Long-term care now costs in excess of $75,000 per year in most cases. This amount is predicted by some to increase at a rate that exceeds inflation, sometimes by as much as 7-9% per year, as has happened for college expenses. Many permanent life insurance policies allow for tax-free early withdrawals of half the death benefit to cover those expenses. That can lead to some peace of mind.

**Income tax free death benefit:** As you probably know, life insurance death benefits pass to beneficiaries Income Tax Free. That is one of the reasons that life insurance is so great. Also be aware of the fact that any death benefit can pass to your spouse income- and estate tax free. Unfortunately, unless you plan on giving the entire death benefit to the spouse, you will have to pay estate taxes on your death benefit, unless the life insurance policy is owned by an irrevocable life insurance trust (ILIT).

**Estate tax-free death benefit:** Death benefits will pass to your spouse income-and-estate-tax free. That is why many people believe that they have no need for an ILIT. But you should ask yourself, what would happen if your spouse died the day after you, or the next year, or within six years.

That is where being well prepared will pay off. We inform our clients the difficulty of passing on the entire death benefit, and typically the client will agree that they are underinsured. The surviving spouse will probably not be able to spend down the estate before they pass away, and the life insurance benefit that passed to the living spouse will be heavily eroded by estate taxes.

**The Con:** The "grantor" may not directly access any cash value build up in an ILIT. The alternative could be an LLC. Or any of several other structures.

**Conclusion:** If you are a young client with a smaller estate, an ILIT may not be appropriate for you. If you have, or are likely to create an estate of more than $11,000,000, and up, which includes any life insurance, then we strongly suggest that you consider an ILIT. If you are 45 years or older with a large estate, and you think you have enough life insurance, double check. Remember that 50% of the life insurance death benefit proceeds that you were counting on could go to the government via estate taxes.

### Section 6: *Leveraged Life (sometimes called "Premium Finance")*

It is in vogue right now (with interest so low) and being pushed by many financial planners. Leveraged life, according to some, is a way to get a "free" death benefit for your heirs. Basically, you borrow money to pay for life insurance premiums. The hope is that there will be enough cash in the policy throughout its life to pay for the interest internally in the life policy until the client dies; this is so you don't have to dip into your personal assets to pay the interest owed on the borrowed funds.

**The Problem:** You are age 70 and divorced or widowed, have a $23-million estate made up of $19 million of real estate and $4 million in stocks. You know you have a huge estate tax problem; but since you retired last year, you also have a limited maximum income of $800,000 a year pre-tax, which comes from real estate rentals, and dividend income on the stock, to maintain your lifestyle and gifting.

The estate taxes, with current planning, are 45% on $13 million, or $5.8 million. You would like to pass all the properties to your children; but in order to do that, you need to buy $5.8 million in life insurance and put that into an Irrevocable Life Insurance Trust (ILIT). The premium on $5.8 million for a 70-year old is in about of $400,000 a year, which would have to be paid after tax.

**The "Solution":** Since you do not have the liquid cash to pay for the premium on the $5.8 million death benefit, you can purchase "Leveraged Life," which *on paper* will cost you nothing. The marketers of leveraged life sell it as follows: XYZ Insurance Company will loan you money for the premium of the life insurance at $400,000 a year, for ten years, for a $5.8 million death benefit policy.

Interest on the loan will be very low, lower than you can get from a traditional bank; let's assume a current rate of 5%. The interest on the loan the first year is $20,000. That amount escalates every year until the 10th year where it levels off. Total interest owed is $1.3 million—if the rates do not climb. That interest is actually paid from the accumulating cash value of the policy. The policy just works. What if the interest rates climb and climb rapidly and dramatically? And what about the principal that must be repaid? Now you could be in trouble.

**Conclusion:** Leveraged life can work fine if the *right client* uses the right company and understands that at some point down the road, there might be a "call" to pay interest and principal on premiums in the policy, because the cash value did not grow sufficiently to pay the interest internally. If a client over age 65 with a large estate wants to look at this topic as an estate-planning tool, we are fine with it as long as you are willing to take the potential risks associated with the financing. For the people who have very large estates, you can afford the risk, and this is often a terrific tool for death benefits exceeding $25 million.

## Section 7: *Life Settlements*

*Should You Consider Selling Your Life Insurance Policy?* For the person reading this—probably not. We wanted to make sure readers knew the concept exists, and we wanted to give you an overview. This topic is probably unhelpful for the younger reader, but may be of interest to the younger reader's parents or grandparents.

The concept behind a Life Settlement (hereinafter LS) is straight-forward. LSs are for the client who no longer needs the life insurance policy that they purchased, and would like to sell the policy for cash so they can use the proceeds for a more suitable purpose.

Buying and selling a life insurance policy has been around for some time, mainly in the form of a "viatical settlement." A viatical settlement is the purchase of a life insurance policy of a terminally ill person who is likely to die within two years.

**Summary:** While the topic of Life Settlements is not in the main stream, it is something to be aware of as yet another tool.

## Section 8: *Reverse Mortgages*

As with Life Settlements, you should be aware of this, even though the application is not likely for you. Reverse mortgages (RM) have become more popular in recent years, as more and more people age. While many advisors have heard of a reverse mortgage, few truly grasp how they work, or their effect on an individual client's retirement plans.

**What is a Reverse Mortgage?** A Reverse Mortgage is a special kind of loan that is easy to obtain if you are at least 62 years of age and own your own home, condo or co-op, with a maximum value of $600,000. A RM converts a portion of the equity of a home into instant cash. The pool of money that is created by a RM can be disbursed in a lump sum or as monthly income payments. And this money is usually income tax free.

One other key feature to a RM is that there are no income-, asset-, or credit- requirements to obtain the loan. That means a client who has poor credit, no income, and no other assets besides a home with equity, could obtain a RM to raise money for a variety of needs.

## Section 9: *Disability Insurance (DI)*

You have probably heard that the disability insurance (hereinafter, "DI") policies available today are drastically different from those available a few years ago. Although this is true, you can still find quality disability coverage if you know what to look for and understand how individual disability income insurance policies are offered. This is the most important and first insurance you should purchase. Because for many, *your most valuable asset is your ability to earn a living.*

**How policies are offered:** DI can be purchased on an individual or group basis. Group insurance is usually provided by an employer or purchased individually from a sponsoring professional association. **Although initially low in cost, group policies have several limitations.**

Group policies are able to be cancelled by the association or insurance company. The rates you are charged will increase as you get older, and premiums are subject to adjustments based on the claims' experience of the group. In addition, group and association contracts often contain restrictive definitions of disability as well as less generous contract provisions.

As a general statement, group policies many times are not worth the premiums paid. Most of the clients using group policies are those who cannot purchase affordable individual policies. Therefore, the premiums, with the limiting language of the contract, are typically not worth paying.

Most insurance companies used to issue **DI** coverage equal to approximately 60% of earned income. Unfortunately, due to adverse claims' experience, insurance companies have decreased the amount of individual coverage available to the insured no matter what they are currently earning. Typically the maximum monthly benefit is now $10,000. We have been able to find policies for our clients that pay several multiples of that amount -- for the right profession. And now, in Florida, the payments have been extended to age 70 from age 65.

### The cost of Disability Insurance

Several factors go into the pricing: your age, sex, health, monthly income benefit, how long the payments will last (a set term of 10 years, or until age 60, 65, or now in many states 70), how soon the payments begin (called "exclusion period") "riders," your occupational classification, and "own occupation" definitions (which *every* surgeon should have).

The younger you are when you purchase disability insurance, the less you will have to pay on a monthly basis. Overall, you may pay a similar total amount. For the middle-aged worker, you can safely assume the annual cost will approximately equal the monthly disability benefit. You will want to purchase a policy as early as possible in your career so that you may lock in lower rates.

The occupational classification assigned to you by the insurance company will have a significant affect on your premium rates as well as the policy provisions made available to you. For example, if you are a physician and perform invasive procedures, you will be placed in the "surgical" category; and the definition of disability made available will not only be more restrictive, the premiums charged will be higher as compared to a non-invasive, non-surgical physician.

### What to look for in a Disability Policy

One of the key features of an individual disability income insurance policy is a renewability provision. This provision spells out your rights as it relates to keeping your policy in force. In general, a disability policy can be Guaranteed Renewable only or both Non-Cancellable and Guaranteed Renewable.

If a policy is Guaranteed Renewable *only*, the insurance company is unable to cancel or change any provisions of the policy up to age 65 as long as you are up to date with your premiums. The insurance company, however, has the ability to increase premiums, with state approval for an entire class of policies in the event of poor claims' experience.

If a policy is *both* Non-Cancelable and Guaranteed Renewable, the insurance company cannot cancel, change any provisions, or increase the premiums for the duration of the policy, up to age 65; therefore, a policy that is *both* Non-Cancelable and Guaranteed Renewable is best because it offers you more protection.

One of the most important aspects of a disability policy is what is the definition of disability. This is especially true for highly skilled professionals who must pay careful attention to the definition of disability found in their policies. For example, if you do not have "own occupation" DI, you may still be eligible to flip burgers and thus not eligible for the claim.

There are three main definitions of "disability":

• Own Occupation" is clearly the definition of choice for most professionals because it has the most liberal definition of total disability available. This type of disability policy pays benefits if you "are not able to perform the <u>material and substantial duties of your occupation."</u>

Therefore, if you were a surgeon, you would collect full disability benefits if you could no longer perform surgery, even if you chose to work in another occupation or medical specialty earning as much or more than you did as a surgeon. We know a surgeon who went back for board certification training in pathology, and retained full DI disbursements in addition to the new professional compensation. **Ideally, you want to purchase a policy with the longest "Own Occupation" period available.**

*Important side note: Own Occupation policies refer to an occupation at the time of disability NOT at the time of purchase.*

- Modified "Own Occupation" – Today, this type of policy is the most popular. Own occupation will pay benefits if you are "unable to perform the substantial and material duties of your occupation" and you must not go back to being gainfully employed in any field. Although benefits are still contingent upon your inability to perform your normal job, this definition will not allow you to continue receiving disability benefits if you are working in another occupation; or for a physician, working in another medical specialty.

- "Any Occupation" - This definition, which is typically found in group or association policies, is the most restrictive definition. Under "any occupation", you will only receive benefits if you are "unable to work in any occupation which you are reasonably suited to by your education, training, or experience."

Unfortunately, the insurance company is the one who will determine whether you receive benefits or not, and many clients, surgeons being the best example, are well educated and -trained and will find it extremely difficult to collect benefits from this type of policy because they will usually be able to find employment elsewhere.

**Hybrid definitions**: Many policies offered to clients today might incorporate an "Own Occupation" with a Modified "Own Occupation" definition. Here, the policy would contain a true "Own Occupation" definition for a limited time period, typically one, two, or five years, and then convert to the more restrictive Modified "Own Occupation" definition previously described.

Although the hybrid definition is not as liberal as a policy with a true "Own Occupation" for the same claim, it is your decision to either continue collecting disability benefits or return to work in another occupation or specialty.

Just because you are physically able to work in another occupation or specialty, does not mean that you will not continue to receive disability benefits. In order for you to have your benefits reduced or eliminated, you would actually have to begin working in another occupation.

**Business Overhead Expense Disability Insurance:** *Protecting Your Business As Well As Yourself*

Most clients do not carry Business Overhead Expense insurance (BOE). The main reason is that they cannot see the value and are too frugal to buy a product they do not understand and do not think they will need in the future. If you are a business owner and are responsible for some or all of the monthly expenses needed to operate your business, you should consider purchasing a BOE policy in addition to a personal disability policy.

A BOE policy provides reimbursement for the expenses of operating your business in the event that you are unable to work due to illness or injury. Usually costs and reimbursements are for a limited time, typically to one year. Some of these cover employee salaries, rent, utilities, certain insurance premiums, and other fixed costs normal to the operation of your business.

The benefit can be sizable, and business partners should not expect the other partners to pick up their pro-rata share of expenses in the event of a disability. The disabled partner will have to dip into his own pocket to pay for these expenses until such time as they are no longer disabled or have their interest in the company purchased.

BOE insurance is fairly inexpensive and is a type of insurance that is a tax write-off due to the fact that the benefit when received will be used to pay for deductible office expenses. No asset protection plan can be complete unless a client has the proper amount and type of disability insurance. We own the maximum the carrier would permit us to purchase.

## Section 10: *Divorce Protection*

*Non-marital property* is what we will address here. True marital property is not likely to ever be protected from divorce. Nor should it, from a moral and policy position. Unfortunately, the story is often more complicated.

Many of you know a friend or relative who was the recipient of an inheritance only to experience the horror of losing half of it to an ex-spouse in a divorce? It happens more than you would think. Imagine the scenario where you are married and your last living parent passes away leaving you with $2,000,000 in real estate and stocks.

You put the money in your "marital bank account" or put the real estate in your and your spouse's name and then go on with life as normal. Then one year later your spouse decides to divorce you. What is the departing spouse entitled to? It depends on the state; but if you have been married for more than 10 years, the chances are significant that your spouse is going to get *half of everything* you inherited from your last remaining parent.

**How do you protect inherited assets in a Divorce?** Unfortunately, there is very little you can do. Even a **prenuptial** agreement may not help. So the planning needs to come from your parents. Typically, parents will leave a fairly liquid estate, usually in the form of a death benefit from a life policy. Real estate and personal belongings are also given, but many times the estate is made up of a nice size life insurance policy.

Either way, the way to protect one's self from losing inherited assets in a divorce is through the use of an irrevocable trust (or an LLC). Your parents create an irrevocable trust so that, when they die, the assets are all poured into it. While you may be the ultimate beneficiary of that trust, during most of your life, the language trust will allow the trustee to disburse some proceeds for many different purposes on your behalf.

**Prenuptial Agreement:** Many clients with significant wealth will use a prenuptial agreement to dictate exactly what each spouse is entitled to in the event of a divorce. Most of the time prenuptial agreements are used in second marriage situations where one spouse has already amassed a significant estate and the other spouse has almost no estate.

The spouse with significant wealth going into the second marriage typically desires to preserve the majority of the estate for his children from a prior marriage, and a prenuptial agreement is a nice way to accomplish that goal. Prenuptial agreements are not an easy topic to discuss with a potential spouse; and because of the touchy nature of the subject, many times wealthy clients who really should have prenuptials do not.

Hindsight is always 20/20; and if you are concerned that your spouse will be awarded more than what you think is fair in a divorce matter, then you should seriously think about a prenuptial agreement *prior to marriage.*

If you are currently married and wish you had a prenuptial agreement, you can see if your spouse will sign a *postnuptial* agreement, which may work the same as a prenuptial agreement. And make sure your spouse or spouse-to-be has engaged legal counsel and representation to avoid claims of coercion or fraud in the inducement.

**Debt Shields on Assets:** If you have already been through a divorce, you know how terrible it can be. To protect accumulated assets, but not to take away from your spouse's property, you may be able to systematically gift and invest in entities owned by other family members, and then "loan" those back to yourself as needed.

**Other Divorce Protection:** This often may be in the form of Trusts, LLCs, or FLPs in which the documents clearly define how the proceeds shall be managed and distributed (or not distributed) in the case of divorce, or any other life-changing event. Every state has different rules. Check with a divorce attorney in your state. For example, a trust or LLC or FLP may have the "HEMS" clause. *HEMS* stands for health, education, maintenance, and support. This could leave an asset intact while providing for the necessary compliance of a divorce decree.

And for further assurance that non-marital property be preserved, be certain there are true business needs for, and multiple non-related parties involved in, the entities. Otherwise, you may be at risk for "fraudulent conveyance" or "civil concealment."

In addition, you may be able to utilize a "poison pill" or "spendthrift" provision, or "buy-sell" agreement built into these entities. A *poison pill* provision may require a large capital infusion to access cash flow or to enact ownership changes, or it may prohibit ownership changes without massive devaluation and dissolution. This benefits no one. Be cautious of a spiteful counterparty (and especially the legal adversary) who may take pleasure in a scorched earth approach. A *spendthrift* provision prohibits any "beneficiary" from exhausting the assets of the entity. A *buy-sell* helps the "owners" to have a predetermined price and terms when there is disagreement as to how to manage the assets and the cash flow, limiting the financial pain of the divorce.

### Section 11: *Generation Skipping Tax*

The Generation Skipping Tax (GST) is not a huge issue for most estate plans because most of the time the majority of the assets in an estate will pass not directly to the grandchildren but instead to the children who, in turn, down the road might pass wealth to the grandchildren. However, if your estate is large enough, using a Generation Skip to pass wealth could save your grandchildren millions of dollars in estate taxes.

The IRS wants assets to flow through as many estates as possible to collect revenue in the form of estate taxes, and so the system is set up to have assets pass to children, where it will be estate taxed, and then to grandchildren where assets will again be estate taxed. If assets were allowed to go directly to the grandchildren, then a whole level of estate taxes would be skipped and the government could lose literally millions of dollars in estate tax just from one client's estate.

If you tried to pass wealth directly to your grandchildren at death without the use of your GST exemption, the transfer would be double taxed both at the estate tax rate and then at the flat GST rate of 45%.

**GST Exemptions:** The exemption rates thresholds vary almost every year. If you gift less than the amounts per spouse allowed at the time of death, you will avoid the double tax hit on the GST.

**Why use a Generation Skip?** The main reason you would use a generation skip and, therefore, the GST exemption, is that you know, when your children die, they will have an estate tax problem. If that is the case, by using the GST exemption, you will avoid having your wealth double estate taxed- first at your death, and then again at your children's death.

### Section 12: *Charitable Gift Planning*

Many clients give because are charitable. For many who are not so inclined, charitable gift planning still could be very important. Most clients do not realize that charitable giving can be client-focused instead of charity focused:

### Benefits of charitable planning:

1. Increases a client's discretionary or "spendable," income;
2. Reduces or eliminate a client's income taxes, capital gains taxes, and estate taxes;
3. Secures a tax free inheritance for a client's chosen heirs; and,
4. Allows a client to leave a lasting family and social legacy, and feel good doing it.

If we told you that we could show you a tax and estate plan with the previous benefits, most would not think we were talking about charitable planning.

**There also are downsides of charitable gifting**: Your gifting purpose may get perverted; you may create a self-serving and self–sustaining administrative corps of employees; your organization may engage in "mission creep"; your gift may create an entitlement mentality in the beneficiaries; your gift may only be subsidizing those who very well could afford what the charity provides; your charitable gifting may actually harm the very people you hope to benefit; too much of your gift may get diverted to non-core activities; and so many more.

There are basic categories of charitable gifts:
• Religious
• Educational
• Social Services
• Health Care
• The Arts (and the arts include museums, symphonies, ballets, and opera companies).

For more on this important estate-planning concept, see *Chapter 3: Income Tax Reduction Strategies: Introduction and Traditional Solutions*

**Section 13:** *Long Term Care Insurance*

*Why Most Clients Should Have It:* Or something like it. Long term care insurance (LTCI) is the most frustrating estate planning topic we instruct on and discuss with clients. In our opinion, LTC coverage is an absolute must in every estate plan of clients with an estate size of over $500,000 and under $20 million; but yet few clients want to purchase it. And fewer carriers are still in the business. The six largest carriers have discontinued selling it. Evidently, the actuaries mispriced them to the point of un-profitability.

**Who is a Candidate for LTCI?** The United Seniors Health Cooperative says you should buy the insurance only if you meet these guidelines, which we completely agree with:

- You have more than $75,000 in assets per person in the household.
- Your annual income is $30,000 or more per person in the household.
- You can afford the premiums without making a lifestyle change.
- You could still afford the premiums even if they increase by 20% to 30% in the future.

**Why do those who are candidates for LTCI need it?** In one simple word, the answer is protection. We suggest that clients purchase LTCI to protect their wealth from the devastating and potentially long lasting costs of long term care. In some areas of the country, the cost of nursing home care or quality around-the-clock in-home care may be $750 per day. And that number is likely to climb. It is a simple matter of supply and demand. There are 10,000 Americans turning 65 every day. One in 8 are likely to need long-term care. With a cohort of some 70 million people over age 70, if only one in 20 need care, the demand will easily outstrip the supply. Then prices must rise.

Additionally, the U.S. Health Care Administration reports that costs are increasing 5.8% per year and are expected to more than triple in the next 20 years. Clients purchase LTCI to protect their wealth not only for their spouse but also for their children. If you do not care about protecting your wealth from devastating long term care costs, then you do not need LTCI.

Not to mention that over 17 states now have "filial liability" laws that allows them to collect from the children of Medicaid nursing home patients. So if you have a parent in Michigan who has benefited from long term care at state expense, and you live in Pennsylvania, watch out.

**Will you need LTCI?** While only a fraction of all long term care is provided in nursing homes, recent studies indicate that 40% of Americans over the age of 65 will need nursing home care at some point during their lives, and 10% will stay in a nursing home for five years or more. Looking at it another way, about 54% of women and 30% of men will spend some time in a nursing home.

Since the majority of clients who call for asset protection or income tax reduction help are males, 50% of those who call and do not take our advice on the purchase of LTCI will actually need long-term care sometime in their lifetime. True, these are average statistics, and may not represent those of us reading this book; nevertheless, the risk is real.

**Why don't High Income or High Net Worth Clients Purchase LTCI?** This may come as a shock to those reading the book; but, as a general rule, people with money are a bit on the frugal side. After all, isn't that part of how you amassed your wealth? We would not be surprised to discover that a good percentage of those of you who purchased this book had to pause before spending whatever you paid for it, because you did not want to waste money on a book you were not sure would be beneficial.

Few of us like the "use it or lose it" factor. And who among us wishes to use it? It is an expense, plain and simple. The price continues to climb, especially for those of us who might wish a high level of service and facility. And it is difficult to find as carriers continue to exit the market. We probably have covered all the objections to LTCI. So what else is there?

**Alternatives to "Losing" Your Premiums for LTCI:** There are new non-LTCI alternatives that work like this. For example, you today deposit a $150,000 premium into an alternative insurance product specifically designed for this use. It may buy you $400,000 of long-term care benefits. If you never use them, your heirs will receive the premium deposited at a minimum. And we can help you set this up in a tax-deductible vehicle.

Also, if you have a sufficiently new (since the Pension Protection Act of 2006) permanent life insurance (PLI), you may be able to access half of the death benefit for long term care needs, completely tax-free. Check to make sure you have the (usually free) rider that allows for it.

With the ability to pay for your LTC needs in a 100% tax-deductible manner, and with the assurance that every dollar you paid in premiums will go to your heirs, income tax-free, most clients who can afford it should exchange their PLI for a newer one with the rider for coverage.

In yet another example, many Fixed Indexed Annuities (FIAs) will **guarantee your monthly payments increase by 50%, 100%, or even 200%** to cover long term care costs for up to 5 years.

A major attraction with FIAs and PLIs as source of funds for long-term care is that your premiums are never "wasted" as they often are in a LTCI policy. And for many of these FIA and PLI contracts, you will not have to become "institutionalized." Though these are best bought with after tax dollars, the benefits can be tremendous. To learn more, and whether you should consider these alternatives, contact the author.

**Conclusion:** We recommend some form of LTCI in almost every estate plan.

**Section 14:** *IRA Protection*

*Controlling Your IRA from the Grave: Protect IRA assets from your children's poor decisions*

More and more wealth over the coming years will transfer between generations as our population ages. Those that know say there will be more wealth transferred from one generation to the next over the next 20 years than in any time in our country's history. Much of the assets transferred will be IRA money.

Many readers of this book will pass IRAs with balances over $100,000 to their children, and many readers will have balances of $1M+. So what's the big deal? You know your children better than we do, but what do you think your children will do with $100,000 - $1,000,000+ cash in an IRA after you are gone?

We hope "your" children will continue to invest the money wisely and use it in their retirement. What many of you should fear is the reality that your children will do things with that money that you would not approve of or would make you roll over in your grave. But don't worry about it, just because it took you 30+ years to accumulate the money, shouldn't your children have the right to burn through that money in a weekend in Vegas?

If your children do not blow it all at once, maybe they will slowly burn through it over a several year period by taking trips around the world, buying expensive cars, throwing lavish parties and otherwise, living well above their normal standard of living. Heck, why would they want to use that money for the grandkid's education when they can buy a new Ferrari to drive around in or sip martinis on a yacht in the Mediterranean?

What if you had the ability to control your IRA assets from the grave, would you? But how can you control IRA assets from the grave? By using a simple Limited Liability Company (LLC), you can. While you may not be aware of this, an IRA can invest in all sorts of interesting assets including an interest in an LLC. There are complicated *prohibited transaction* rules. Check with a specialty IRA custodian, such as my friend Glen Mather's "NuView IRA".

You do need to know, however, that there is a specific way an IRA needs to buy the LLC interest. Once the money is funded into the LLC, the manager of the LLC will control what happens to the LLC assets, not the IRA owner. In fact, the IRA owner cannot be the manager of the LLC.

When you think about it, it makes sense, doesn't it? You may be saying to yourself, this doesn't prohibit my son or daughter in the above example from distributing the IRA and getting the money, does it? It does. When the IRA distributes assets, what is it distributing? It is distributing the LLC interest.

An IRA distribution DOES NOT remove the money from the LLC. So your son or daughter in the above example now has ownership of the LLC interest, yet the manager of the LLC still controls the money, including distributions to pay estate and income taxes. If the LLC manager has enough discretion in the LLC operating agreement, the manager does not have to take money out of the LLC for any reason he does not feel is appropriate.

What's not appropriate? The list is long and would probably include a week long bender to Vegas, a Ferrari, a new 60 foot speed boat, diamonds for a part time girlfriend, and so on. Hopefully you are getting the drift.

The LLC structure acts similarly to an irrevocable trust (IT) after a client dies. You are probably familiar with how ITs are used to make sure children spend inherited money wisely. The LLC structure with an IRA basically does the same thing. A client will setup this structure inside their IRA and have a trusted person or institution act as the managing member of the LLC.

Direction will be given to the manager of the LLC through a well-written operating agreement. The manager, not the child or heir, controls the money in the LLC. In addition there is the more simple stretch IRA. It can last until your grandchildren die. You can arrange for a distribution to be made to them on your birthday. They will remember you fondly. Your accountant can check out <u>IRS Publication 590</u> [http://www.irs.gov/pub/irs-pdf/p590.pdf], or we can help you set this up.

**Section 15: *Family Limited Liability Companies (FLLCs); Family Limited Partnerships (FLPs) and Limited Liability Companies (LLCs) Lower Estate Taxes by Using FLLCs, FLPs and LLCs***

It is sad how few clients who may benefit from FLPs, LLCs, and FLLCs actually have them. For purposes of this section, we will use FLP as an interchangeable acronym for Family Limited Partnerships and Limited

Liability Companies. FLPs are not a primary estate-planning tool, but FLPs can nicely supplement an estate plan and have the possibility of saving your heirs millions of dollars if properly implemented.

**Lifetime Gifting:** As you are probably aware by now, parents currently can gift to their children approximately $14,000 per spouse per child each year without incurring gift tax. Many clients choose not to utilize gifting, because they know that once money or property is gifted it cannot be taken back. A parent does have some discretion as to how the gift is used if the money is placed in an irrevocable trust.

What type of client ideally would use gifting to reduce estate taxes? Individuals or couples with $11,000,000 estates or over. That is about 8% of all wealthy clients over the age of 60. If you die in 2015 with less than this amount, then you will avoid all estate taxes. A properly constructed FLP permits you to enjoy substantial discounts the IRS recognizes such as limited "marketability" and control, resulting in an acceleration of you gifting

**How Does an FLP Work?** An FLP is a limited partnership whose members are all family. An FLP is similar to a corporation, except that the FLP usually owns family assets like a house or vacation home or brokerage account. A client who is concerned with asset protection and estate taxes could benefit from a FLP, and then "capitalize" the FLP by contributing cash or an asset or multiple assets.

Typically this may mean a piece of real property; although a brokerage account sometimes can get discounts up to 20% of their value. Eventually the children will end up owning the majority of an asset they would receive anyway when the parents die through gifting of the interest in the FLP and through discounting of the stock.

We arranged ours early on, with no discounting. We had nothing to discount yet. We gifted "seed capital" to our young sons' irrevocable trusts, which were the 98% "owners" of the FLP. This FLP then invested that seed capital into an affiliated and closely held business that generated much value. That asset is now permanently out of our estate. All the while, we are the general partners and control the assets and the cash flow, and we have HEMS provisions for us. And we also have in place a buy-sell agreement for when we are gone.

**General vs. Limited Partner Interest:** Usually an FLP is formed by an older generation family member who contributes some assets to the FLP in return for General Partnership units and Limited Partnership units. Usually, the general partners have a 1% interest in the FLP and limited partners have a 99% interest. The parents are then able to gift Limited Partnership units to their children and grandchildren or their trusts, while retaining the General Partnership units that control the FLP. General partners will **retain control** over the assets in the FLP, whereas limited partners do not have any meaningful control over the assets.

**Discounting of the Assets in a FLP** – For many, the concept of using a FLP merely for discounting the interests, though enticing, could be a mistake. While many times you might enjoy asset discounts from 20% to 40% of their normal market value (except when using a **"Freeze" Partnership** which can obtain upwards of a _90% discounts_), we would caution you to avoid excess. After all, the purpose of any entity must be above and beyond tax reduction scheming for the IRS to consider its legitimacy.

FLPs have three legitimate discounts available:

• The first discount is because the limited interest in the partnership is no longer marketable in the open market – it can only be available to an exclusively defined person (the "limiteds").
• The second discount is a result of a "minority interest" owned by the children or their trusts—the , meaning that the limiteds have no voting right.
• The third discount comes from limiteds' lack of direct management control.

**Multiplying the Discounts:** *How to Receive a 90% Discount on an FLP*

*"Freeze Partnerships":* An Interesting Planning Opportunity

The concept of a "Freeze Partnership" is again receiving attention as an alternative to the traditional FLP structure. A "Freeze Partnership" has two classes of interests: a preferred interest and a common interest. This could get complicated. I hope your eyes don't get that glazed look in them. Here goes.

The preferred interest is typically a limited partnership interest, but could be the general partnership interest in very rare circumstances. The preferred interest is considered "preferred" because it is entitled to preferred dissolution rights. The preferred interest holder has a fixed dissolution value based on the value of the property initially contributed to the partnership.

There are typically preferred income rights as well, which means the preferred interest holder is entitled to receive preferred distributions of net cash flow from the partnership equal to a set percentage of the value of the dissolution value. As a practical matter, preferred interests operate very similarly to preferred stock in a corporation.

The "common" interests in the partnership are subordinate to the preferred interests with regard to dissolution and income rights, but the common interest holders tend to have voting and managerial control over the partnership. The common interest holders will share proportionately in the partnership's income distributions but only to the extent that the preferred interest holders have received the preferred income or dissolution payments.

*Example:* A Preferred Family Limited Partnership is formed in which $2,000,000 worth of assets is contributed to the partnership. In return for the contributions, the parents retain a preferred interest equal to a $1,000,000 dissolution value and a 10% preferred income distribution and the balance of the interests are common interests and are either sold or gifted away by the parents to their children or trusts for the benefit of their children.

In this case, the preferred interest (the parent) is entitled to the first $100,000 of distributable income. Once this $100,000 is distributed, the balance of the distributable income will be distributed to the common interest holders (the children) based on each partner's pro-rata ownership of the partnership.

If upon the death of the preferred interest holder the partnership is liquidated, the preferred interest holder's estate will include the full $1,000,000 liquidation value; but the balance of the assets and all the appreciation from the date of inception would be allocated and distributed to the common interest holders (the children).

The planning implications of using preferred family limited partnerships are: First, because the liquidation values of the preferred interests are "frozen," the common interests (the children) will receive all of the growth and appreciation of the assets held by the FLP. This allows for the possibility of a large wealth transfer to the common interest holder.

Because common interests are subordinate to preferred interests in most respects, especially with regard to cash flow, it is possible that the common interests would be subject to valuation discounts for gift or sale purposes. Thus, depending on the types of assets that the FLP is intended to own, there are substantial planning opportunities to use the preferred and common interest structure to provide significant wealth transfer planning benefits.

For example, suppose the assets held by the FLP are capable of producing more than the $100,000 of income as set forth in the above example. For demonstration, suppose that the assets held by the FLP produce $150,000 worth of income, thus leaving $50,000 of income remaining after the preferred distribution has been made.

Assuming that the FLP would make tax distributions to each of the common interest holders equal to the tax they owe on the $50,000 of income, the balance of the income not distributed could be used to purchase life insurance or other assets to increase the overall value of the FLP.

Thus, if a $1,000,000 life insurance policy could be purchased with the remaining cash in the FLP after the preferred and the tax distributions are made to the preferred and common interest holders, and the preferred interest holder died the next day, *all of the assets in excess of the frozen $1,000,000 liquidation value would be allocated to the common interests holders(the children)*.

Oftentimes, a Preferred Limited Partnership has multiple classes of interests, so the planning can be very creative. The ability to use the preferred and common interest FLP in connection with a family's overall wealth planning can present substantial planning opportunities. In the following schematics, keep in mind the following assumptions: The mother capitalized the FLP with $2,000,000 and her son capitalized on the FLP with $20,000.

The mother is issued a preferred interest representing 49.5% ownership and a non-preferred interest equaling the same 49.5% interest. The son has a 1% non-preferred interest but is the managing member of the FLP. Also assume that the FLP interests receive a 30% discount for the various restrictions put in place via the FLP documents.

**An Interesting Example for a $25 Million Estate**: Please assume there is no need for immediate income from the FLP; assume $10 million in liquid assets; assume client uninsurable; assume parent 70, child 45; assume desire for liquidity prior to death of parent.

Parent is preferred, non-managing limited partner; child is non-preferred general partner who controls the assets contributed. Each contributes. Child contributes $100,000. Parent contributes $10 million. Because they are related parties, parent's return can be limited to the long-term Applicable Federal Rate (AFR) at current rate of 2.74%.

FLP purchases 2 separate life insurance policies on the *child's life*. "Preferred" policy used to pay back parent for contribution at a simple interest rate. Remaining money purchases high cash value, low death benefit policy on child's life over 7 years for maximum efficiency and for future tax-free withdrawals. When child needs cash, policy "loans" are taken. No income tax due.

Child receives "special allocation" from FLP equal to policy loan amount. Upon death of child, preferred policy repays parent or parent's estate. No gift taxes. Parent transferred $10 million into FLP. $7.5 million into cash value policy ($1.1 million per year premium payment) for $16 million death benefit.

Remaining $2.5 million uses 5% or $125,000 per year to purchase the $10 million owed. Parent owns FLP units that only pays upon child's death. Child's life expectancy is 90. Therefore current value of FLP units to parent must be discounted dramatically. Even a small discount results in a significant decrease in parent's taxable estate.

Most attorneys who understand this strategy are comfortable with at least a 6%-14% discount. Therefore, if parent died in year one, the value of the FLP interest in parent's estate, using a 8% discount would be $3 million, not the $10,000,000 she capitalized the FLP with. This is because the FLP units are not liquid and will not payoff until the child dies.

The calculation needed is to find out the current value of a future interest and, when discounted, the number becomes very low. The reason typical 20-40% FLP discounts are **not** used is due to the fact that the mother's interest is "preferred" and, therefore, the value of her interest cannot be discounted to the same degree as FLP interests in a "traditional" FLP set up for estate planning purposes.

Even if mother dies in the near future or twenty years down the line, there will always be a sizable discount in the value of the FLP interest, due to the fact that the interest is always going to be discounted based on her son's projected life expectancy.

**Summary of the preferred non-manager/non-preferred manager FLP/LLC structure:** This structure is one of the most powerful, and little known, and therefore under-utilized estate planning techniques in the industry. It requires very little legal structure and manipulation. It is very flexible, depending on the needs of the clients, and can significantly reduce the size of a taxable estate and can also create a situation where a young heir can have access to income and gift-tax free loans from a life insurance policy years before a parent passes away.

**Conclusion on FLP Planning:** Besides the fact that all of a client's major assets should be in an LLC, FLP, or FLLC for *asset protection* purposes, if a client intends on passing wealth to his children upon death, the FLP is a terrific way to do so in a manner that can significantly lower the estate taxes the children will have to pay on the death of their parents.

**Section 16:** *Closely Held Insurance Companies (CIC)* *http://www.mysummitwealth.com/wp-content/uploads/2012/10/CIC-Monograph-Final-2.pdf*

**"ART" (Alternative Risk Transfer) for Business Owners:** Business is risky. Most business owners are self insuring much of the risk. By creating and owning your own insurance company, you can better manage the risks. And it is one of the most powerful asset protection tools. A properly setup CIC can transfer out of a client's estate, overnight, tax deductible dollars, without gift taxes and without estate taxes. CICs also happen to be very powerful income tax reduction or planning tools; to the extent there are limited number of claims—which you can control to a large degree. And they are commonly used.

**A CIC is a Small Business Insurance Company** (IRS Sec 831(b)) established to insure the risks of its parent company or a group of companies. In the simplest form, a CIC is an organized plan of self-insurance that operates just like the typical Insurance Company which calculates risk, issues policies, collects premiums, pays expenses, and establishes reserves to pay future claims.

**In short, a CIC is an excellent way to self-insure, and to establish a large capital pool for risks. Though each contract usually runs in 12-month stretches for premium payments, these CICs are best used when multi-year (we recommend 2-7 years) commitments are anticipated. If there is a bad year and premium payments stress the business, the premium may be "made up" in arrears. The premium is deductible. And in the event that no loss occurs (that is, no judgment or settlement is paid on the risk), the capital may be accessed, when properly structured, in a lump sum, or slowly over time at the owner's discretion, by the CIC owner tax-free (only the <u>growth of the capital</u> may be taxed), when structured properly.**

To the extent a CIC reduces net income (because of the *deductible* insurance expense under Rule 162), there is a subsequent and necessary *reduction of income taxation*. And to the extent that there are limited claims paid, the owner of a CIC should have substantial reserves available and accessible, and (though this should never be its primary purpose), thus may also enjoy substantial income tax reduction benefits.

If your CPA and your attorney are uncomfortable with a CIC, we will help educate them for you. We have a library of supporting articles from academia and the professions. And there is an entire "Captive" industry with its own association and monthly publication available for subscription.

One reason for their discomfort is that their clients who may benefit from one, represent such a small slice of their practice. They have not had the need to familiarize themselves with this tool. And, there may be the self-serving and self-preservation aspect: they may fear, the "why didn't you bring this to me before?" conversation. We can help them with this too.

For more on income tax reduction strategies continue to the next chapter.

**For more on this subject, see *Chapter 3: Section 10: Why Profitable Closely Held Businesses Should Consider a CIC***

# Chapter 3

# Income Tax Reduction Strategies:

## *Introduction and Traditional Solutions*

The preceding section on **CIC**s should be quite intriguing. It has the *secondary* beneficial effect of substantially reduced income taxation. (The primary use is to transfer your business risk). Do not let its obscurity frighten you away. It is simpler and more common than you think. And like almost every strategy discussed in this book, it is not for everyone (you must qualify: as a business owner, with sufficient gross revenues, and free net cash flow to fund the premium payments), and it requires attention to detail, and specialty professionals to develop and maintain it in compliance.

And, if the following comment from your CPA sounds familiar to you, then you are like most of the high-earning clients in America: *"Put money in your 401 (k)/Profit Sharing Plan and pay taxes on the rest. To take home more money, make more money."* We find that most CPA's are not proactive in saving their client's money on taxes.

Most CPAs simply process historical tax returns or consult on what is going on this year, and they are so overwhelmed that they do not make the effort to work on a true income tax reduction plan for the future. Again, we can help.

The traditional income "tax reduction" solutions are simple, and you have heard of every one of them. They are as follows: A **401(k) Plan** is a qualified retirement plan in which an employer permits an employee to defer receipt of part of his or her compensation by contributing that part to his or her account in the 401(k) Plan. <u>For more information on this topic see **CHAPTER 1: Section 5: *Qualified Retirement Plans (ERISA Department of Labor Governed Plans***</u>

401(k) plans are voluntary for an employee, and can be opted into by a prospective employee. Once enrolled, there will be an automatic payroll deduction for the employee. Many large companies choose to offer a match, as a benefit to the employee. We see a lot of companies matching 50 cents on the dollar up to 6% of pay, thereby capping any potential match at 3% of payroll. The maximum payroll deduction for 2015 is about $18,500 with a $5,500 catch up provision for those ages 50+.

The fallacy here is that you are postponing the tax owed, and the future tax rate. Many believe tax rates will be higher in the future. When asking tax professionals: "if a client put $100,000 into a qualified retirement plan, tax-deductible, and he is in the 30% bracket, how tax did he save?", frequently the response $30,000. That would be incorrect. We do not know what tax bracket, nor the tax rate of that bracket you will be in upon distribution.

A **Profit Sharing Plan** is a qualified retirement plan where the annual contribution limits are 25% of pay or about $52,000. A combined 401(k) Profit Sharing Plan allows an employee or owner to "max out" the pension plan contributions; although it can be very expensive for a business owner to max out because it may require a large amount of money to fund for the employees participating.

A **Money Purchase Plan** is a defined contribution plan. A Money Purchase Plan is one in which the employer is required to make an annual contribution to each employee's account regardless of how much money the company makes each year. Contributions are usually specified as a percentage of annual compensation and in 2007 were capped at the lesser of about $52,000 or 25% of an individual's annual salary.

A **"New Comparability" Plan** came about with the final 401(a) 4 regulations, in the Pension Protection Act of 2006, allowing defined contribution plans to be tested for discrimination based on benefits, just like a defined benefit plan. An allocation formula can be utilized that creates separate allocation levels. This formula is allowed by permitting "averaging" of projected benefits, similar to the old comparability rules, in a plan providing for two levels of allocations, one for the staff and one for the principals.

The basis of the testing is comparing what the contributions of the staff will grow to at retirement age, with what the contributions for the principals will grow to at retirement. The results are divided by the cost of an annuity and expressed as a benefit for testing purposes. This is an appropriate plan design in a situation where a small business wants to discriminate in favor of the highly paid participants.

It is our opinion that, if you are looking for a 401 (k) Profit Sharing Plan that is the most discriminating, one where the owners of the company have to contribute the least amount of money for their employees, you need to implement a New Comparability Plan.

A **Defined Benefit Plan** is the old-school qualified retirement plan that funds for a retirement benefit in the future for its employees based typically on years of employment, wages, and/or age. Defined Benefit Plans are funded solely by the employer and were in vogue 20-plus years ago when the rules on funding benefit plans were not nearly as stringent as they are today.

Due to a change in the law back in 2000, Defined Benefit Plans have become more in vogue again. Defined Benefit Plans calculate an amount owed at a future time. The Department of Labor does not care if your company doesn't have the funds to pay the future benefit when the time comes.

Legally, a company is obligated to pay the future benefit; and if the company does not have the money, it better go out and borrow the money to pay the benefit in order to stay out of trouble with the DOL. Because of this future funding requirement, Defined Benefit Plans are typically funded with guaranteed annuities.

Income Tax Deductible **IRAs** are not applicable for 99% of high-income clients who have some kind of qualified plan.

A **Simplified Employee Pension (SEP-IRA)** is a traditional IRA set up by an employer for a firm's employees. An employer may contribute up to $52,000 or 25% of an employee's compensation annually to each employee's IRA. SEP plans are usually set up in smaller companies where the owner is looking to provide something for the employees at the lowest cost, while still allowing the owner to contribute a decent amount of money.

If a person creates a SEP-IRA, he must also include all eligible employees. Eligible employees include anyone who earns more than $500 and has had any service in three of the past five years.

A **S̲avings I̲ncentive M̲atch P̲lan for E̲mployees' IRA (SIMPLE IRA)** is a "simplified" version of the Department of Labor-controlled, ERISA-derived 401(k) plan; and one that only pertains to employers with 100 or fewer employees. One of the best aspects of this plan is that nondiscrimination testing usually found with 401(k) plans does not apply. A SIMPLE is the plan of choice for many small employers due to some of its administrative aspects.

A SIMPLE plan also gives the employees the chance to postpone current income taxes (and the tax calculation of future withdrawals, which could be much higher in the future, so be careful) by reducing the amounts received in their paychecks. The employer, you, in general must match up to 3% of payroll, dollar for dollar.

Or you could consider **the Solo 401(k).** A Solo 401(k) allows a business owner with NO employees, except a spouse, to contribute to both a 401(k) and a profit sharing plan so the total contribution in

2007 could have been $52,000. And, unlike a SEP or SIMPLE or any other IRA-like non-qualified retirement vehicle, life insurance can be purchased in the Solo 401 (k), or any other 401(k) for that matter. However, it is difficult to imagine the scenarios where you would want to have the death benefit be subject to income taxes.

A Solo 401(k) can also include a loan provision where the owner/ employees may borrow up to half of the account balance from the Plan up to a maximum of $50,000, *which ever is lower.* This loan must be re-paid within 6 months to avoid penalties and tax. This added liquidity can be very important to a small business owner who has a bad year and needs cash. As the client essentially borrows money from the Solo 401(k), all the interest goes back into his account.

By contrast, a SEP or SIMPLE-IRA cannot offer this important feature. A retirement plan is unable to discriminate in favor of "highly compensated employees" in contributions or benefits. That does not mean that everyone will receive the same contribution. When designing a **"Next Level" profit sharing plan,** pension plan providers will often offer three tools that can be incorporated to best meet the company's goals and budget.

These include the following:

1. "Integration" with Social Security
2. Age-Weighting the Contribution
3. New Comparability Classification Plans

In **Integrated Profit Sharing Plans,** employers are already sponsoring at least one retirement plan that is funded jointly by the employers and employees. This is known as the *Old Age & Survivor Benefit* of Social Security. The government acknowledges this by allowing you to "integrate" your qualified retirement plan with your Social Security contributions.

The benefit of this approach is that it allows the employer to guide additional benefits to highly compensated employees while lowering them for lower paid workers. Under an Integrated Profit Sharing Plan, compensation is broken out into two parts-the amount above the integration level and the amount below the integration level.

The integration level typically is the Social Security Taxable Wage for the applicable year. The employer can offset their contribution to Social Security by giving less to the base compensation and more to the excess compensation.

A Profit Sharing Plan Integrated with Social Security is great for a company who wants to make greater contributions to highly compensated employees who are either younger or the same age as other employees in the company. The final regulations governing nondiscrimination introduced an old pension plan concept to profit sharing plans.

As you already know, the contribution cannot discriminate in either contributions *or* benefits. So, if you were to give everyone 20%, it would clearly be nondiscriminatory. Giving each the same theoretical retirement benefit though is also nondiscriminatory, as with a defined benefit plan. Why is **Age-Weighting** a profit sharing plan helpful?

For basic reasons: because older employees have fewer years until retirement, it is necessary that they have larger contributions than younger employees to receive the same benefit level. While the design chart shows that this is a favorable plan for the owner, in operation though, it can prove to be inconvenient.

Older persons will definitely receive higher contributions. Employees who have the same job title, and who are basically receiving the same wages, will get very different contributions unless they happen to share the same age. Because of these details, this plan tends to be less popular than the next option, **New Comparability.** We believe that this may be one of the most exciting options in pension plans, this "Next Level" design allows the administrator to allocate significantly greater contributions to specific classes of employees.

This plan combines both the integration and age-weighted rules, but uses weighted averages to determine the contribution. This plan is ideal for principals who:

- Are older and earn more than most of their employees;
- Want the biggest possible share of the plan contribution allocated to their own accounts; and,
- Desire the contribution flexibility of a profit sharing plan.

This type of plan goes by different names: "super-integrated," classification plan, group allocated plan, and, more commonly, "new comparability." Since the plan was finalized in the Code in 1993, it feels disingenuous to call the plan new; so we prefer to call it super comparability since it it is a very flexible plan that is capable of steering extra benefits to certain groups of employees.

The great thing about New Comparability is that it is highly customizable and is easy to match to a business. Groups can be created for different profit centers, subsidiaries, sister companies or, most commonly, by job class, any clearly identifiable group really. Some common examples include:

| | | |
|---|---|---|
| 1. Owners | 1. Sr. Partners | 1. Executives |
| 2. Non-Owners | 2. Ir. Partners | 2. Managers |
| 3. All Other Employees | 3. Employees of Subsidiary A | |
| 4. Employees of Subsidiary B | | |

Sponsors are able to get very creative when creating clearly identifiable classes that are appropriate for their business organization. It is important to note that when you are creating different classes, you do not have to give different contributions in any given year. In one year you could give each class zero, and then choose to give 25% of pay to everyone in the next.

You get to choose, as long as the contribution satisfies testing each year. The way it works is that the amount of contributions you give to the bottom group will determine the amount that you will give to the other groups. If, on average, your preferred groups are older than the bottom groups, albeit should be possible for you to leverage modest contributions to the rank and file employees into substantial contributions to the other groups.

A great new plan is the "New Comparability" Profit Sharing Plan. This plan enables the sponsor to target groups of employees for larger contributions while lowering cost for the rest of the employees while satisfying nondiscrimination testing.

What this means is that if the preferred employees are older than the average age of the non-preferred employees, the plan is able to divert a large amount of the benefits to the older group. A **Super-Charged Safe Harbor 401(k) plan** (SCSH) combines a "safe harbor" 401(k) plan with a new comparability profit sharing feature.

The results are often dramatic and compelling. Another goal is to keep the employee benefit cost reasonable or minimal, if possible. This SCSH 401(k) accomplishes these objectives by first awarding a flat 3% "safe harbor" to all eligible employees. This is the ONLY required employer contribution each year. By awarding this safe harbor, both the owner and the key employee may defer the maximum with Average Deferral Percentage (ADP) testing. By including a new comparability profit sharing feature, the owner can dramatically skew added benefits to himself and his key employee with discretion.

Thus, the safe harbor and the new comparability provision combine to offer a SCSH. A new retirement account was signed into law on August 17, 2006, within The Pension Protection Act. This is a common component of a typical 401(k) plan. The major difference is that funding of a **"Roth" 401(k) Plan** is with AFTER-TAX dollars.

While this design is similar to the Roth IRA, it has higher funding limits and no limit on earnings to contribute. With a Roth 401 (k) plan, the money contribute grows without tax and is distributed without tax.

Will you grow more wealth funding a Roth 401 (k) or will you grow more wealth in a traditional 401 (k)?

**The answer** is ... **it depends.** We know that you do not want such an indecisive answer, so we can safely say that most individuals would be better of using the Roth plan.

**Who should use a Roth 401(k)?**

- Individuals retiring in the same or a higher tax bracket.
- Individuals retiring in a tax bracket within 10% of their current tax bracket.

Say you are currently in the 40% tax bracket but will likely retire in the 30% tax bracket, using a Roth plan would be better for you than using a tax deferred retirement plan. We are going to illustrate for you the benefits of a Roth plan and when it is appropriate to use one. The following examples will show the economics of a Roth 401 (k) plan for an individual in the 40%, 30% and 15% tax brackets when both contributing to a Roth 401(k) and when removing money from it later in retirement.

We chose to use a Roth 401(k) plan in the example because we want to illustrate using a $100,000 contribution, which would be in excess of the contribution limit for a Roth and traditional IRA, but which we will use for simplicity. For this example, assume that you are a 45-year-old client contributing $100,000 to a Roth 401 (k) plan each year for 20 years and that you will be taking distributions from the plan from the ages 66-85

Since your annual contribution is nondeductible, depending on what income tax bracket you are in, you would pay the following taxes:

- $100,000 x 40% = $40,000 in taxes
- $100,000 x 30% = $30,000 in taxes
- $100,000 x 15% = $15,000 in taxes

You should assume that the investment returns would be 7% over the life of the plan. We want this illustration to show how much money an individual would be left with after tax using a Roth 401 (k) plan and with a traditional 401 (k) plan.

If you funded a traditional 401(k) plan with $100,000, you would have saved this amount of taxes ($40,000 in the 40% tax bracket, $30,000 in the 30% tax bracket and $15,000 in the 15% tax bracket). So in order to run an appropriate comparison we will allow.

1. $100,000 to grow tax-free and be withdrawn tax free from the Roth 401(k) plan.
2. $100,000 to grow tax-deferred in the traditional 401(k) plan.
3. $40,000, $30,000 and $15,000 to be invested into a taxable side fund for the traditional 401(k) plan.

When investing money in the stock market in taxable side funds, capital gains and dividend taxes must be figured into the equation. The following are what we will assume for the annual blended *effective* tax rates for the side fund.

- 25% for the client in the 40% tax bracket
- 20% for the client in the 30% tax bracket
- 15% for the client in the 15% tax bracket

Because we want this example to be as accurate as possible, we will also add in an annual mutual fund expense of *only* 0.6% annually on the money as it grows (even though the average mutual fund Net Expense Ratio is more than double that at 1.25%, according to Morningstar. **[http://corporate.morningstar.com/US/documents/researchpapers/Fee_Trend.pdf]**. So how much could you expect to receive in retirement from your Roth 401(k) plan? $125,000 from the plan income tax-free every year for 25 years (70-95).

If you had a regular taxable 401(k), you could expect to receive the following ages 70-95 after-tax. Here is the comparison of what you could receive:

- $75,000 in the 40% tax bracket
- $87,500 in the 30% tax bracket
- $106,250 in the 15% tax bracket

The previous numbers must be added to the side account that you would have funded with the extra dollars you would have saved in income taxes when you funded a deductible 401 (k) plan. You could receive the following amounts, after taxes from ages 66-85.

- $37,500 in the 40% tax bracket
- $30,000 in the 30% tax bracket
- $15,937 in the 15% tax bracket

If we add the regular tax-deferred 401(k) plus the taxable side account, you would receive the following from ages 66-85:

- $112,500 in the 40% tax bracket
- $117,500 in the 30% tax bracket
- $112,187 in the 15% tax bracket

Since you would receive $125,000 from a Roth each year, you would be better off with a Roth regardless of you income tax bracket.

So what happens if a client moves up in tax brackets in retirement? The client will do better using the Roth 401(K) plan.

**Employer Matching Contributions:** If you are an employee where there is a match to your contributions into the 401 (k) Plan, you should take advantage of that up to the maximum amount. It's tough to pass up putting a dollar into an investment and then having an employer match that with 50 cents or even dollar for dollar. It covers the future taxes upon distribution.

But for our clients, who are the Highly Compensated Employees, in the higher marginal income tax brackets, we suggest you only contribute up to the match. The taxes upon withdrawal could be more costly than the current deduction and the deferral.

**Summary on Roth Plans vs. Traditional Income Tax Deferred Retirement Plans:** Roth plans work better for readers who do not drop in income-tax brackets by more than 10% from the time of funding until the time of retirement. Also, if you remain in the lower tax brackets, using a Roth is nearly a wash.

**Other Solutions** really are not so much solutions but more line item deductions that business owners often "write off". Those include: automobile expenses, cell phones, health insurance, life insurance, and, typically, anything else that can legally be deducted through a corporation via a normal IRS Section162 business deduction.

We don't blame the typical CPA for not being proactive, it is not what we general pay for, and time is a factor for every professional; yet, in order to fully service clients, **advanced planning advisors** like us need to do more to educate the other professionals on the issues that are most important to our clients.

The number one issue for most high-income clients is that they would like to put more money somewhere through their corporations in a tax deductible manner and would like to do so, if at all possible, without having to put significant amounts of money away for the staff.

**Section 1:** *Non-Qualified Deferred Compensation Plans (NQDC)*

Traditional Non-Qualified Deferred Compensation plans (NQDC) have been around for many years. Small business owners rarely run into the concept due to the fact that NQDC plans are not a good fit for owner/employees. While NQDC might not be prevalent in the small business and professional practice market, when starting to talk about income tax reduction or deferral, NQDC is a nice place to start since the concept has been around for years and is the most conventional and traditional type of "deferred compensation" plan in the marketplace.

**How does NQDC work?** Simply stated, a NQDC plan is an arrangement whereby compensation earned by an employee in one year is paid in a later year. That money (that normally would have been paid as compensation to the employee) is invested by the employer on behalf of the employee. At a future time, the employee receives that "deferred compensation." **plus** the growth on the money accrued through the investments, while it was deferred.

Usually deferred compensation plans pay the employee over a period of years, rather than in one lump sum. Also, NQDC plans can be implemented in a *discriminatory* manner for the benefit of key executives, which is why at first glance the topic might intrigue a small business owner. In 2004, NQDC plans were turned on their heads by Congress with the passage of The American Jobs Creation Act of 2004.

This law made prior NQDCs painful because of the new restrictions and taxes.

**The 162 Bonus Plan** is a fancy term for a company simply giving a bonus to a key employee at the end of the year. These plans are deductible to the employer and can have contractual language that goes along with them if the employee does not stay with the company for X amount of years, the employee must re-pay some or the entire bonus to the company.

The problem with the 162 Bonus Plan is that the employee has to pay tax on the bonus. So the employee doesn't see a $100,000 year-end bonus as a bonus; he sees it as a $60,000 bonus after paying $40,000 in income taxes.

**The 162 Double Bonus Plan** gives an employee a bonus at the end of the year and then another 'bonus" to pay for the taxes on the first bonus. See the following chart for the math on the double bonus plan:

| Bonus Plan | 100,000 |
|---|---|
| Tax Deduction | 40,000 |
| Net Cost of Bonus | 60,000 |
| Double Bonus | 66,667 |
| Tax Deduction | 26,667 |
| Net Cost of Double Bonus | 40,000 |
| Gross Cost: | ($166,667) |
| After-Tax Cost: | ($100,000) |

You can tell from the above numbers these are not very effective or less expensive.

**Who might use NQDC plans?** C-Corporations, usually with multiple owners and professional managers, who are looking to retain key employees.

**Do NQDC plans work in small companies?** For a small company, especially one that is privately held, when you run the numbers, there is little benefit to implement a NQDC plan. Here is an egregious example:

A CPA referred a client with a tax-deductible SADI (Supplemental Accident and Disability Insurance) Trust. Tax-deductible dollars went into the trust. $500,000. The trustee then purchased a deferred Fixed Indexed Annuity (FIA). It was a very good annuity that performed well. The client was told he could remove $700,000 in 10 years, or a tax-free income of $45,000 per year for life.

While it is a fact the annuity had that kind of excellent performance, the trust provision was another story. The SADI was sadly not on the up and up.

Unfortunately, the trust clearly states the beneficiary, the CPA's client, who also was the business owner, can ONLY receive any financial benefit upon complete disability as defined by the IRS. The seller of this plan, the trustee and the trust document preparing company were one and the same -- all referred by the annuity sales agent. These people promised the purchaser that he could claim disability if had a "scratch on his eye." Not true. He must be extricated from this entity if he is ever to see the asset again.

Needless to say, the trust preparing company, the trustee, and sales agent all have been raided by the FBI, and prosecuted or otherwise appropriately punished. The purchaser is also punished. But not by the authorities. He must pay back taxes, and possibly interest and penalties. He should have known better. But he wanted to believe in unicorns.

The annuity was great. Its wrapper—not so much. Once again, paying for an insurance product with paying some income tax, at least one time prior to purchase or upon distribution, is a non-starter.

We, along with the CPA, were successful in mitigating some of the penalty and interest on behalf of the client, who has learned his lesson. He now has regained possession of the asset, though he had to relinquish that annuity, and uses our strategies.

**Leveraged Bonus Plan (LBP)**

A 162 Leveraged Bonus Plan works like a 162 Double Bonus Plan except that, with LBPs, rather than the company making a "grossed up" second bonus to cover the entire cost of taxes lost on the first bonus, the company will give a second, smaller bonus that can be used to cover the interest cost of borrowing an amount that replaces the taxes lost on the first bonus.

The employee borrows an amount equal to the tax paid on the first bonus. LBP is essentially an individually owned executive benefit program that is funded with universal life insurance owned by the employee. A portion of the premium is paid through a loan made by a third-party finance company.

**Section 2:** *Defined Benefit Plans and 412(i) Defined Benefit Plans*

*The Perfect Retirement Plan for Business Owners over 50 who Have Little or No Money in a Qualified Plan or IRA or are Looking for "Guaranteed" Investment Returns*

Most of us do not like paying income taxes. While we all will, nothing says we must give the IRS a "tip." When navigating your way through ERISA Plans, Department of Labor, and Internal Revenue Service rules and regulations can be complicated and arcane or Byzantine, if not dangerous. The key for many business owners is finding the plan that provides the maximum deductions and benefits for the owner (called "plan sponsors"), with the minimum contributions for the employees.

A basic 401(k) offers very little in the way of annual deductions. They are *Defined Contribution Plans*.

Profit Sharing Plans can increase that up to about $52,000; but, generally speaking, you have to put in a significant amount of money for your employees in order to get a benefit. *These are elective on annual basis.*

A Money Purchase Plan may offer you deductions of $52,000 as long as you contribute the same percentage of each employee's compensation to his account; and unlike most Profit Sharing Plans, the Money Purchase Plan is *mandatory* every year.

Generally, a Defined Benefit Plan allows for much bigger deductions for employees who are getting a late start on their retirement planning. For example, a 50-year-old client who makes over $170,000 per year and is just starting to make contributions to a newly formed Defined Benefit Plan may contribute an additional $70,000 or so, tax-deductible each year. How is this possible?

**The basics of Defined Benefit Plans:** Defined Contribution Plans, like 401(k)s and Profit Sharing Plans, *restrict* but do not *define* your contributions. Of course, every client will have a different amount available in his plan at retirement, depending on the investment results. The government restricts the amount of income benefit you may enjoy every year, not the asset growth.

Further, there is no guarantee on how much will be available for retirement unless the investments inside the plan are all guaranteed with fixed investments.

In a Defined Benefit Plan, the amount you will retire with is set or *defined*, based on your salary and year of retirement. Under IRS approved and actuarially reviewed assumptions, you are allowed to put money away on a tax-deductible basis (by effectively taking a payroll reduction) to achieve that goal.

Of course, if the plan shoots for 8% growth in your investments, and you only get 6%, there will be much less available in retirement. To make up for this risk, the government allows you to alter the amount each year based on the returns on the investments in the previous year.

There is also a possibility your investments may exceed the assumed rate of return. If that happens, you will not be allowed to deduct as much in annual contributions in future years.

Because of the annual costs of the actuarial review, Defined *Benefit* Plans are more costly than the Defined *Contribution* Plan alternatives. If you are over the age of 50 though, and do not have much in the way of retirement plan savings, the tax deductions will more than offset the additional $500-$1,500 per year in administration costs-not to mention you will be able to save more for your retirement.

**How to deduct greater than $100,000 per year:** *412(i)* **Defined Benefit Plans**

A 412(i) Plan is a unique type of Defined Benefit Plan. This plan works almost exactly the same way as the typical Defined Benefit Plan. However, there is one major twist: the income benefit in retirement, which is **"Guaranteed!"** That's right. If you construct a 412(I) Plan to give you a monthly benefit $10,000 per month in retirement, it is guaranteed to be at least that high.

How is this done? The 412(I) Plan buys annuities from insurance companies that offer guarantees of 2%, 3%, 4%+ a year. With a 2% or 3% return guaranteed, the IRS allows you to use the 2% or 3% return in your calculation of the future value of the plan.

Because the regular Defined Benefit Plans assume a non-guaranteed return of 6%-8% when determining the amount of tax deductible contributions the owner can make and the 412(i) Plans use a much lower 2%-3% return, the 412(i) Plans allow for significantly more in tax deductible contributions annually.

**Why would anyone want lower returns? You would not, of course.** Nor are you getting lower returns. You are just *guaranteed a lower return* with the upside potential of greater returns. The annuities in the 412(i) Plan may still give you 4%-7% or more per year. In fact, the 412(i) Plan's investments are more likely to give you more than the 2%-3%.

We only use the guaranteed amount in our *actuarial calculation*. This allows us to help some 60 -year-old clients to make *$400,000+ in tax-deductible contributions* per year into a 412(i) Plan.

Furthermore,
- **You save significant income taxes in your prime earning years,**
- **You get a guaranteed return on your investment,**
- **You have the upside of the market, and**

- **You do NOT have to have any employees to start a 412(i) Plan.**

This plan works very well for most professionals and small business owners. To fund a 412(i) plan for an owner when there is a sizable amount of staff, may not be cost effective. Call us to determine if you are eligible.

**Life Insurance vs. Annuities:** Because 412(i) Plans need guaranteed return investment vehicles, <u>the only two allowable options are annuities and life insurance</u>. A 412(i) Plan can use a combination of life insurance and annuities, as long as the amount of life insurance used does not exceed 49% of the planned contribution amounts.

**Pros and Cons of using life insurance in a 412(i) DB Plan:** In order to "max out" a 412(i) Plan, the client would need to purchase the maximum amount of life insurance in the Plan. On the flip side, if you were allowed to fund the same amount of money into an annuity, you would have significantly more money to use in retirement.

Let's look at an example. If you are age 55, making a $400,000 a year, and have three employees, ages 25, 30, and 34. You could contribute in a tax-deductible manner $206,000 to a 412(i) DB Plan each year for seven years IF you use annuities only. Alternatively, you could contribute in a tax-deductible manner $245,000 a year into a 412(i) DB Plan each year for seven years, if the $142,000 purchases an annuity product and $103,000 funds a life insurance policy.

Why wouldn't you opt for a 412(i) Plan that uses life insurance if you can put more money away? It is because the returns inside the life policy are likely to be lower than the returns of the annuity. Why? Because, with annuities, there may be no life insurance costs.

Is there a point where the deduction just for the sake of a deduction doesn't make sense? If you do not need additional life insurance for estate planning, you probably should not be using life insurance in a 412(i) DB Plan.

## Discrimination

Many employer-owners (who usually also are the "plan sponsors") want to enjoy the maximum benefits for the minimum costs. Many clients may not recognize that a poor way to solve this problem is to create a "separate company" for the owners to receive their income, and implement a qualified plan only in the new company, which has no other rank and file employees. This is a non-starter (see below in bold). There are rules that allow for discrimination in favor of the highly compensated employees. We will help you understand and optimize them for you.

**Related Employers:** A huge issue in making sure that a plan satisfies nondiscrimination testing is the inclusion of all "related employers" as joint sponsors. The reason being that many small employers may own or control more than one business.

While it may be attractive to adopt a 412(i) Plan to benefit only one group of employees, without covering related employees, this may not be possible under current pension laws as a plan must meet specific coverage and participation rules. *[IRS §410(b) and §401 (a-26)]* Generally, **all the employees of businesses *under common control* are aggregated for nondiscrimination testing, vesting and top-heavy rules.**

### Parent-Subsidiary Controlled Group

1. One business must own at least 80 percent of another business.
2. If the two businesses in item #1 together own 80 percent of a third business, the third business is also a member of a parent-subsidiary group.

### Brother-Sister Controlled Group

1. Five or fewer persons own in combination at least 80 percent of the stock of each business, and

2. The same persons own more than 50 percent of each business, counting only identical ownership in each business.

3. A person's stock ownership is not taken into consideration for the 80 percent test in item #1 above unless the person owns some stock in each business. *[IRC§J563(a)]*

4. Attribution rules for stock ownership of spouses and certain family members may apply. *[IRC §J563(d)]*

Example:

| Owner | Business 1 | Business 2 |
|-------|-----------|-----------|
| A | 40% | 50% |
| B | 70% | 30% |
| C | 20% | 0% |

Result: Businesses 1 and 2 are members of a Brother-Sister Controlled Group because A and B own at least 80 percent of both businesses and more than 50 percent of both, counting only up to 40 percent ownership for A and 30 percent ownership for B. Because C owns no stock in Business 2, C is disregarded for the 80 percent ownership test.

## Combined Group

1. Consists of three or more businesses, each of which is a member of a parent subsidiary or a brother-sister group; and,

2. One company is both a parent of a parent-subsidiary group and a member of a brother-sister group.

## Affiliated Service Group

1. Consists of a service organization and an affiliated organization which is at least 10 percent owned by highly compensated employees of the organization, and

2. The affiliated organization performs services for the service

organization, which account for at least 5 percent of the gross receipts of the affiliated organization. *[IRe §414(m)]*

Example: You own 100% of a Medical Practice. You also own 20% of X-Ray, Inc., a firm whose employees provide radiology testing services to the Medical Practice. 50% of X-Ray, Inc.'s gross receipts are on account of services provided to Medical Practice. Result: Medical Practice and X-ray, Inc. are members of an Affiliated Service Group.

## Legally Discriminate with "Carve-Out" Planning

Most clients and their advisors are not familiar with Carve Out planning. It is really the new wave of legal discrimination when using qualified plans. If you are thinking of implementing a defined benefit plan or 412(i) defined benefit plan or if you already have one, you should strongly consider a Carve-Out Plan as a way to save the business money on its contributions to the plan for the employees. Explaining the technical details behind why Carve-Outs work is outside the scope of this book, but the following example for a "hypothetical" Dr. Jones will illustrate to the readers how powerful Carve-Out planning can be.

## A "Next Level" Retirement Plan for Jimmy Jones, DMD

*Step 1: Determine Your Goals and Budget*

Meet Jimmy Jones, a successful doctor of dental medicine with a small but thriving practice. He had been using a SEP-IRA plan to meet his retirement needs because he was told it was the cheapest and best option. As many "baby boomers" nearing retirement are now learning, a SEP-IRA may fall far short of actual retirement income needs.

Dr. Jones' goals are to receive the maximum retirement benefit allowed by law and to retire by age 62. He wants to make sure though that his employee-benefit costs do not get out of control. He is able to commit

$200,000 a year to his tax-deductible plan and sleeps better at night knowing that the assets in his retirement plan are protected from the claims of creditors and potential litigants.

*Step 2: Analyze Potential "Safe Harbor" Solutions*

An initial study reveals that Dr. Jones may certainly improve his retirement security by turning to a Defined Benefit Plan. That's because the tax-deductible contributions are not limited to $52,000 as with his current SEP-IRA. Interestingly, the cost of Dr. Jonse' traditional Defined Benefit Plan is more than triple his SEP-IRA contribution, while the attributable cost for his younger employees is lower.

Although he and his wife, Janet, receive the majority of the benefits, he is troubled by the benefit cost attributed to his younger employee, Sally Sue. Employees who do not have one year of service or who are younger than age 21 can be excluded, while all other eligible employees need to be considered for non-discrimination testing.

There are two tests that must be satisfied every year. The first is relatively basic, at least 40% of the otherwise eligible employees need to be covered in the Defined Benefit Plan. The second rule is slightly more involved; the ratio of rank-and-file employees benefiting in *each* plan must be at least 70% of the ratio of the owners, their family members, and other highly compensated employees.

If there is more than one family member in the business, a *plan sponsor* has the option of creating non-discriminatory classes of employees to either include in the plan or exclude them.

What do you do with the excluded employees? Because the excluded group will often include important assets of the business, it is recommended that they be included in a separate plan.

*Step 3: Consider Advanced Design Services as Necessary*

Dr. Jones likes the defined benefit plan idea but is concerned about the added expense and potential confusion that may come with operating two plans for two different groups of employees. He would like to pursue an alternative that can accomplish a similar objective using one plan, if possible.

After consulting with a Summit Asset Protection Group, LLC advisor, Dr. Jones is referred to a qualified pension plan administrator, who prepares a "Next Level" Defined Benefit Plan alternative. By using a "New Comparability" approach that places the employees and spouse in one class and the doctor in another, he can specifically design his plan to meet all of his objectives.

This design is most efficient when there are others who can be included in the more modest benefit group. A "New Comparability Plan" allows a client to craft a plan specifically to meet their retirement goals and business needs.

Using this design, clients are able to accomplish their objectives, while at the same time providing meaningful benefits to everyone eligible. Dr. Jones' plan formula could look like this:

1. Dentists who are Owners: 6.71 % of final average salary times years of future service
2. All Other Employees: 2.00 % of final average salary times years of future service.

The minimum monthly accrued benefit for any employee earning less than $37,500 in a year will be $111 for that year. Complex testing must be made each year to ensure that your plan is nondiscriminatory. For this reason, the client must supply employee census and other plan data to the actuarial firm immediately after the end of each plan year.

This will allow more time to calculate and discuss alternatives if your plan does not pass testing due to a change in employee census. The added administrative time and expense of this oversight and testing should be outweighed by the reduced employee benefit cost if this "Next Level" option is appropriate for you.

**Conclusion:** Defined Benefit Plans and 412(i) Plans are nice options for the right client in the right corporate setting with the right financial makeup to income-tax defer significant amounts of money into a qualified retirement plan. The right corporate setting is that of a small employer with as few employees and owners as possible.

The right financial makeup would be a client who does not have a sizable IRA or traditional pension plan balance. If you are over the age of 50 and would like to fund significant dollars into a "guaranteed" retirement plan, then you should strongly consider using a 412(i) DB Plan. If you would like to see an illustration for how a 412(i) plan would work in your company, please feel free to give us a call.

**Section 3:** *Funding Qualified Retirement Plans vs. Cash Value Life Insurance*

Please remember that if you have accumulated $1 million in a traditional, income tax-deductible and deferred 401(k), you have a "partner". The IRS. For most of our clients, the IRS will take $400,000 and leave you $600,000.

OK. What if you double that to $2 million? Then the IRS claims $800,000 and leaves you $1.2 million. And it does not matter when or how you take the money.

**The fact is that the longer the time frame for you to withdraw the money, the more the IRS gets.** That is because over time, you are likely to grow the amount in the account through our good investment management. So is it better to pay the tax now or to defer it later? The answer will be revealed shortly.

*This Section of the book will show you with "real world math" whether it make senses for you to over-fund a tax deferred qualified plan, or an after-tax Roth 401(k), or if you should build wealth funding a low-expense high cash value life insurance policy. This discussion does not address the double tax dilemma of over funding a qualified plan.*

**Complicated Nature of this Section of the Book:** This Section of the book is not going to be the easiest to read. We do not believe that the subject matter is that confusing; but because of the multiple comparisons and charts and graphs, it will possibly be a bit disorienting for some readers.

While the details that support our conclusions are in this book, we also have summaries with the conclusions. So, if you want, you can read this section over a few times to focus in on the details, or you can skip straight to the conclusions. We recommend seeing the details that support the numbers; but, the important thing is that you know the outcome of the calculations, which will be very interesting and may be eye opening for some readers.

The chapter will illustrate a client who wants to build wealth for retirement. The material:
1. Illustrates how much after-tax retirement income you will have available using a **Roth 401(k)** plan.
2. Illustrates how much after-tax retirement income you will have available using a traditional/deductible 401 (k) plan.
3. Compares what you have available from a Roth and traditional 401(k) plan to what you could receive if you funded a high cash value life insurance policy with after tax money.

**Roth plans:** The maximum contribution amount to a Roth 401(k) plan as a salary deduction in 2015 is $19,500. To simplify, I will use $15,000 as the annual contribution as the baseline for all the examples in this chapter. The following illustrates a Roth 401(k) plan for a client who is in the 40%, 30%, and 15% income tax brackets, both while contributing to the plan and distributing from it.

For the purposes of this example, assume that the client is 45, contributing $15,000 to a Roth 401(k) plan each year for 20 years. They then take distributions from ages 66-85. The client will have to pay the following taxes on contributions to a Roth.

The amount of tax depends on your income tax bracket. We have given the numbers for several brackets, so that you can choose which one is most applicable to your own:

- 40% tax bracket = $6,000 tax
- 30% tax bracket = $4,500 tax
- 15% tax bracket = $2,250 tax

All of the examples in this chapter assume a commonly held expectation of a 7% investment return over the life of the plan (please remember we are not predicting that for you). For a comparison example using a traditional 401(k) plan, you will invest an amount of money equal to the taxes you would have saved had you implemented a "standard" non-Roth 401(k) plan.

In other words, if you funded a traditional tax-deductible 401(k) plan, you would NOT have had to pay the additional taxes listed above when funding a nondeductible Roth 401(k) plan. Therefore, when comparing numbers to fund a Roth 401 (k) plan, you would have to fund into the *side fund* an additional $6,000 if you are in the 40% tax bracket, $4,500 in the 30% tax bracket, and $2,250 in the 15% tax bracket.

When many advisors discuss a side fund, what they might actually be talking about is a typical investment account. When clients are actively invested in the stock market, taxes must be taken into account. The following are the assumed annual taxes in the side account:

- 25% for a client in the 40% tax bracket
- 20% for a client in the 30% tax bracket
- 15% for a client in the 15% tax bracket

All right, now that you have an understanding of some of the variables, let's see how we do describing retirement planning using these various options:

1. How much can you receive in retirement from your Roth 401(k) plan?

Clients who contribute to a Roth or any 401(k) plans typically use mutual funds as the primary investing tool. Typically the cost of an average mutual fund will be 1.5%. To make this a conservative example, I am only going to assume a 0.6% annual mutual fund expense. Remember, the client is funding $15,000 a year into his Roth 401(k) plan for twenty years, from ages 45-65.

The answer is: you could remove $56,541 from the Roth 401(k) plan income-tax free every year for 20 years starting at age 66 and withdrawing the money until age 85.

2. How much can you receive in retirement from your traditional tax deferred 401(k) plan?

If you instead funded a regular income-tax-deductible and -deferred 401(k) plan, the following is how much you could receive from ages 66-85 *after-tax*. Remember that money, when withdrawn from a traditional 401(k) plan, is fully income taxable in the year received. You could remove annually from ages 66-85 the following, depending on the client's income tax bracket in retirement:

- $33,925 in the 40% tax bracket
- $39,579 in the 30% tax bracket
- $48,060 in the 15% tax bracket

As we like to do, we would like you to be able to see how money grows for yourself. The $39,579 after-tax withdrawal from the traditional 401(k) plan must be added to the *side account* you would have funded with the extra dollars he would have had from funding an income-tax-deductible 401(k) plan.

From the side account, you could receive the following *additional amounts* after-tax each year from ages 66-85:

- $16,533 in the 40% tax bracket
- $13,206 in the 30% tax bracket
- $7,031 in the 15% tax bracket

Totaling the numbers: To compare numbers for the various options available to you, simply total the amount you can withdraw after-tax from the traditional 401(k) plan plus the after- tax side fund. From a regular 401(k) plan plus side account, you would receive, after-tax, the following from ages 66-85:

- $50,458 in the 40% tax bracket
- $52,785 in the 30% tax bracket
- $55,091 in the 15% tax bracket

**Which** one wins? A Roth beats out a traditional tax-deferred 401(k) plan. Since you would receive $56,541 from a Roth each year, you would be much better off with a Roth if you were in the 40% bracket, better off if you were in the 30% bracket, and slightly better off if you were in the 15% income tax bracket.

Therefore, if you are currently participating in a traditional 401(k) plan at work, you might copy this section of the book and give it to your employer to help the employer understand the benefits of a Roth 401(k) plan over a traditional plan.

3. 401(k) plan funding vs. cash value life insurance and Roth 401(k) plan funding vs. life insurance.

**Our recommendation:** If you are in the high tax bracket while you are earning and in the high tax bracket while you are withdrawing, the Roth is for you. Farmers in Wisconsin where I went to college used to say that you are "**better off paying tax on the seed than the harvest.**"

Additionally, IRS Publication 590 permits a "Roth Roll Out". This lets you convert to a Roth over time, rather than all at once. Doing a Roth roll out correctly can mean that you get to **spread out the tax dollars over time, and you never have to jump into the next highest tax brackets** either. This can save you additional tax dollars.

If, on the other hand, you are in the high tax bracket while earning, but have a modest lifestyle and will be in a low income tax bracket while withdrawing or "distributing", then *perhaps* a Roth is not for you. How does any one know what the tax brackets will look like in the future? And who among us believes that tax rates are going down?

**The Comparison of 401(k) or a Roth to High Cash Value, Low Death Benefit and Low Expense Permanent Life Insurance:** Now that we have some baseline numbers to work with, we can now compare them to repositioning money into a low expense cash value life insurance policy instead of a traditional or Roth 401 (k) plan.

When you position wealth in a cash value life insurance policy, you do so after-tax just as in a Roth 401(k) plan.

Therefore, in this life insurance example, you need to pay a life insurance premium of $100,000 a year from ages 45-55, and then *borrow* money "tax-free" against your policy cash values from ages 70-94. For illustration purposes, we will actually assume a little less than a 7% rate of return on the cash in the life insurance policy. That may be unrealistically high, but it is what many currently illustrate.

The policy we will be using for these examples is an Equity Indexed Universal Life Insurance (EIUL) policy that mirrors its growth to the S&P 500 index. If you did in fact maximally-fund a low-expense, non-MEC EIUL policy in the amount of $100,000 each year from ages 45-55, how much could you borrow against your life insurance policy cash values, income tax-free from ages 70-94?

**$170,00** a year! Wait a moment… Is this possible? How can a cash value life insurance policy funded with after-tax dollars possibly outperform a traditional 401(k) plan or the new and better Roth 401(k) plan? No one is more of a skeptic than yours truly. Skepticism can easily be overcome or re-affirmed when you look at the numbers for yourself.

The following spreadsheet comes directly from an insurance company's software.

**Income Tax-Free, and "Death Tax"-Free Assuming a $100,000 Premium for Ten Years, or $1 Million Total Premium**

| Age | Annual Premium | Total Premium | Cash Value | RR on Cash Value | Death Benefit | Tax Free Withdrawals | Total Tax Free Withdrawals |
|---|---|---|---|---|---|---|---|
| 46 | 100,000 | 100,000 | 76,831 | -23.17% | 2,776,837 | 0 | 0 |
| 50 | 100,000 | 500,000 | 500,239 | .02% | 3,697,706 | 0 | 0 |
| 55 | 100,000 | 1,000,000 | 1,215,265 | 3.52% | 4,855,517 | 0 | 0 |
| 65 | 0 | 1,000,000 | 2,195,564 | 5.13% | 4,021,989 | 0 | 0 |
| 75 | 0 | 1,000,000 | 2,589,411 | 5.35% | 3,751,534 | 170,000 | 1,020,000 |
| 85 | 0 | 1,000,000 | 1,855,735 | 5.24% | 2,787,866 | 170,000 | 2,720,000 |
| 94 | 0 | 1,000,000 | 157,950 | 4.93% | 815,150 | 170,000 | 4,250,000 |

**Income Tax-Free, and "Death Tax"-Free Assuming a $50,000 Premium for Twenty Years, or $996,746 Total Premium**

| Age | Annual Premium | Total Premium | Cash Value | IRR on Cash Value | Death Benefit | Tax Free Withdrawals | Total Tax Free Withdrawals |
|---|---|---|---|---|---|---|---|
| 46 | 50,000 | 50,000 | 39,947 | 20.11% | 1,188,282 | 0 | 0 |
| 50 | 50,000 | 250,000 | 255,432 | 0.72% | 1,680,526 | 0 | 0 |
| 55 | 50,000 | 500,000 | 617,544 | 3.81% | 2,299,174 | 0 | 0 |
| 65 | 49,349 | 996,746 | 1,727,891 | 4.98% | 3,650,305 | 0 | 0 |
| 75 | 0 | 996,746 | 1,774,069 | 5.30% | 2,574,789 | 170,000 | 1,020,000 |
| 85 | 0 | 996,746 | 529,897 | 5.23% | 1,141,611 | 170,000 | 2,720,000 |
| 94 | 0 | 996,746 | 335,068 | 4.90% | 716,768 | 0 | 2,885,055 |

The differences between the two: the premiums total the same $1 million. The top is over 10 years, the bottom is over 20 years. In the top example, you get to take out $1.19 million more, tax-free. This a great example of the power of compounding.

To *summarize* the past few pages, you could invest in a Roth 401 (k) plan, traditional 401 (k) plans, or you could re-position some money into a cash building life insurance policy to build a retirement nest egg. We assumed you could position $15,000 into a Roth 401(k) plan or cash value life insurance after-tax.

Compared to a 401(k) plan, we had you tax-deduct $15,000 into such a plan and, depending on your income tax bracket, fund money into a *side fund* so you have the same out-of-pocket costs when funding all the various options.

We then created three charts so you could review the outcomes for yourself. We created one chart for you in the 15% income tax bracket, one chart for the 30% income tax bracket, and one chart for the 40% income tax bracket.

Remember that your tax bracket doesn't matter when taking money out of a Roth 401(k) plan or from a life insurance policy as there are no income taxes due on either, except to the extent that you have other taxable income in retirement. Then, if you have income from these, it does not count to your overall tax liability. And what would have been a larger amount of taxable income is now lower, and possibly even in a lower bracket.

We know of a client who needs to live on about $800,000 per year. He is in the highest bracket, and likely would also be so in retirement. He decided to re-positioned substantial amounts of money into a life insurance policy (because he was ineligible to place those amounts into a Roth).

Now he will receive almost **$500,000 per year in tax-free** loans from the life insurance for his retirement, lowering his overall taxable income to only $300,000 and thus also *lowering his marginal tax bracket*. And he gets to *avoid the newly imposed "Medicare Surtax" of an additional 3.8%* (currently) on higher incomes. A big win for him!

Your tax bracket *really* matters when taking money out of a taxable/traditional 401 (k) plan, or any other taxable account.

**The following chart summarizes the outcome:**

| "After-Tax" Retirement income; Ages 70-94 | |
| --- | --- |
| Regular 401 (k) (15% tax bracket) | $55,091 |
| Regular 401 (k) (30% tax bracket) | $52,785 |
| Regular 401 (k) (40% tax bracket) | $50,458 |
| Roth 401 (k) | $56,541 |
| Life Insurance Policy | **$170,568** |

This above chart and supporting math may be fascinating to some, and irritating to others. The numbers, based on the assumptions, show that Roth or a life insurance policy can increase your income by about 12% per year.

How much extra risk would you have to take to **receive an *extra* net of tax 12% return**? Who knew that funding a cash-value life insurance policy as an after-tax investment could possibly work out better than investing at the same pre-tax rate as a 401(k) plan or even a Roth 401(k) plan? Tax is a Big Threat to your wealth. Lowering it can mean substantial gains to you.

Also keep in mind, in my example, that you also had a sizable initial death benefit ($759,000), which would pay income-tax free to your heirs upon death. The death benefit far exceeds the cash values in the 401(k) plans. Also, keep in mind that you would have to pay a 10% penalty to remove money from your 401(k) plans before the age of 59, and may not withdraw funds from the Roth until that age either. Not so with the life insurance.

With a life insurance policy loan there is no such penalty. Also, keep in mind that you did not have to worry about the cash in your life insurance policy declining in a down market because there is the annual lock-in feature in the life insurance policy. Also consider that there is no **contribution requirement limiting** the amount of money you can fund into your cash value life insurance policy.

**Issues to Consider:**

Issue: If you die before retirement, are you better off with a 401(k) plan, Roth 401(k) plan, or cash value life insurance?

Answer: Cash value life insurance - this is because a large death benefit will be paid out to the beneficiary. This payment will be income tax-free and it also may also be estate-tax free.

Issue: When do you have access to the money in either kind of 401(k) plan or a cash value life insurance policy?

Answer: You have access to the cash in all three; but with the Roth and the regular 401 (k) plans, there are negative tax consequences if the money is removed before age 59.5. With a cash value life insurance policy, you will be able to access the cash in two ways immediately:

1. You can "surrender" the policy for the cash surrender value ("CSV"). This can work okay for readers if you use a high cash value life insurance policy that you fund for only 5-10 years instead of 20.
2. You can access the cash through tax-free loans. Again, this can work okay if you use a high cash value policy.

For either 1) or 2), without a high cash value life insurance policy, in the first 10 years you will be limited in the amount of cash you have access to.

**Summary:** We know that there are a lot of numbers and assumptions and tax brackets that are dealt with in this Section. For many, you will have a bit of a headache after reading this chapter; and we certainly understand why. What you need to take from this chapter is that putting your blinders on and funding a traditional 401(k) plan at work may be easy, but is not always in your best interest.

There are other options that you'll want to look at when deciding which way is the best to grow your wealth. If you are going to fund a 401(k) plan or IRA, you should fund a Roth. The numbers are unmistakably clear. For those who understand how a low-expense, maximally- funded, life insurance policy works as a retirement vehicle, many will prefer to fund such a policy instead of funding a 401(k) plan.

It sounds counter-intuitive, we know; but again, the numbers are what they are. The bottom line is that there is no "right" answer or one perfect tool when it comes to building wealth. Nor is there a "bad" tool. You've heard the saying, "different strokes for different folks." It's the same in the manner you choose to accumulate your wealth.

For those who don't mind risk (of market losses, reverse dollar cost averaging in distribution, bad timing, and tax rates), you will not mind having your money in a 401(k) plan. For those who are averse to risk, you may prefer the safety of *appropriate* cash value life insurance policies, which have minimum guarantees and a low death benefit.

Which option should you use to build your wealth? We could not say for certain unless we looked at your specifics; but we hope that after you have read this book you will be equipped with the knowledge and information to make the best decisions for yourself as to how you want to grow your wealth.

## Section 4: *Charitable Planning*

High-income and high-net-worth clients by nature seem to be more giving people than the general public on a percentage basis. For those who are not charitably inclined, some of these strategies still may be attractive.

There are many different ways for you to gift money to charity, i.e., Charitable Remainder Annuity Trust (CRAT) Charitable Lead Annuity Trust (CLAT), Family Foundations, and Charitable Gift Annuities (CGA); among many others.

Let's first define these.

A **CRAT** allows for a current income tax deduction for your large gift to charity. In return, you get a taxable income stream from the assets, for a period of time. At the end of that period, the "remainder" stays with the charity.

A **CLAT** allows for a current income tax deduction for your large gift to charity. So far it is the same. The difference here is that over a period of time, the *charity* gets all the income generated. After that defined period, your *beneficiaries receive the remainder*, usually income and estate tax-free.

A **Family Foundation**, because they are private (and thus may not raise outside funds) can be expensive. For that reason, many prefer "Donor Advised Funds" that may work in a similar fashion, but are administered by a larger tax-exempt entity, like a public foundation. You get a current income tax deduction for a very large gift. You get to decide who gets how much for how long, within certain limits.

An extensive review of charitable strategies is beyond the scope of this book. We will delve into one such strategy that has significant appeal to many clients for variety of reasons.

**Charitable Gift Annuity (CGA)**

**CGA Quick Facts - Client is the donor:**
- A charitable gift annuity is a contract between a donor and a qualified 501(c)(3) public tax-exempt organization.
- The donor makes an irrevocable gift to the charity and in return receives a promise of lifetime income.

- A lifetime income is paid to the donor or to donor and spouse at an agreed upon rate
- Once reserve or reinsurance requirements to make donor payments have been satisfied, the charity is able to use whatever remains from the original gift to use for its charitable purposes.
- Some charities allow a portion of this "charitable remainder" from the CGA to pass into a client/donor's Donor Advised Fund (DAF).
- A CGA is useful because it can provide lifetime income at a high rate that is guaranteed by the charity and also provides an immediate tax deduction for the donor.

**CGA Program Overview:**
1. You gift an asset to a charity for a current year income-tax deduction
2. Your deduction may "carry forward" for four more future years to use it up
3. Charity purchases a commercial annuity and a life insurance policy from the asset
4. Commercial annuity pays income to the charity
5. Charity assigns that income to donor/you
6. You gift *a portion* of the annuity income to an ILIT
7. ILIT buys additional life insurance to replace value of the original gifted asset
8. You enjoy current income, a tax deduction, and get to replace the asset value
9. At your death, life insurance proceeds pass income and estate-tax-free to your heirs
10. And, the remainder of the gifted funds and the additional life insurance proceeds go to the charity.

**Guaranteed Benefit Income Protection:** When entering into a CGA contract, most donors want to make sure the charity will be carful in protecting the funds that will be used to pay the lifetime income to the donor. Charities are required to maintain certain reserve requirements and may also be mandated to invest funds according to strict parameters depending on state requirements.

Just because there are reserve requirements, it is still vitally important to work with a reputable charity that knows how to implement a CGA. One that can be trusted not to mismanage the money that is partially to be used to pay a "guaranteed income" to the donor or his heirs. Most of the time, a charity will use a single premium immediate annuity (SPIA) for the life of the donors from a highly-rated commercial insurance carrier.

**Charitable Benefit:** Once a charity has met its payment obligation to a donor, it is able to use the remainder of the gift to fulfill its charitable objectives. Some charities allow all or a portion of this remainder to be designated for a Donor Advised Fund (DAF). Typically the DAF is funded at the death of the donor.

This permits the donor to have input in an *advisory capacity* as to how the charitable funds are distributed and is a great way to establish a legacy. In other words, the charity will purchase an *additional life insurance policy* on the donor with what remains supposed to go to the charity.

You utilize life insurance because a large guaranteed death benefit will ultimately pass to the charity. Many clients want their children and grandchildren to engage in charitable giving. A good way to do that is through a CGA where the charity will apportion a part of the death benefits from a life policy purchased with the proceeds from the gift to the charity to be used in a DAF.

The DAF is one the client sets up in advance of death where the client's heirs would help direct how the death benefits will be used in a charitable manner. When you use a DAF, the children and grandchildren will not receive the money but are able to watch the money go to the charitable entities that the client felt were important.

**Substantial Tax Benefits:** A CGA can assist in tax management in three ways.

First, when transitioning the ownership of a highly appreciated capital to a charity in exchange for a CGA, the donor does not realize a lump sum capital gain. The capital gain is reduced significantly and then spread out over the donor's life expectancy. This means that a portion of the donor's CGA income will be taxed at the *lower capital gains tax rate*.

Second, a substantial *immediate income tax deduction* occurs, which can be used to offset current and future income taxes up to a certain amount based on adjusted gross income that can be carried over up to five additional years. The amount of the tax deduction is based upon the projected value of the ultimate gift to charity.

Third, when you transition an asset to a CGA, it removes the asset from the donor's taxable estate. This has the potential of greatly *reducing potential estate taxes*. Depending on the asset, transitioning an asset can also *avoid income with respect to decedent (IRD) taxation* at estate settlement.

**Wealth Replacement:** Many clients who do not have a charitable may not appreciate a CGA. For clients who are unsure if they want to use a CGA or not, one way to rationalize using a CGA is to implement a "wealth replacement" strategy. Wealth replacement is a fancy term for buying a life insurance policy, with the entire income stream flowing to the donor Client from the CGA.

The general idea is that a client will gift an asset to charity, get an income tax deduction, and use the income from the charity to buy a life insurance policy inside an Irrevocable Life Insurance Trust. ) Normally, you would want to purchase the policy inside an ILIT so the death benefit will pass income- and estate-tax-free to the heirs.

Example: Assume that you have an estate of $15 million at the age of 60. The $15 million estate is made up of a home worth $2 million, a brokerage account worth $5 million, an IRA of $2 million, a vacation condo worth $3,000,000, and a rental property worth $3,000,000. The rental property has a basis of $1,000,000.

Assume you still work as a surgeon where you makes $700,000 a year. You have three children and five grandchildren, and you and your spouse would like to leave something to charity so you can teach your children about the power of donating by involving them in charitable giving through the DAF.

You decide to implement a CGA, and it would work as follows:
1. You gift the $3,000,000 rental property to a charity that sells the property for $3,000,000.
2. You receive an income tax deduction for his tax return of $3,000,000. This deduction could be increased substantially if you waited to receive income payments from the CGA. Also, if you are older when making the gift, the income tax deduction would be larger.
3. A. The charity buys a single premium lifetime annuity on you and starts paying you $125,000 in income each year until your death. The first year, $60,000 of the payment is taxable to you at the long-term capital gains rate of 20%, $55,000 is treated as ordinary income, and $5000 is tax-free. The taxable consequences of CGA payments to you change during your lifetime and are not discussed for the sake of brevity. The tax consequences to each person will vary widely; and if you are a candidate for a CGA to fund your charitable goals, please feel free to give us a call to create a specific example for your individual situation.
4. The charity also buys a $5,000,000 Second-to-Die Life Insurance Policy on you and your spouse that will fund the DAF at the last spouse's death.
5. You take $45,500 from the income you receive from the CGA each year and gift that to an ILIT where a $5,000,000 Second-to-Die Life Insurance Policy is purchased and where the death benefit will be able to pass onto your heirs, income-and estate-tax-free.
6. When you and your spouse die, $5,000,000 will pass to your heirs, income and estate-tax-free. The DAF will be funded at the second spouse's death and that money will be used in the DAF for charitable purposes with the involvement and direction of your heirs.

Summary of benefits:
- You helped a charity by gifting it a $3,000,000 asset;
- You received an immediate deduction for your current and future income taxes;
- Your heirs did not lose the asset, but actually will receive more, due to the fact that a $5,000,000 life insurance policy in an ILIT was purchased with the income from the CGA;
- You removed a $5,000,000 asset from your estate for estate tax purposes;
- And at your deaths, your heirs became involved in the DAF that was funded with another life insurance policy that was purchased and owned by the charity.

**Distinguishing CGAs from the Most Commonly Recommended Charitable Solution (the Family Foundation):** Family Foundations (herein after FF) for many "charitable experts" are the tool of choice for their high-income, high-net-worth clients when it comes to charitable planning.

What are the Advantages of a Family Foundations (FF)?

1. Total control of the money gifted to any variety of charities. While a client's heirs can have significant input on how a CGA is distributed, a FF gives the family total control over assets in the FF.
2. Total control over the how the foundation is to be managed.
3. The donor's children have an opportunity to participate in the giving process, and become vital members of the community. They may even receive some small compensation for their efforts.

The main difference between a FF and a CGA is cost. This is also a function of the size of the estate. If your estate will be larger than $25 million after passing assets and income to your family, you should consider an FF.

The setup cost of a CGA is ZERO and the setup cost of a FF is between $20,000 and $45,000. More importantly, **when a client contributes to a FF, there are additional limits on the deductions**

**a client can take against his personal income.** The limit differences on the income tax deduction a client can take between FF and a CGA are as follows:

Income Tax Deduction for Donor
Cash Gift 50% of Adjusted Gross Income
Property/Securities 30% of Adjusted Gross Income
Family Foundation
30% of Adjusted Gross Income
20% of Adjusted Gross Income

Charitable giving *sounds simple*: "just give your property or money away, enjoy a deduction, and provide wealth replacement for the heirs, via a life insurance death benefit and everyone is happy".

The sentiment is false. The reality is that setting up a charitable giving program is similar to buying life insurance. If you use the wrong advisor, he will likely end up working on what is best for himself, and will not be as concerned with what is best for you or the charity that you care about.

For most of our clients, if you are looking for a simple way to fund your desire for charitable giving, you should consider a CGA. You can remove a low basis asset from your estate and pass an equal amount of wealth to your heirs, while at the same time funding a charity your heirs will be able to work with to help others who are less fortunate.

**Preservation Charitable Trusts**

Preservation charitable trusts come in two general varieties, both regarding real estate property: historical and open-space. In the historical preservation trust, the entity owning the property wishes to preserve it for important historical reasons. In the open-space trusts, the entity owning the property wishes to protect the land from future development. Each, however, wish to optimize the value and enjoy the cash use of that value through a "liquidity event".

Here is how it works. Family owns a farm near a large future development. Family wants the cash from the value, yet still wishes to preserve the open space. Family sells to a trust. Trust finds investors. Investors buy $50,000 unit-shares in the land. Investors and trust agree to not develop, and to not sell to developer, but to donate the land to the public. Due to the higher developed value, usually 4 times the original purchase price by qualified and reputable appraisers, investors receive $200,000 charitable deduction from current income tax. Very powerful.

The questions come up: Is this legal? Or will we get audited? Or how can this be? In short: yes, no, and here is how. The left in the Congress likes to preserve properties from development or destruction. The right in the Congress likes to preserve tax deductions. The local community desires to preserve. The IRS allows for charitable deductions. Only the Trust would liable to get an audit. Every thing seems to be on the "up and up." Of all the clients we know who have bought these, not one has been audited, and not one dollar of deduction has been disallowed.

**Section 5:** *Section 79 Plans*

*A Simple Plan to Take a Sizable Deduction for an Individually Owned Life Insurance Policy:* Section 79 Plans have been around for some time and are making a comeback as topics like 419 Plans have lost favor in the "deferred compensation" market. The plan as devised before the recent proposed 412(i) regulations was more tax favorable, but even now in its current form the plan may be *attractive for certain clients.*

But be cautious. In the tax code under Section 79, is the basic outline, entitled "Group Term Life Insurance". Traditional Section 79 Plans are sold as a way to provide additional employee benefits. Over the years, like with many topics, promoters have figured out how to use the tax code to make it seem more attractive.

**A Section 79 Plan:**

- Allows for a current tax deduction on contribution to the plan.
- Allows for tax -deferred growth.
- It provides for a flexible, unlimited-funding window for key participants.
- Employee participation requires a minimal funding outlay.
- There are no minimum age requirements to withdraw income.
- The plan provides a non-taxable, on-demand income stream.
- Transfer of assets at the participant's death is income-tax-free to heirs.

**How does it work?** Basically, a Section 79 Plan allows an employer to purchase life insurance on employees in a tax-deductible manner. Usually the employees are encouraged to opt for $50,000 in term life insurance and the key employees to opt for a permanent, Universal Life Insurance Policy (UL).

In these plans the life insurance premiums enjoy a corporate deduction; for the universal life policy (UL), the employee will have to recognize the premium as income for some portion of the deductible premium made by the employer. This results in a "Phantom Income Tax." Phantom income tax occurs when you pay **a tax on income not realized**.

**Conclusion about Section 79 Plans post-412(i) proposed regulations:** While the proposed 412(i) regulations have reduced the financial viability of Section 79 Plans, the plan may still be a viable option for the right client to fund a cash building UL policy in a tax favorable manner, which then can be used for supplemental retirement benefits or for a client looking to tax deduct life insurance for estate planning purposes. Many insurance carriers in 2015 have prohibited the use of their policies within Section 79 Plans. In general, stay away. There is no obvious benefit, especially when you compute the tax owed.

### Section 6: *Employee Stock Ownership Plans (ESOPs)*

Many think the "O" in ESOP stands for Employee Stock Option Plan it is really Ownership Plan. An ESOP is a government "qualified" benefit plan that is designed to transfer ownership in a company to the employees.

That means you must comply with the Department of Labor's ERISA rules as well as the IRS. Many of these are in trouble right now.

**What is an ESOP?** An ESOP is a special kind of **employee benefit plan,** governed by ERISA that enables **employees to acquire beneficial ownership** in their company without having to invest their own money. The owner who makes the transfer takes out a loan for the appraised amount. Then that loan is paid by the new owners, the company's employees.

First, an ESOP is required by law to invest primarily in the securities of the sponsoring employer. This means that employees will have a stake in the company where they work. ESOPs are also unique because of their ability to borrow funds.

Because of this uniqueness, "leveraged ESOPs" can be used as a technique of corporate finance. On of the most frequent uses for an ESOP is to buy out the shares of a departing owner of a closely held company. Therefore, in reality, even though an ESOP is an employee benefit plan, they are rarely implemented unless the main beneficiary is the key owner.

It is possible for an owner to defer tax on the money they have made if the ESOP holds at least 30% of the company's stock. You can use pretax corporate dollars to fund the purchase.

**So how does an ESOP Work?** A company setting up the ESOP creates a "trust" to which it makes annual contributions. These contributions will then be allocated to individual employee accounts within the trust. These allocations can be formulated a number of different ways. The shares of company stock and other plan assets allocated to employees' accounts must "vest" before employees are able to access them.

Vesting is where employees are entitled to more of their accounts over time. The least permissive vesting schedule is 20% after three years, increasing by 20% per year until the employees are fully vested after seven years of service.

**Uses of ESOPs:** The two most common uses of ESOPs are 1) to purchase from the retiring owner stock in a closely held company and, 2) as an extra employee benefit or incentive plan. Two-thirds of all the ESOPs now in existence are used for this purpose.

There are too many closely held companies out there who have no plans, or incomplete plans, for continuing the business after the departure or retirement of the founder or major shareholder. If the company were to repurchase a retiring or departing owner's shares, the proceeds would be taxed as capital gains. A sale to another company would also be taxed as capital gains. And finding a buyer is not always easy, even for a profitable closely held company. (See my book, *PayDay*) **http://www.amazon.com/ Payday-Congratulations-Business-Prepare-Protect-ebook/dp/ B00SN90HWG.**

An ESOP can provide a ready-made market for the equity of any major shareholder including the owner, and also provide job security as well as a benefit for employees. An owner of a closely held company that is a C Corporations incurs no taxable gain on a sale of stock to an ESOP, as long as the plan owns 30 percent or more of the company after the sale, and the sale's proceeds are reinvested in "qualified" securities within a 15 month period beginning three months before the date of the sale.

This tax-free rollover is the most tax favored way for an owner of a closely held company to sell his or her stock and, thus, encourages the owners of closely held companies to help create new owners through ESOPs.

## Types of ESOPs:

Non-Leveraged ESOPs

This first type of ESOP does not require the use of any leverage to acquire stock. The employee sponsor funds it. New shares are issued to the ESOP and **a deduction is taken by the corporation**.

Another option would be for cash to be put into the plan as cash flow allowed or from another shareholder. Generally, a non-leveraged ESOP is established to promote growth of the sponsoring company by creating tax deductions from the newly issued shares, thus improving cash flow and reducing taxes.

Steps:
- Company makes a tax-deductible contribution of cash or stock to the ESOP.
- ESOP purchases stock from company or shareholders.
- Company increases its cash flow and net-worth or shareholder receives liquidity for company stock.

Example: If the company contributed new shares of stock to the ESOP to fund the ESOP, the company receives a "deduction" for the fair market value of the stock. If we assume the stock in a typical contribution was valued at $50,000, the company would receive a deduction for the contribution of stock to the ESOP.

The deduction will allow the company to pass through more money to the shareholders in the year of the contribution. Remember, the company's cash flow was not lessened by the contribution of newly issued stock.

Leveraged ESOPs

A leveraged ESOP borrows money from either a bank or other lender. If the leveraging is being used to buyout the stock of a retiring owner, the ESOP will acquire those existing shares. Two tax incentives make borrowing through an ESOP a great option for companies that might otherwise never consider financing their employees' acquisition of stock.

Since ESOP contributions are tax deductible the corporation repaying the loan is able to deduct interest from taxes in addition to the principle. This can significantly reduce the cost of financing for the company by significantly cutting the pre-tax dollars to repay the loan. .

Example: The client is an owner of a closely held business with an interest in the company worth $10,000,000. The client has no ready market for the sale of his company, and he would also like to sell the stock with no current income tax or capital gains taxes. The best way to help this client is with the creation of an ESOP which will purchase the owner's stock for a "fair market value."

| "On The Street" ESOP Sale | Scenario A Discounted Sale | Scenario B Premium Sale |
|---|---|---|
| A. Selling Price | $16,000,000 | $20,000,000 |
| Cost Basis | $1,000,000 | $1,000,000 |
| B. Capital Gain Tax | $3,000,000 | $0 |
| C. Transaction Cost | $2,000,000 | $3,000,000 |
| Net Proceeds from Sale | **$11,000,000** | **$16,000,000** |
| D. Company Loan | $0 | $20,000,000 |
| Repayment Deductions | $0 | All Interest & Principal |

You can readily appreciate the attractive nature of an ESOP for a seller. This illustration shows a company with a "fair market value" of $20,000,000, but no readily viable buyer at hand. Thus, the attractiveness of an ESOP.

If the fair market value is $20,000,000 and the seller would have to discount the sale price by 20% to $16,000,000 in order to sell quickly, the seller will have "lost" $5,000,000. The ESOP allowed the seller to enjoy an **extra 45%** of the net proceeds. In addition and, as with any ESOP transaction, the seller is able to use a Section *1042 rollover* to defer the capital gains with the sale of the stock.

Rather than discounting the price for a sale, or if a seller does not want to wait for a buyer, or simply wants to transfer ownership in the company to the employees, you could choose to implement a leveraged ESOP.

While a leveraged ESOP can be a very powerful tool to help clients sell their business and fund their retirement in a tax favored manner, they will not work for companies that cannot *qualify for an ESOP loan* due to lack of assets to pledge as collateral and/or a lack of cash flow to service the debt on the loan.

*So sometimes the seller takes on the risk of the loan by personally guaranteeing the loan. And to make the risk even greater, if the $20 million valuation is "inaccurate" or contested, the "tort" lawyers may be waiting to pounce on the seller, too.*

**Seller Financed ESOPs (the most common ESOP for small businesses):** If the corporation does not have the cash flow to fund the ESOP or the loan, and the seller is unwilling to take on the debt guarantee, where does the money come from?

Many small companies will not qualify for a loan and those that can, may not want to for the typical reasons companies do not want to have sizable loans on the books. A way for a company to create a non-leveraged ESOP without a loan from a traditional lending source is to have a seller-financed ESOP.

The seller of stock is typically the owner of the company. Instead of being paid with borrowed money, the owner takes back a note payable from the ESOP to the seller as payment for the purchased stock. One risk here is the ESOP may not repay the note to the seller.

A seller-financed ESOP allows the company owner to collect the interest on a note payable from the ESOP and allows much more flexibility should the company have problems funding the principal and interest payment on the note to the ESOP every year.

**Tax Deferral Dilemma:** Another problem arises with a seller-financed ESOP: the seller MUST invest the sale proceeds from the stock in "qualified replacement property" (QRP) within 12 months of the sale. If the installment note payable to the seller from the ESOP is due to pay over a several year period, the seller still must fund the QRP within 12 months for the entire proceeds of the sale.

Few sellers have the liquidity to fund the QRP without actually receiving the funds from the sale of the stock; and so many times a seller financed ESOP will still involve a loan from an outside lender and the use of "Floating Rate Notes" (FRNs). FRNs are beyond the scope of this book, as few of you will have a business to sell to an ESOP.

We feel it is important that you at least have an overview of what an ESOP is, and the different types, and how they work, and what the risks may be. For more information, contact the author.

**Conclusion:** ESOP "experts" too often state that the transaction is an easy one to understand. The previous material should have illustrated that an ESOP as a plan might be easy to understand, but the specifics of the plan are quite complex. As a succession-planning tool for certain small business owners, an ESOP has advantages that no other plan can offer.

Clients are allowed to sell their C-Corporation stock to an ESOP, tax defer all the proceeds with qualified replacement property, and, if the client dies before taking the money out of the QRP Trust, the heirs will receive a "stepped up basis" on the stock. Clients who can fully understand ESOPs, their benefits, and application to various business owners will be far ahead of the game when it comes time to evaluating the best way to transition out of their business.

## Section 7. *Owner Debt Option Plans (ODOPs)*

**What about an ODOP?** An "Owner Debt Option Plan" is a *non-qualified, non-regulated* way to extract loads of cash from the business **Income Tax Free**, over and over again, while still retaining control. The risks are lower than an ESOP, while the cash extraction is not quite so great due to certain debt-to-income ratios required to maintain compliance with bank covenants. This section is excerpted from, "*Payday! You Sold Your Business, Now What? How to prepare for and maintain your sudden wealth*".

An ODOP is regulated by you. It works in a similar fashion to the ESOP without the regulatory risk: you retain the equity. You go to the bank and borrow the funds; your business makes the payments. The payment is an interest only note with a balloon in 7 years. You place the borrowed money into an asset protected low yield, low risk account, in which the money compounds tax-free. You may access the money any time, for any reason, usually tax-free.

For example, say your business has $10 million in sales, and $1M in EBIDTA, with a $700,000 net free cash flow. Your business borrows $3Million. You place the $3 million into the ODOP account. Payments for interest and principal at 7% interest will be around $500,000 per year.

The original $3Million you borrowed will have grown also to say $3.6Million in your ODOP account. If you have done this, you may have reduced the risk associated with a sale. And you have increased the total amounts available to fund your needs and desires.

Assuming your business is still growing, why not do it again? At the end of the 7 years, if you have a 10% Compound Annual Growth Rate of profit (CAGR), your profits will have doubled, along with your net free cash flow to over $1.4Million.

You borrow another $3Million and do it again. At the end of the next 7 years, your $6.6Million will have grown to say $8Million. You still will have owed $6Million. Your profit has doubled again. You role over the note to a fixed 10 years amortizing payment of interest (at say 9%) and principal, your monthly payments will equal $76,005 (annual $912,060) with your profit now $2.8Million, $2Million net free cash flow.

Your ratios are good, your cash flow is sufficient to handle the debt, and to leave more for you to do what is best. You will have more than $10Million in your bank that you can access tax free, at any time and for any reason at the end of this term. If you could have sold your business for 6 times EBIDTA originally you would have wound up after tax and expenses of somewhere in the neighborhood of $4.2Million. And you would no longer have owned the business. This is a way to have your cake and eat it too.

### Section 8: *Tax-Advantaged Alternative Long Term Care Coverages Options*

*Reduce Your Taxes Today AND Provide for Potential Long Term Care Costs Tomorrow:* None of us likes paying any more in costs and taxes than necessary. As advisors for high-income clients, we are always exploring new ways for you to reduce your income taxes and estate taxes.

With increased life expectancy due to advancements in medicine, there is a greater chance that you may suffer a debilitating illness that may require significant Long Term Care. In some areas of the country, the cost of nursing home care or quality around-the-clock in-home care may be *$450 per day*.

What if you could enjoy asset protection and wealth transfer all done in a tax-deductible manner? A tremendous opportunity exists to fund a LTCI policy through your business to protect your wealth, and to transfer money out of the business in a tax-deductible manner.

The IRS Section 162 provisions allow owners of small companies to tax-deduct the premiums for long term care insurance, to provide a vehicle for funding a potential huge future liability, with present tax-deductible dollars. If you are serious about having a complete estate plan that protects your heirs, LTCI should be one of your planning tools.

Except now it is difficult to find these. Many of the leading insurers (at least 6 as of this writing) of long-term care policies are no longer "writing" them. Apparently, their actuaries under-priced them, creating too much risk to continue. And they were already expensive to begin with.

### Section 9: *Voluntary Employee Benefit Plans (VEBAs); Welfare Benefit Plans (419A) 06 and A (05 Plans); IRS Dramatically Alters the Use of 419 and VEBA Plans*

Generally speaking, the IRS does not like ANY plan *primarily designed* to mitigate income taxes. If you go through the history of qualified plans, when they first rolled out, the IRS deemed many of them "abusive tax avoidance plans".

In the good old days of the 1980s 419A (f) (6) plans, reputable advisors used vendors to administer plans to help small business clients implement "death benefit only" plans. These death benefit only plans would fund "cash value" life insurance policies owned by the 419A (f) (6) trust, and would receive a sizable tax deduction. If the death benefit was set up correctly, it would pass to the heirs income and estate tax free at an employee's death.

And, then, abuse did come into the picture. Because large annual premiums were commonplace with these plans, new "better" TPAs came into the business and "stretched" the Internal Revenue Code (IRC) to make even more marketable/salable plans. This helped millions more in premium dollars to flow into plans many considered "abusive."

Marketers of the plan flaunted it in the IRS's face. The IRS, in turn, asked congress to pass very negative regulations essentially killing the use of 419A(f)6 and (5) plans, as well as multiple-employer VEBAs. **The phoenix rises** As many in the life insurance industry were licking their wounds over the loss of this neat sales tool which was very beneficial to clients, some TPAs were able to use VEBAs and 419(e) plans because Congress had not included them when they passed new regulations that essentially shut down multiple-employer plans.

**The same old story.** Not that it should surprise you, and it didn't us, but just like multiple-employer plans, single-employer VEBAs/419(e) plans also became much abused and were flaunted in the face of the IRS, so in October of 2007, Revenue Ruling 2007-65, and Notices 2007-83 and 2007-84 were issued by the IRS.

Essentially the Revenue Ruling and Notices did away with the deduction to fund such plans with cash value life insurance, which come out tax free to the employee. Many unfortunate clients fell prey to the unscrupulous sellers of these abusive plans. And then paid a heavy price. The best way to explain the effects of the new IRS commentary is to do so through a little question and answer session.

**FAQs regarding the New IRS Actions to Curb 419 and VEBA abuses:**

**Question:** *Are the IRS Notices and Rev. Ruling the same as case law or statutory law?*
**Answer:** Not when a client is in the court system. A tax court is able to decide as to the "law" and the outcome for the client.

**Question:** *Are businesses allowed to make a tax deductible contribution to a 419 or VEBA plan if the trust takes the contribution and purchases cash value life insurance?*
**Answer:** This is the question that everyone wants to know. In the IRS's opinion it is clear that no deduction is available for contributions to purchase cash value life insurance.

**Question:** *Can an employer "carve-out" and only offer benefits to employees they deem necessary?*
**Answer:** According to current IRS guidelines the answer is definitely not. All eligible employees must be included.

**Question:** *If you believe that the IRS guidance is incorrect, must you follow it?*
**Answer:** The technical answer is no. Having said that, the IRS clearly states its opinion. Anyone who chooses to not follow this guidance and is put in front of a court that agrees with the IRS will lose their lawsuit, and will have to deal with the listed tax transaction penalties among others.

**Question:** *Are all 419NEBA plans now listed tax transactions?*
**Answer:** No. It appears that only plans that use cash value life insurance have been added to the listed tax transaction list.

**Question:** *If we were to sell a 41ge or single employer VEBA today, how would I sell it? This is also a popular question.*
**Answer:** We would only be selling 419 Plans for pre- and post-retirement medical benefits.

**Question:** *Would we sell cash value life insurance to fund the plans?*
**Answer:** We believe you can use cash value life to fund the plans, the real question is should you? We believe the answer is no and that we'd rather see clients use annuity only VEBAs.

**Summary:** These plans had been terrific tools used by small business clients to take sizable business deductions to fund for death benefits that would pass income and estate tax free to employee beneficiaries and to fund for post-retirement medical expenses where the benefit would inure to the employees in a tax-free manner.

Unfortunately, the abuses with these plans became too great and the IRS took action. The IRS may have gone too far with their notices. Until case law comes down and a judge rules on the new notices, using 419(e) or single employer VEBAs fund for anything other than post-retirement medical benefits, we suggest you avoid them for now.

**Section 10:** *Why Profitable Closely Held Businesses Should Consider a CIC*

While large companies have long used CICs to manage risks and gain tax advantages, it is only recently that medium to small businesses have begun to take advantage of them as well. Certainly, CICs *can* be ideal tools for businesses and their owners if established and maintained properly and if suited to their economic needs. The following is excerpted from my "monograph," **The ART (Alternative Risk Transfer):**

The Executive Summary To Take Back Control...
And Become Your Own Micro-Insurance Company
The Captive Insurance Companies (CIC)

The benefits of a micro-captive (< $1.2 million) include:
• Direct access to reinsurance
• Control over insurance coverage
• Deduct up to $1.2 million per year, per business entity
• Wealth Accumulation on Surplus
• Manage excessive compensation as defined by IRS guidelines
• Creditor protection
• Wealth transfer (gift & estate)
• Creation of a family estate planning bank
• Creation of a profit center
• Business succession planning

Business is risky. If a business were to buy insurance to cover every contingency, chances are that the insurance company would profit, but the business wouldn't. This reality creates a planning opportunity in situations where the business (or its stakeholders) owns its own insurance company, if only because insurance companies are subject to favorable state and federal income tax treatment.

Separately from the tax planning opportunities, forming a captive insurance company adds financing mechanisms and managerial focus to a business' risk retention strategy. Economically, captive insurance is self-insurance housed in an incorporated pocketbook. The organizational formality of incorporating the self-insurance pocketbook (and treating it as an insurance company) tends to influence a business' decisions about which risks to retain vs. which risks to buy insurance for from a commercial insurance company. In this light, a captive insurance company is generally a risk management tool that happens to come with potential tax advantages.

Captive insurance planners have a tendency to emphasize the non-tax reasons for forming a captive insurance company, as it is taboo to discuss the tax advantages. The anxiety is misplaced, although certainly a non-tax business purpose and economic substance are essential for qualifying a self-insurance pocketbook as a captive insurance company for tax purposes. For insight into the "taboo," see the article by Randall Beckie and Phillip England, "When the Tail Wags the Dog," Captive Review (2009).

**A CIC is a Small Business Insurance Company** (IRS Sec 831(b)) established to insure the risks of its parent company or a group of companies. In the simplest form, a CIC is an organized plan of self-insurance that operates just like the typical Insurance Company which calculates risk, issues policies, collects premiums, pays expenses, and establishes reserves to pay future claims.

Every business has to self-insure multiple risks that are excluded in the basic traditional commercial insurance contract. If a captive insures these particular types of risk, the planner and the captive owner should be prepared to concede upon IRS examination that such risk is not an insurable risk in the commercial markets.

Some examples of these risks are: loss of license for professionals (doctors, lawyers, CPAs, financial planners, etc.), loss of key supplier or key customer, legal defense, or audit defense liabilities – though not for medical malpractice or other types of Errors and Omissions, which are commercially available. A captive can qualify as an insurance company if more than 50% of its premiums qualify as "insurance premiums", as distinguished from self-insurance deposits.

If a business incurs a loss because of one of the aforementioned risks it is very possible that the business could suffer a very large monetary penalty as a result. Captives are useful mainly for financing risks that the business has otherwise already decided to retain.

Captives are formed for several reasons which include but are not limited to: 1) reducing total insurance costs; 2) protecting against uninsured risks not covered by traditional insurance; 3) controlling risk by setting coverage desired by the business owner; 4) providing greater control over claims; 5) income tax planning; 6) wealth building; 7) estate planning; 8) asset protection.

There have been captive insurance companies in the U.S. since at least 1961, and it took until 2001 for the IRS to acquiesce to the favorable tax treatment of them. Almost 5000 companies in the U.S., including more than 44 of the Fortune 100 Companies and 75% of the Fortune 500, utilize these structures to decrease the cost of their insurance premiums, underwrite coverage's that are much more comprehensive to protect their particular interests, and protect certain assets from lawsuits. They also use this "mechanism" to build wealth on a tax-favored basis.

On a smaller scale, many physician practices are beginning to use a Captive to decrease the cost of their Malpractice Insurance coverage for any administrative charges caused by unwarranted regulatory audits, as well as protecting their assets.

Industry experts estimate that companies with favorable claims history, instead of less favorable loss histories, can recognize significant savings on their cost of business insurance using a Captive Insurance Company. Captives that are set up correctly can receive up to $1.2M in payments from your business tax free, fully deductible to your business under IRS Section 162 of the code as a necessary business expense.

Through our strategic alliances, we can help provide "turn-key" services that begin with the initial feasibility study, continue through formation, and include full captive management services. Your team includes captive managers, CPAs, attorneys, underwriters and other professional staff. Because of our collaborative approach, we are able to deliver efficient and affordable captive management services, and avoid the confusion resulting from multiple firms, each providing only a portion of the management service.

In the past, many professionals either were unaware of CICs or avoided them because of their expense. In recent years, competition has lowered the threshold for using these powerful tools, creating great value and great opportunity. Of course, you must "respect the entity" by doing it properly and complying with the guidelines.

**What is a CIC?** Remember, a CIC is a legitimate insurance company, licensed to write insurance in the U.S., registered with the IRS, but typically "domiciled" in one of several states: Vermont, Delaware, Kentucky, South Carolina, and our current preference Utah. Or you may use an offshore jurisdiction, such as the British Virgin Islands. Most offshore CICs have lower capitalization requirements, but an added layer of administration.

**So how does a CIC work?** CICs are very basic. An individual, company, or trust sets up its own insurance company and funds it. Once setup, the CIC functions just as most insurance companies you are probably familiar with function. The CIC sells insurance coverage to various businesses, uses the premiums to invest and pay necessary claims, and if needed, purchases reinsurance to cover catastrophic losses.

As long as there are not to many claims, the CIC over time will accumulate significant money. Depending on the CIC structure, the income will be taxed in different ways during the wealth accumulation phase as well as the payout phase to the CIC owner when money is needed.

## Types of CICs

While there are three types of CICs, we will only discuss in this book, the primary tool our clients utilitze:

Small Insurance Companies - Insurance companies with annual premium income of less than $1.2 million are considered to be "small" CICs. It is possible for them to elect to be taxed only on investment income. Income from premiums paid into the CIC is tax-free. Investment income earned on the funds held inside the insurance company is taxable at ordinary C corporation rates.

Due to significant abuses with 501 (c) captives, Congress recently changed the laws to make 501(c) (15) captives not nearly as advantageous and most new captives are setup as 831(b) s.

**CIC as a risk management tool:** A CIC primarily has risk management benefits. The main benefit from a corporation's standpoint is to supplement its existing insurance covers. For example, a trucking company might lower its workers compensation coverage and pick up excess coverage with a CIC. Many auto dealers use CICs for their warranty work, and often at great profit.

**The "Other" insurance coverage:** Generally speaking, when a small business sets up a CIC, the types of coverage purchased are ones in which the CIC owner hopes never have claims. Following are some other coverages:

- Loss of License Insurance
- Excess Mental Health Expense Reimbursement
- Health Insurance Difference in Conditions Expense Reimbursement
- International Travel Accident
- International Travel Medical Expense Reimbursement
- International Travel Disability
- International Communicable Disease Medical Expense Reimbursement
- International Kidnap/Ransom Investigation Expense
- Tax Audit Defense Legal Expense Reimbursement
- Criminal Defense Legal Expense Reimbursement
- Regulatory Investigation Defense Legal Expense Reimbursement
- Injunctive Relief Defense Legal Expense Reimbursement
- Bankruptcy Legal Expense Reimbursement
- Key Supplier Loss Expense Reimbursement
- Key Customer Loss Expense Reimbursement
- Product Recall Loss Expense Reimbursement
- Market/COGS Fluctuation Loss Expense Reimbursement
- Currency Risk Loss Expense Reimbursement
- Research and Development Expense Overrun Reimbursement
- Regulatory Legal Expense Reimbursement
- Sexual Harassment Coverage

All in all there are approximately 30 potential coverages, and many businesses find they purchase coverage for 7-19 different risks that otherwise were not covered.

**No loss of control:** The CIC structure allows for complete control by the business owner subject to disclosure. There is no need for the owner to trust any other person or entity with his assets.

**Avoiding the land mines:** "Pricing the risk" by an actuary is the greatest land mine. To create a CIC structure properly, using professionals who have expertise in the area is critical - especially the actuaries, attorneys, accountants, and insurance managers involved. You do NOT want to go with a firm you found on the internet or heard about at a fly-by-night seminar.

This is one area where "doing it right" is the only way to enjoy the CIC's benefits while staying out of trouble with the IRS. Because you WILL get audited. Getting and maintaining "clean" books will be a secondary benefit, then.

Example: Let's look at an example of how a captive can be beneficial to a small business owner: You, age 45, are a successful business owner with gross revenues of $10 million and profits of over $1.3 million (on which you pay income taxes to the tune of $500,000 per year).

Your business currently pays $200,000 annually in insurance premiums for various property and casualty insurance. You set up a *bona fide* 831 (b) CIC to help control insurance costs *and reduce income tax*. You raise the deductible on your current insurance policies with the traditional insurance companies.

You insure the deductible through your newly setup CIC. Once your deductible is higher, your traditional insurance premiums are reduced by $50,000 a year. You use the $50,000 of savings to insure the $50,000 deductible through your captive. In addition, you obtain new types of insurance coverage from your CIC that you could not or had not previously purchased from a traditional commercial insurance company.

The new coverage includes business interruption, terrorism, employment practices and fire damage to your tracts of timber. These are legitimate business risks that you have, whether you choose to insure for them or not. The premiums for this coverage are $750,000. You don't mind paying the $750,000 because the cash will be held inside your own captive insurance company.

Under Internal Revenue Code section 162, you may deduct all the premium payments. At a 40% income tax rate, this **saved you and your companies $520,000 of income tax**. And under section 831(b), the $750,000 of premium income received by your insurance company is also free of federal income tax. You repeat this every year for 4 years.

**CIC for wealth building/retirement planning:** You have placed $3 million into your CIC. This amount has grown by 5% per year, or $600,000 more. And **you can access this completely tax-free** if structured properly. At worst, you pay long-term capital gains *when you distribute* the money.

**CICs and Estate Planning:** Captive insurance companies also can be one of, if not the most powerful wealth transfer tools available to affluent business owners. How? If the CIC, upon setup, is owned by a client's children or a trust for the benefit of the children, when a premium payment is paid from a business to a CIC, the client is effectively moving a tax deductible dollar out of his estate literally overnight.

The effect is to avoid gift taxes and estate taxes. In the earlier example, your adult daughter could own the captive insurance company. Your businesses could pay premiums into the captive for legitimate insurance coverage. This also would help reduce your estate because the cash would be transferred to the captive insurance company owned by your daughter.

To say that a CIC is a powerful and tax favorable wealth building tool would be an understatement. They are terrific for the "right" client.

*Summary of Captives:* a CIC is an excellent way to self-insure, and to establish a large capital pool for risks. Though each contract usually runs in 12-month stretches for premium payments, these CICs are best used when multi-year (we recommend 3-7 years) commitments are anticipated. If there is a bad year and premium payments stress the business, the premium may be "made up" in arrears. The premium is deductible. And in the event that no loss occurs (that is, no judgment or settlement is paid on the risk), the capital may be accessed, when properly structured, in a lump sum, or slowly over time at the owner's discretion, by the CIC owner, tax-free (only the growth of the capital may be taxed).

**Conclusion:** CICs can be one of, if not the most powerful income and estate tax planning tools a business owner has at his disposal. They are not for everyone due to the costs and the fact that some very small companies may not be able to purchase enough legitimate insurance to make the CIC financially viable.

If you are a small to medium sized business owner looking to reduce income and potentially estate taxes through the purchase of legitimate business expenses, then you should strongly consider a CIC. For help on this topic, please feel free to contact one of the authors. Also, please see the links below for more information.

**For more on this topic please see** *Chapter 2: Section 16: Closely Held Insurance Companies (CIC)*

The following table shows how frequently and by how much the income tax thresholds have changed. This should give you pause, and highlight the importance of income tax reduction.

| Income Thresholds 1973 to 2014 | | | | |
|---|---|---|---|---|
| 1973 | 14.00%c | $ 1,000 | 70.00% | $ 200,000 |
| 1974 | 14.00% | $ 1,000 | 70.00% | $ 200,000 |
| 1975 | 14.00% | $ 1,000 | 70.00% | $ 200,000 |
| 1976 | 14.00% | $ 1,000 | 70.00% | $ 200,000 |
| 1977 | 14.00% | $ 3,200 | 70.00% | $ 203,200 |
| 1978 | 14.00% | $ 3,200 | 70.00% | $ 203,200 |
| 1979 | 14.00% | $ 3,400 | 70.00% | $ 215,400 |
| 1980 | 14.00% | $ 3,400 | 70.00% | $ 215,400 |
| 1981 | 14.00% | $ 3,400 | 69.12% | $ 215,400 |
| 1982 | 12.00% | $ 3,400 | 50.00% | $ 85,600 |
| 1983 | 11.00% | $ 3,400 | 50.00% | $ 109,400 |
| 1984 | 11.00% | $ 3,400 | 50.00% | $ 162,400 |
| 1985 | 11.00% | $ 3,540 | 50.00% | $ 169,020 |
| 1986 | 11.00% | $ 3,670 | 50.00% | $ 175,250 |
| 1987 | 11.00% | $ 3,000 | 38.50% | $ 90,000 |

| Income Thresholds 1973 to 2014 | | | | |
|---|---|---|---|---|
| **1988** | 15.00% | $ 29,750 | 28.00% | $ 29,750 |
| **1989** | 15.00% | $ 30,950 | 28.00% | $ 30,950 |
| **1990** | 15.00% | $ 32,450 | 28.00% | $ 32,450 |
| **1991** | 15.00% | $ 34,000 | 31.00% | $ 82,150 |
| **1992** | 15.00% | $ 35,800 | 31.00% | $ 86,500 |
| **1993** | 15.00% | $ 36,900 | 39.60% | $ 250,000 |
| **1994** | 15.00% | $ 38,000 | 39.60% | $ 250,000 |
| **1995** | 15.00% | $ 39,000 | 39.60% | $ 256,500 |
| **1996** | 15.00% | $ 40,100 | 39.60% | $ 263,750 |
| **1997** | 15.00% | $ 41,200 | 39.60% | $ 271,050 |
| **1998** | 15.00% | $ 42,350 | 39.60% | $ 278,450 |
| **1999** | 15.00% | $ 43,050 | 39.60% | $ 283,150 |
| **2000** | 15.00% | $ 43,850 | 39.60% | $ 288,350 |
| **2001** | 10.00% | $ 6,000 | 39.10% | $ 297,350 |
| **2002** | 10.00% | $ 12,000 | 38.60% | $ 307,050 |
| **2003** | 10.00% | $ 14,000 | 35.00% | $ 311,950 |
| **2004** | 10.00% | $ 14,300 | 35.00% | $ 319,100 |
| **2005** | 10.00% | $ 14,500 | 35.00% | $ 326,450 |
| **2006** | 10.00% | $ 15,100 | 35.00% | $ 336,550 |
| **2007** | 10.00% | $ 15,650 | 35.00% | $ 349,700 |
| **2008** | 10.00% | $ 16,050 | 35.00% | $ 357,700 |
| **2009** | 10.00% | $ 16,700 | 35.00% | $ 372,950 |
| **2010** | 10.00% | $ 16,750 | 35.00% | $ 373,650 |
| **2011** | 10.00% | $ 17,000 | 35.00% | $ 379,150 |
| **2012** | 10.00% | $ 17,400 | 35.00% | $ 388,350 |
| **2013** | 10.00% | $ 17,850 | 39.60% | $ 450,000 |
| **2014** | 10.00% | $ 18,150 | 39.60% | $ 457,600 |

Source: Circle of Wealth Money Trax

## TOP TAX BRACKETS
### Average is 58.43%

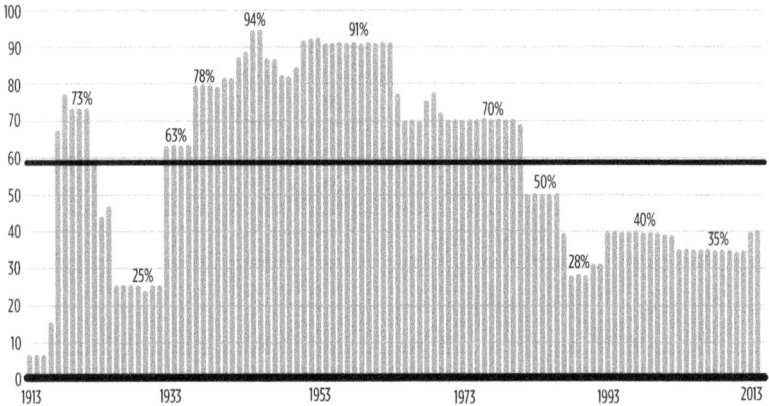

*Notice the highest income tax bracket was 94%! And the average highest income tax bracket is 58.43%. No wonder so many of us believe that income tax rates are likely to climb. No wonder we worry about high-income earners putting money into qualified plans. You would deduct at a low rate, only to remove at a higher rate. Not a good idea.*

http://www.mysummitwealth.com/wp-content/uploads/2012/10/
avoiding-medicare-3-8-tax.pdf

http://www.mysummitwealth.com/wp-content/uploads/2012/12/
Changing-Thresholds-vb-1.pdf

http://www.mysummitwealth.com/wp-content/uploads/2012/12/
Tax-History-vb.png

**Summary and Thoughts on Income Tax:** *Reduction*

We did not have space in this book to put some of the more outlandish topics that, in our opinion, are straight-out illegal tax-avoidance plans. Chances are good that in the next several years you will run into a plan that is not above board. We would like to end this section of the book with a few comments we hope readers will take to heart when reviewing "income tax reduction" plans:

1. Always have an independent advisor look a plan over before moving forward. Your local advisor many times will not be qualified or have time to review a complicated tax transaction; and, if that is the case, find another unbiased advisor to help review any income tax reduction plan.

2. Make sure someone or an entity pays tax on the money you are deducting into an income tax reduction plan. If you are saying to yourself, "isn't the point of an income tax reduction plan to avoid paying tax", the answer is NO. Tax avoidance is illegal. With all of the tax topics discussed in a favorable light in this book, someone or some entity pays personal or corporate tax on the money at some point.

3. If you do not feel comfortable even after your advisors say a plan is technically sound, do not do it. It is better to sleep soundly at night than worry about whether the IRS is going to come get you.

4. If you get pitched an income tax reduction plan and cannot find anyone you know to review the plan, please give one of the authors a call. We would be happy to give you our opinion. Also, if you would like more information on any of the topics covered in this section of the book, please feel free to contact us as well.

5. Finally, when trying to reach Critical Capital Mass, a properly and conservatively planned "income tax reduction" plan can help you attain CCM years earlier than conventional post-tax investing.

# Chapter 4
# Personal Finances

Personal finances are just that - personal. Some clients like to have their money actively traded in hopes of getting 20+ percent returns in the market. Others like to invest fairly conservatively in order to protect their principal, understanding that with conservative investments 10+ percent returns annually probably are not going to materialize.

Others do not have money to invest because they spend every penny they make. This section of the book is not going to give you stock tips for where to invest your money. Much of this section of the book is excerpted from the book on personal financial planning, "Smart Choices for Serious Money," available at Amazon, or call 407-656-2252 for your copy.

**Section 1:** *Life Insurance*

According to Nick Murray, the advocate of stocks for all investors, "life insurance is the backbone of financial planning." And this book on asset protection planning must also include financial planning to be complete.

The regulators frown on using the words "investment, savings vehicle, deposits" instead of *premium payments* when describing the money you pay for life insurance. Let's use the proper terminology.

If there is a way to fund a life insurance policy in a tax favorable manner like through a Section 79 plan, or possibly by borrowing funds from your

Captive Insurance Company, we might recommend looking into the feasibility. By and large, the IRS dislikes tax-deductible life insurance premiums, so beware.

Bank-Owned Life Insurance is a large industry. Banks own life insurance as a substantial portion of their capital requirements. They know a little about money. Life Insurance can often work out as a nice *tax-free* mechanism to store and cash. We already described how life insurance works in simple terms in Chapter One, Section 4. Here we will explore how to optimize life insurance in great detail for you.

THE MOST SUCCESSFUL CEOs AND PERSONAL FINANCIAL EXPERTS MEET THEIR CAPITAL EXPENSE NEEDS AND KEEP WINNING FINANCIALLY, USING LIFE INSURANCE. IN PARTICULAR, HIGH CASH VALUE, LOW DEATH BENEFIT, LOW EXPENSE LIFE INSURANCE.

Most of us, at least on occasion, have large capital expense needs (from business equipment, cars, to college education, and more). **Most important of all, from a capital standpoint, understand that you finance everything you purchase.** This is a very simple, yet very important concept that most fail to grasp.

So, I repeat: *You finance everything you purchase.*

Here is how. You either forego interest and returns when using your own money or you pay someone else interest to use their money. In doing so, you lose what that foregone interest or return could have earned; we can call this your "opportunity cost."

When repeated, this behavior becomes very expensive.

Whenever you borrow money and there is a fixed payment schedule, you pay something called amortizing interest. Each payment includes a little more principal and a little less interest. This continues until the payments of principal, plus the interest, equal the term of the loan.

Thinking of leasing a car or equipment? Please do not be fooled into thinking that leasing equipment is less expensive. It is not. It is much more expensive than common bank financing, no matter what the lease "factor" is.

When quantifying the imputed interest rate, most capital leases are in the 9-15% range. Leasing may be good for your cash flow; however, it is not less expensive. Compounding the issue of utilizing inefficient or expensive resources, too many of you mask your financial mistakes with your high cash flow.

Think about it, have you ever made a financial decision where the results were unexpected or disappointing? You are a smart, sophisticated and savvy business professional. Why does this happen? Could it be that you based your decision on misinformation, missing data, myths, or misconceptions?

There is a better way. Let's explore this further by first returning to the amortizing discussion.

REMEMBER THIS: COMPOUNDING INTEREST ALWAYS OUTRUNS AND OUTPERFORMS AMORTIZING INTEREST. It works best over time and works great when it is uninterrupted, untaxed, and undeleted. You may say you knew this already, yet are you practicing this in your business decisions? Is there evidence of this knowledge in your behavior when funding your capital equipment needs?

There is an alternative for making that capital purchase through leasing or paying for it out of your own pocket, one that is used by the smartest investors and consequentially, some of the most successful CEOs.

IT BEGINS WITH BUILDING YOUR "COLLATERAL CAPACITY." Do not be alarmed if you are not familiar with this term, because if it were common, you would already be doing it – and so would your competition. Building your collateral capacity usually takes place in an asset protected account.

We will call this account your **Private Capital Reserve Strategy** (PCRS).

IMPORTANT NOTE: PCRS IS A STRATEGY, NOT A PRODUCT.

Also, it is a savings strategy, not an investment. This strategy creates conditions necessary for your account to grow and to compound without delay taxation. With this strategy, you are using dollars for which you have already paid tax. You can access this account for any reason, at any time, without penalty, and with no tax. The account will continue to grow and to compound, while you retain liquidity, use, and control of the money. There are limitations.

CONSIDERING THE SAFETY OF THIS STRATEGY, YOUR POTENTIAL FOR GROWTH WILL BE LOWER THAN THE MARKETS. You also will not take on the risks associated with the markets. In fact, your money is always there and your principal protected. As long as you follow a few simple rules, you can never lose your money. While you neither take on the market risk nor access the comparable potential for growth, you will get competitive rates of return.

Currently, many accounts are paying 3-4.5% <u>tax-free, with a guarantee</u>, usually on the order of 1-2%. These rates could go up and they could go down. However, you will never lose the money in your PCR. As you build your PCR, your account continues to grow. Another potential limitation is time.

IT TYPICALLY TAKES FOUR TO NINE YEARS TO BUILD A REALLY EFFECTIVE CRITICAL CAPITAL MASS IN YOUR PCRS.

How does it work? After you have built your collateral capacity sufficiently, say by saving $100,000 per annum, you will have approximately $745,000 in seven years. This money will continue to compound at a solid rate.

Now, let's say you need to purchase a new equipment with a price tag of $375,000. The equipment has a technological life of five years. Had you leased this, the payments might cost you $8,500 per month and it would likely be near obsolete five years from purchase.

Now that you will pay cash (not your cash), you have negotiated the price down to $350,000. This is already a savings of $25,000. That savings can earn a significant amount of interest for you, adding again to your already growing collateral capacity; however, for the sake of staying focused on this article, we can discuss that another time.

Put simply, you lien your PCR to access the cash, saving you money off of the top and buying you tons of opportunity in the future. Then what? You reduce the lien by paying it down and you choose the amount you should have paid had you leased the equipment—the same $8,500 per month for 60 months.

## WHAT IF YOU SKIP A PAYMENT?

Not a problem. This is not a *structured* loan. You can skip payments for a very long time if you must. It is better, though, not too. Soon you would have the original $700,000 in your account, plus the interest it earned, plus the amount you used to reduce the lien, totaling a whopping $1,050,000.

You can access this account for any reason, at any time, without penalty, and with no tax. You build your personal wealth and security by using the safe and tax-advantaged (IRS section 7702) compounding effect of the insurance carrier dividend payments (which are always dependent on the claims paying abilities of the carrier). We prefer you use only highly rated companies.

**To review:**

1. You have all the money you put into the account
2. You have all the payments you would have paid to a bank or leasing company
3. You own the equipment.

You can achieve this by simply utilizing the power of the velocity of money multiplier to your benefit.

RATHER THAN BENEFITING THE BANKS or the leasing company, you build your personal wealth and security by using the safe and tax-advantaged Private Capital Reserve Strategy. We're talking about your firm and your passion. Doesn't it make sense to pay yourself for growing it? For more on how to use this to your advantage, contact the author.

**Section 2:** *Section 529 Plans*

*Another Sensible Way to Save for a College Education:* Because readers of this book are typically in a group of high-income parents, you have created a two-fold problem when it comes to paying for your children's education. First, because you are "high income," your children believe, by right, that their parents must pay for college. To make matters worse, even some courts have agreed that you MUST pay for your child's college education. Yuk. We will see if that holds up on appeal.

Second, because high-income parents are in the highest income-tax bracket, it costs them an extra 40% or more to pay for college. Are you looking for a way to save for your child's or grandchild's college education including tuition, books, and room and board? Do you like the idea of money growing INCOME-TAX-FREE?

Are you looking for a college savings plan that allows investments far beyond the $500 Educational IRA? Would you be interested in reducing your taxable estate **without** paying a gift tax and **without** giving up control of the money? We created this section to introduce you to the Section 529 Plan.

These plans have been around for some time. You probably have heard of the original plan that allows you to put money into an account with the state for use at a later time **IF** your child goes to a school in the state where the money was contributed. Further, that school must be a state-run school, not a private school.

The new Section 529 Plans have been tweaked by Congress to allow you to contribute to a 529 Plan, have the money grow, and then take out the money income-tax-free as long as when the money is taken out, it is used for college tuition, room and board, and books. Unlike the old plans, the money in a 529 Plan can be used to pay for ANY two or four year school that qualifies, anywhere in the country.

With the average cost of a four-year education being $47,000 for a public school and over $100,000 for a private college, it is no wonder parents are having trouble sleeping at night. Factor in inflation, and the numbers jump to $115,000 and $250,000 respectively in 20 years. That means the cost to someone in the 40% tax bracket in 20 years will be $190,000 pre-tax to pay for an $115,000 four-year education, and over $400,000 pre-tax to pay for a $250,000 four-year education.

We all hope the cost of education does not go that high, but we use the 20-year projections to illustrate why you need to deal with the topic today. What can be done? As we have stated, the new Section 529 Plans are really the only viable option we know where a parent or grandparent can immediately put a significant amount of money away tax-deferred every year to protect against this problem.

If you have friends who are trying to put two children through college, ask them if they would have contributed 10-15 years earlier if there was an opportunity to do so into an income-tax-free vehicle where the money could come out and the gains would NOT be taxed. We all can do compound math, but we think an example will be helpful.

If you put $10,000 away into a Section 529 Plan starting in 2007 for five years and that money grew at an assumed 8% until 2021, you would have approximately $136,000 of which $86,736 would be growth. Normally, the growth would be taxed. With the new 529 Plans, the growth is not taxed, thereby freeing up an extra $34,694 if you were to take the money out in one lump sum in the tax bracket of 40%.

The five-year example would allow your child to take out $35,000 a year income-tax-free for four years and $19,905 income-tax-free in the fifth year to pay for tuition, books, and room and board. Remember the money left in the 529 Plan continues to grow at 8% while in the plan. Contrast this with the fact that you will have to find $58,333 a year pre-tax for four years and $33,175 in the fifth year pre-tax to provide the same value.

**In a nutshell:** You can contribute $10,000 post-tax a year for five years now while you are making a good income; **or** you can find approximately $58,333 pre-tax a year for four years and $33,175 for the 5th year starting in year 2021 when we have no idea what you will be making in this ever uncertain world.

**Side note for grandparents:** If you are a grandparent and you are trying to figure out a way to shrink your estate via aggressive gifting, charitable giving, or trusts in general, you should consider funding a Section 529 Plan for your grandchildren. It is a terrific way to immediately transfer wealth out of your estate while at the same time still having access to the money.

**Asset protection:** We have talked with several different companies that offer 529 Plans, and we cannot find one that will go on record and state that money in a 529 Plan is asset protected. There are some states that have language in their 529 statutes that try to make their 529 Plans protected from creditors, but no one knows for sure if that will work.

Our official position is that a 529 Plan is not asset protected; and we suggest that if you are worried about asset protecting a 529 Plan, you use a state that has language attempting to asset protect their 529 Plan even though we're not certain if that language will hold up in a court of law.

## Section 3: *Annuities*

Have you seen the ad, "I hate annuities and you should too"? How foolish. How sad. That is like saying, "I hate hammers," or "I hate cars." When would you hate a car? When you are flying to Europe. Or when you are going up the road of Telluride to find mountain goats, or big-horn sheep.

Annuities, like everything else you can purchase, are just a tool. Misapplied, or the wrong annuities may not be helpful -- or even worse. In the appropriate situation, using the proper annuities, there can be very powerful and enjoyable results. In fact, they are considered a "new asset class" by Drs. Milevsky, Babbel, and Pfau (professors at the University of Ontario, Wharton Institute at University of Pennsylvania, and the American College, respectively). [http://blogs.cfainstitute.org/investor/2013/06/11/the-us-retirement-crisis-essential-reading-and-resources-2/]. Annuities have been shown to lower risk and improve returns in your investment portfolio. We call the *fixed* variety the "**True Alternative Asset Class™**"

Annuities have been around since Roman times, in some form. They currently are used to transfer risk to an insurance company that ensures your income. They work by pooling the risk of several people to ensure income for a long time (10 years, 20 years, for your life, for the life of you and your spouse, and many other varieties). While if you "outlive" your own principal, you are a net winner; if you die before receiving all your capital back, you may not be a net winner.

Thus, annuities are contracts where the insurance carrier primarily returns your own capital, plus any returns the insurance company earns on your behalf, for as long as the contract remains in force. *All the returns accumulate tax-deferred.* Depending on who or what entity owns your annuity, the taxability of that income generally is beneficial: the return of your own capital is tax-free, and the gains are taxable. If your 401(k) or IRA owns it, all the income is taxable (since none of your premium was taxed yet. If your Roth owns it, all the income is tax-free.

Overall, the longer you hold the annuity contract, the better off you will be. And the longer you can receive the income benefits from your annuity, the better off you will be.

**Annuities come in two basic types.** *Fixed and Variable.* Fixed annuities may either be Immediate and Deferred. Fixed annuities pay a commission to an insurance agent, and are regulated by the insurance commissioners. Variable annuities pay a commission to registered securities representatives like stockbrokers, and are regulated by the securities industry.

*Immediate annuities are fixed* contracts with an insurance company where you pay a *fixed premium*, and they agree to pay you back your money, in *fixed amounts*, starting right away, for a defined, *fixed period of time*. If you die before you have received your anticipated full benefits, the insurance company, in most cases, gets to keep your premium. Immediate annuities therefore often pay a much higher monthly benefit (say 7.8% for a 70-year old) than deferred annuities (a 70-year old may receive 5.5%).

*Deferred annuities* are *fixed contracts* where you pay a *fixed premium*, that is allowed to grow for a period of time at your choosing, and then they pay you back your money plus the growth with a *fixed minimum amount*, for a defined *fixed period of time*. Deferred annuities may pay you a slightly lower monthly benefit than immediate annuities. This is often because in most cases, if you die before receiving your full benefits, the remainder is passed to your heirs. Thus, your premium is never "wasted". Deferred annuities come in different flavors. The growth may be fixed, or the growth may be tied to an index.

*Variable annuities* have *variable growth and the payments may be variable.* That means your principal may be at risk, and your income payments may also be at risk. We are not big fans of these because of the costs and the risks. If you pay an insurance to take on the risk to pay you income, it makes little sense to take back that risk. We will discuss more on this a little later. <u>If you own a variable annuity, contact the author to discover your options.</u>

**Variable Annuity (VA) Fees:** A variable annuity is simply an insurance wrapper around an investment that allows it to grow tax-deferred. This carries the usual fee from the insurance carrier (about 2% per year). In addition, you get to invest in mutual funds, sometimes those that have no other method of distribution. The mutual fund expenses run about 1.5% on average. Then there are other "riders" and fees. So you must make at least 3.5% just to stay even. We have seen some VA fees north of 4.7%. How can you possibly gain with that headwind? The thrill for the client seems to be tax-deferred growth; but when you look at a variable annuity closely, are you really getting what you hope and pay for? It depends.

**No guarantees. This is HUGE.** There are no investment guarantees. If the stock market tanks, so does the value your variable annuity. Most have no principal protection. Many will have minimum income guarantees once you decide to make your income election, or "annuitize" your annuity. Because of the opportunity for losses, these payments are substantially lower than for fixed annuities. A 70-year old may only be guaranteed 4% income on the original premium (vs. 5.5% for a fixed indexed annuity).

**Tax Advantages?** Too many mistakenly think a VA is some wonderful tax haven for money. In fact, you may pay more taxes on money coming out of an annuity than with traditional after-tax investments in a brokerage account. Alternatively, investments in your brokerage account would be taxed when you sold at the long-term capital gains rate of 15-20%. In a VA, you get a blended tax rate where all of the gains that come out of the annuity are treated as ordinary income.

Many salespersons sell products and investments based on the myth that clients will be in a lower tax bracket when you retire. We believe for most of our clients you will never be in a lower tax bracket; and, therefore, when money comes out of the variable annuity, you will pay income tax rates on the gains.

We feel more comfortable with a *fixed annuity* since you have a guaranteed rate of return. With a *fixed indexed annuity,* the fees are lower than in a VA because your money is NOT invested in mutual funds. Instead, with an FIA, the insurance carrier buys long-term "options", or LEAPS, on the stock market indices. So, if the markets go up, you get the gains, minus the cost of the options; if the markets go down, the insurance carrier is out only the cost of the option. Thus, you will never lose money.a

**Conclusion:** Variable annuities can work IF the stock market does not tank before you need to access your money and IF you are in a lower tax bracket after you retire. Variable annuities with the guarantee rider can also work for you if you know for a fact when you put your money into the annuity that you will at some point annuitize the contract.

All annuities are a form of insurance vehicle, specifically designed to "exhaust an estate." (As opposed to life insurance, which is designed to "build an estate"). Annuities are typically funded after-tax and are allowed to grow tax-deferred. We are going to explain the three most common types of annuities and give you our opinion of who is a candidate for each type. There are two main reasons companies continue to sell billions in annuities every year.

1. **Risks of stock market meltdowns** - When the stock market is down, annuity sales go up; and when the stock market is up, annuity sales go down. The reason is fairly simple - when the market is doing well, investors do not think they need the security of the annuity to guarantee their principal investment or the need to find a guaranteed return product. However, while you are in the "distribution phase" of your financial life, the "sequence of returns" can be critical and devastating. *Annuities protect you against this.*
2. **Guaranteed Income for Life** - With investors who are already in, or getting near retirement, many choose to put money in annuities

with the guarantee to protect against not having enough money to live on in retirement. It is one thing for a young investor to choose an annuity to protect a long term investment; but it is quite another for an older investor who might run out of money due to a lack of funds. You can *never run out of money*. Like Social Security.

If an older investor plans on retiring soon, you will be counting on some rate of return on your assets to live on when in retirement. If the stock market goes down significantly and the wealth of a client is not "principal protected", you might not be able to retire as planned; or, if in retirement, you might have to cut back significantly on your lifestyle due to financial constraints. Or, even worse, you might have to go back to work.

This is the reason that most of you should consider buying annuities. In fact, the U.S. Government, in 2014 allowed and now encourages annuities in your retirement plan. It is about time! **Ben Bernanke** (whether you like him or not is not the point), **as the head of the Federal Reserve who oversaw the Great Financial Meltdown of 2008 and its recovery, held over 90% of his money in annuities.** That should tell you something.

There are millions of Americans wishing they had put their money into guaranteed annuities prior to the crash of the stock market in 2008-2009. If protecting your income stream in retirement is important to you, then you should consider one of the annuities discussed in the upcoming pages.

**Investment returns of immediate fixed annuities:** The annuity company typically invests the money fairly conservatively. Many times, the investment returns mirror interest rates and are invested in conservative bonds. Overall, you will typically get the lowest rate of return with a fixed annuity due to the trade-off of a guaranteed annuity payment. This, again, is offset by higher monthly incomes. Why? You share risk with some who may not live long enough to receive the entire premium back.

**What types of payouts are available? More on Period Certain -** You can purchase a fixed annuity that pays you over a period certain such as 10, 15, or 20 years. Depending on your goals, a fixed payout period might be just what you are looking for. The annuity company, when entering into the contract with you, will promise to pay X amount for 10, 15, or 20 years, as negotiated.

You can budget for and *count on that money no matter what happens to the stock market or what the economy does.* When the payment period is over, there is no more money due to the client. You already received back your entire premium plus its returns. What if you die before the end of the term? Most period certain annuities will continue to pay the monthly or quarterly benefit to the beneficiary of the contract.

While some period certain annuities will immediately pay the balance to the beneficiary while others will continue to pay a monthly benefit for that initially designated period. With the lump-sum payout option to the beneficiaries at the annuitant's death, the monthly or quarterly annuity payment while living likely will be lower than the continued payments. Why? Because there is less time for your returns to accrue.

Features (good and bad) of Annuities:

Liquidity—They are not that liquid. Once you have made your premium payments, many types of annuities will allow only a penalty-free 10% withdrawal. Anything greater can lead to "surrender charges". If you think you might want your money sooner than 10 years after purchase, don't buy an annuity.

Surrender charges - If you withdraw more than the 10% from your fixed annuity in a lump sum there will be surrender charges for up to ten years after your purchase. This is actually for your own protection. Imagine if everyone but you wanted out at one particular time. There may not be enough money for the insurance company to honor its contractual guarantee to pay you. The surrender charges are like early withdrawal penalties in CDs. They discourage market timing by others, and they protect your contract.

Once you buy a fixed annuity, you should stay in it for at least as long as you want to avoid the surrender charge for giving up the annuity, or "1035" tax-free exchange to a different annuity. If yield rates go up by 5% for new fixed annuities in the year following your purchase, you will basically be forced to wait until your surrender charges evaporate to move your money to a different annuity.

Fees – Annuity fees come out of the returns your contract accrues. These fees are also attractive to other insurance companies if yours is unable to stay in business. This is good for you too. Another company will be happy to take over your contract.

Commissions – These are a cause of much debate. The annuity company has to make money, and the agent who sold you the annuity is also getting paid a nice commission. Though the commissions do not come from your premium deposit. All of your premium goes to work for your contract. The commissions come from the insurance carriers operating income.

The insurance companies' best distribution mechanism is through insurance agents. If they could eliminate that expense, you can bet they would. Immediate annuities usually pay about 2% of the premium. Deferred annuities can pay a lump sum 7%, or the commission can be a 1% "trail" for the life of the annuity, and anything in between.

What would the fee be if you had invested rather than purchased an annuity? If your agent is also an investment advisory representative, and if you were to stay with the registered investment advisor, you most likely would stay with that firm for more than 7 years. So the agent/investment advisor is effectively working for free on that asset amount after that period of time. Your real estate agents' commissions are usually 6%. These are competitive.

Guarantees – These are based on the companies' "ratings" and their "claims paying abilities". In addition, the internal fees are attractive to other carriers if yours is unable to honor its contract. Moreover, your premium often "resides" in a separate account. And finally, the insurance carrier has required reserves to cover the contracts as well as "re-insurance". Many states also have State Guaranty Associations that function like the FDIC that covers your CDs, only they are often better financed. Florida does not permit agents to present this fact to you. The insurance commissioners do not want this to be the deciding factor in your purchase decision.

Low rates - One major drawback of a fixed annuity is the fact that you might get stuck with low rates. In 2015, interest rates were almost at historic lows. Low interest rates are great for home and business loans – especially fixed loans like mortgages; but the return rates on fixed annuities follow those interest rates, and yields from fixed annuities in 2015 were pathetically low. Thus the indexing option can be very attractive.

**Guaranteed (FIAs) Fixed Indexed Annuities:** *Why the "New" Annuities can save you Money vs. Traditional CDs, Savings Accounts, and Rollover IRAs. Explaining the Simple but Confusing FIA.*

After the stock market "crash" of 2008-2009 where many segments of the markets went down over 50%, clients started realizing that the stock market really doesn't return 10%+ every year. Millions of people lost billions of dollars in the market over that three-year stretch, and now those same clients are looking for alternative investments with principal protection.

The "new annuity" is a nice but confusing option for the client to protect their investment dollars while still trying to participate in market growth. What is the number one principal protected investment used by clients? CDs. Why Certificates of Deposit? CDs are simple – there is a guaranteed return on the investment, and the investment can be changed at the end of a term of months or years.

CD rates typically under-perform the equity markets, as does any "fixed" return investment vehicle. Clients dislike the low return rates, especially because they are aware that they have to pay income tax on the return on an annual basis and would like to have something better. The problem, as we have demonstrated is that most variable investments have no principal guarantees.

**What about Fixed Indexed Annuities (FIAs)?** FIAs marry the **best of a fixed and guaranteed annuity and the potential growth of the markets with a principal guarantee.** And perhaps more importantly, FIAs allow the client the potential to profit from upswings in the market, but do not put a client's money at risk.

These are insurance products with complicated features we will simplify for you. There are "spreads", "participation ratios", and many riders. Spreads refer to the amount the insurance carrier will charge you in up markets for the cost of their options. Participation ratios refer to the amount of upside you will get when the markets go up. Most of the time you can expect between 50-75% participation.

In addition, there may be "caps" where the insurance company recoups some of the option expenses by limiting your upside. We prefer uncapped, high participation, low spread FIAs. They are available to independent agents.

**The Ugly Part of FIAs. Or, What is not fixed, that insurance carriers can change?**

1. The Caps - Most companies offering hard annual caps reserve the right to change those caps on an annual basis. They will always have a bottom cap threshold that they cannot go below. Clients need to understand this so they do not get upset when in a down market the 9% cap moves down to 7%. We prefer uncapped FIAs.

In some instances companies will have multi-year caps. Instead of having a cap each year, companies will have caps over a multiyear period. So a company could have a two year 15% cap, where the client will not be credited more than 7.5% a year for the two-year window.

2. Participation Rate - Many companies reserve the right to change the participation rate annually. A FIA might start with a 100% participation rate in an up market; however, if that market turns, that rate can be adjusted down to whatever minimum threshold is specified in the FIA contract.

One FIA with no "caps", and only a 2.5% spread in the current market has a 65% participation rate-- that has been reduced recently, with no advanced warning, from a 70% participation rate.

3. Spreads—due to the cost of guarantees on your principal, and the costs of the options, the carriers charge a spread. That is another fee. But only when the markets go up, and your account climbs greater than the spread plus the participation.

Putting these numbers all together: If you have a 2.5% spread, with a 65% participation ratio, the market index must climb greater than 3.9% before you get to enjoy any increase. A 3.9% market index increase X 0.65% participation, minus 2.5% spread = Zero. Under the same scenario, if the market index goes up 20%, you get 65% of that or 13%, minus the 2.5% spread, which nets you 10.5%. By the same token, *if the markets decline by 5% or 50% your account balance remains unscathed.*

**Practical application for FIAs:** There are really two types of investors for whom FIAs work best - those who have money in bonds, CDs, and other "fixed" products, and for those who place importance on maintaining principal in an investment portfolio. In other words, almost all investors.

**CDs vs. FIAs:** The typical scenario: say you have $200,000 in a CD or savings account. Most people like to keep money in a CD or savings account because they can have easy access to it in case of an emergency. Say that you do not end up needing any of the money for ten years; and at the end of the tenth year, you have a sum of $250,000.

If you had placed your money in an indexed annuity with a minimum guaranteed return rate of 1% but possible higher returns of 4%, you would have approximately $300,000. You have not paid taxes on the gain yet, because it grew tax-deferred for that 10-year period. And you could have removed up to $25,000 per year as needed, penalty-free, and tax-free.

If you do not need the cash in the short term, you can continue to let the money grow tax-deferred until retirement; and then you could "turn on the income" guaranteed for life .

**Guaranteed Lifetime Benefits Riders:** Through purchasing a "rider" with various names, such as "Guaranteed Income Benefit" you get income for your entire life, and even the life of your spouse. This rider often has a fee of 0.6-.95%. Some companies allow you to have flexibility with this rider. This rider's cost will have a drag on the cash value left to your heirs if you die before enjoying all the income benefits you expect.

In recent years, the percentage of guaranteed income offered has been in decline. Two big reasons for this: 1) increasing life expectancy. The "average" life expectancy of a couple aged 62, has a 60% chance of at least one person living to age 92, and a 30% chance of at least one living to age 97. Of course, you are not average. Your life expectancy is likely to be longer. And 2) Low long-term interest rates. With 10 Year Treasuries at around 2.2%, and 30 Year Treasuries at around 2.9%, it is difficult to support higher income amounts.

The guarantees can be "banded" or "annualized" increases. Banded means if you are in the age band of 65-70, or 70-75 years of age when you turn on your income stream, as of this writing, you may receive 5% or 5.5% respectively. Annualized, you might have 0.1% annual increases. For example, at age 65 you might get 5%; 66 –5.1%; 67 –5.2%; and so on. These amounts have been lowered in the past 10 years by a full 0.5-1%.

**Surrenders:** Both CDs and FIAs have surrender charges and periods. The longer the "surrender", the greater the returns. There are no good long-term investments we know of that are also good short-term investments.

Thus, the surrender is truly a non-issue. It is unlikely you will need all $250,000 in the short-term. The purpose is to have access to the liquidity ($25,000 per year as emergency funds) and long-term repayment. The longer the term of the repayment, the higher the repayment amounts, due to longer compounding and tax deferral.

**Rollover IRAs:** Retiring clients, or those who are close to retirement, should consider FIAs as a way to safeguard their wealth while still taking part in the gains from any upward growth in the stock market. Rollover IRAs appear to be very popular, but many roll into mutual funds with no principal guarantee. While you do not need a tax-deferred vehicle (annuity) inside a tax-deferred vehicle (IRA), *FIAs are still a great way to preserve principal* in retirement so you do not suffer your portfolio going backwards.

**Conclusion:** FIAs can be very beneficial to clients who seek to maintain principal on investments for a long time, while still participating in the upside growth of the stock market. FIAs try to get you the best of both worlds. In our opinion, they do a good job as long as you understand that, in a steady up or big bull market, the FIA account balance will lag behind traditional stock or mutual fund investments.

### Section 4: *Equity Harvesting or Debt Shields*

Everything you believe to be true about this may not be. Advanced apologies if your head is about to explode due to "cognitive dissonance" (where you hold two completely opposing ideas simultaneously). Just stay with it while you read this. You may get more clarity.

Equity harvesting is a concept that has been around for many years, but only recently is it completely derided. This may be one of the most misunderstood, under-utilized, and controversial concepts we present. The idea behind equity harvesting is simple: borrow money on an asset you already "own free and clear", and reposition the cash into a wealth-building vehicle that will grow tax-free and can be removed tax-free in retirement.

Ah, but you say, "debt is bad". We agree. Debt is bad, unless it is mortgage debt or some other kind that is income tax-deductible. Is it truly debt if you have the capital, but choose to use "other peoples money" (OPM)? We make a case that it may not be.

*We define true debt as "the purchase of anything that requires you to utilize anticipated future revenues to cover the costs of the purchase".*

Ah, but you "pay cash" you say? Well, please understand that **you finance everything you purchase**. Repeat after me. *"You finance everything you purchase".* Why? You either borrow someone else's money and pay interest, or you use up your own capital and forego interest. There is no other way. That is reality.

Equity harvesting is the most efficient way to utilize your locked-up capital. **Because equity earns nothing**. Zero. Never has. Never can. Never will. In fact, it is more likely to lose value due to the ravages of inflation.

Here is an example of why equity earns nothing. You and your twin own identical waterfront houses, each worth $1 million. Your twin paid 100% cash. You have 100% mortgage. Which house goes up or down in value as the markets change? Think carefully. That is correct. They both vary exactly the same, regardless of any debt. So then, how much did the equity in your twin's house earn when the values climbed? Zero.

Let's say you own an appreciating asset like a rental property. Let's also say you have no debt on it. Now let's say you want or need some of that capital. How do you get it? Only two ways; 1) you can sell the property; though you may not want to. And 2) you can ask the lenders, to loan you your own money back, for a price. Is that attractive?

Here are some questions for you, dear reader:

1. If you had the opportunity to borrow money with an interest rate of less than 4% to relocate elsewhere, would you?
2. If you were able to write off the interest on the loan, would that be helpful to you?
3. Would it be helpful if the place you invested the borrowed funds was a tax favorable environment where the money was able to grow tax-free and was able to come out tax-free, at any time, and for any reason?

If reading the above questions has not created an interest in this topic, we suggest you take the time to re-read the questions again. From a financial standpoint and when done right, the concept of **borrowing your own money** to reposition in a tax-favorable manner, and then being able to write off the interest on the borrowed funds, is a great strategy.

And, as you continue to read, you will see that even if you cannot write off the interest, using Equity Harvesting to invest can be a terrific wealth-building tool. What if we made the example more real world? By real world, we mean that we will assume a small spread between the lending rate on the life insurance policy loans and the crediting rate on the cash inside the policy.

| Age | Annual Premium | Total Premium | Cash Value | IRR on Cash Value | Death Benefit | Tax Free Withdrawals | Total Tax Free Withdrawals |
|---|---|---|---|---|---|---|---|
| 46 | 100,000 | 100,000 | 76,831 | -23.17% | 2,776,837 | 0 | 0 |
| 50 | 100,000 | 500,000 | 500,239 | .02% | 3,697,706 | 0 | 0 |
| 55 | 100,000 | 1,000,000 | 1,215,265 | 3.52% | 4,855,517 | 0 | 0 |
| 65 | 0 | 1,000,000 | 2,195,564 | 5.13% | 4,021,989 | 0 | 0 |
| 75 | 0 | 1,000,000 | 2,589,411 | 5.35% | 3,751,534 | 170,000 | 1,020,000 |
| 85 | 0 | 1,000,000 | 1,855,735 | 5.24% | 2,787,866 | 170,000 | 2,720,000 |
| 94 | 0 | 1,000,000 | 157,950 | 4.93% | 815,150 | 170,000 | 4,250,000 |

**Do nothing:** Let's re-examine how much better you did by using Equity Harvesting versus doing nothing. In the real world, doing nothing means spending every penny you have and not saving. In this book and our examples, doing nothing means allocating the money you would have used to pay interest on a loan to a brokerage account to build wealth and comparing that to how much wealth you can build by Equity Harvesting and funding a cash value life insurance policy. The following is a summary chart listing the previous numbers. The numbers for Loan I come from the life insurance illustration where we assumed NO spread between the interest rate on the loan and what the S&P 500 credits in the policy; Loan 2 is with a 1 % spread on the borrowing rate; and Loan 3 is with a 2% spread on the borrowing rate.

| After-Tax From | Tax-Free Brokerage Account | Loan 1 | Loan 2 | Loan 3 |
|---|---|---|---|---|
| From ages 66-90 | $19,038 | $23,000 | $26,800 | $30,000 |
| Total for 25 years | $475,950 | $575,000 | $670,000 | $750,000 |
| Improvement with EH | | $95,000 | $194,050 | $274,050 |
| % Improvement with EH | | 20% | 41% | 58% |

**Summary of the first example:** This chart should really crystallize the benefits of Equity Harvesting for you. With very conservative assumptions, Equity Harvesting improved your cash flow by 20% in retirement. With a 1% spread on the borrowing rate, cash flow improved by 41%; and with Loan 3, which is what most "experts" think will happen, your cash flow improved by 58%.

That's the power of Equity Harvesting. Also remember that the equity indexed life insurance policy you used is a conservative wealth-building tool due to the fact that the policy has an annual growth guarantee and locks in upside gains annually. You also have a nice death benefit to protect the family; and if the past 20+years is any indicator of the future, you should end up with over $100,000 more in tax-free dollars from your Equity Harvesting plan than simply funding a brokerage account.

What about the home mortgage deduction? The interesting thing about the previous example is that it worked even though you did not write off the interest on your home equity debt. Having said that, as a general rule (Title 26 Section 163) limits the deduction on home equity debt to $100,000 of new debt.

That leads many to believe that they can borrow $100,000 from their home and reposition that into cash value life insurance to build a retirement nest egg and write off the interest. Unfortunately, Section 264(a) 3 does away with the deduction if the borrowed funds are positioned directly into a cash value life insurance policy.

What we want you to take away from this section of the book is that there ARE ways to write off interest on $100,000 of borrowed funds even if that money is repositioned into a cash value life insurance policy. The ways to write off that interest, however, are outside the scope of this book. If you have an interest in this topic, the authors will be happy to talk with you about it.

How will writing off the interest on the loan affect the financial viability of Equity Harvesting? From what you have already read, you can see that it works well even if you don't write off the interest on the loan. Now, let's assume that you can use one of the ways to posture your $76,500 of home equity debt as tax-deductible.

Because readers will be in several different tax brackets, we are going to show you the numbers for the 15%, 30% and 40% tax brackets. We are also assuming that you itemize your deductions on your tax return. If you were in the 15% income tax bracket, you would get a $5,737 deduction on your taxes when you pay the interest expense on the $76,500 loan.

The "real" cost to you is not $5,757 but instead is $4,876. Therefore, when we create the financial comparison between Equity Harvesting using life insurance and doing nothing and investing money in the stock market, we will allow $4,876 to grow instead of $5,737. If you were in the 30% income tax bracket, your real cost to borrow the money annually would be $4,015.

If you were in the 40% income tax bracket, your real cost to borrow the money annually would be $3,442. Let's see how much money you could take out of a brokerage account after tax from age 66-90 in the three different tax brackets:

In the 15% income tax bracket he could remove $16,181 from ages 66-90 for a total of $404,525. In the 30% income tax bracket he could remove $13,324 from ages 66-90 for a total of $333,100. In the 40% income tax bracket he could remove $11,442 from ages 66-90 for a total of $286,050.

Let's see how Equity Harvesting, using life insurance with the numbers from earlier examples, compares to post-tax investing in the market with the money you would have had to allocate to the interest expense. For the following chart we used only the most conservative numbers when you access tax-free loans from his life insurance policy.

You will see that the numbers are quite significant.

|  | Brokerage Acct. (15%) | Brokerage Acct. (30%) | Brokerage Acct. (40%) |
|---|---|---|---|
| From ages 66-90 | $ 16,181 | $ 13,324 | $ 11,442 |
| Total for 25 years | $ 404,525 | $ 333,100 | $ 286,050 |
| Life policy from 66-90 | $ 575,000 | $ 575,000 | $ 575,000 |
| Improvement with EH | $ 170,475 | $ 241,900 | $ 288,950 |
| % Improvement with EH | 42% | 73% | 101% |

Because we know you are curious, we thought we would show you the difference with the other two higher amounts that you could borrow from your life insurance policy if there is an interest rate spread in a positive fashion when you borrow it in retirement. With a 1% spread, you could borrow $26,800 each year from ages 66-90 for a total of $670,000.

| | Brokerage Acct. (15%) | Brokerage Acct. (30%) | Brokerage Acct. (40%) |
|---|---|---|---|
| From ages 66-90 | $ 16,181 | $ 13,324 | $ 11,442 |
| Total for 25 years | $ 404,525 | $ 333,100 | $ 286,050 |
| Life policy from 66-90 | $ 670,000 | $ 670,000 | $ 670,000 |
| Improvement with EH | $ 265,475 | $ 336,900 | $ 383,950 |
| % Improvement with EH | 66% | 101% | 134% |

To say that Equity Harvesting works better if you can write off the interest would be an understatement. While we believe there are ways you can posture yourself to write off the interest on home equity debt, if you simply borrow money from the home and reposition it into a cash building life insurance policy with the contemplation of borrowing from it, the interest is not deductible.

As you have seen, that's not the end of the world; but I'm sure you like the last set of numbers much better where we show you being able to write off the interest. When we tell clients and advisors that Equity Harvesting is nearly a "no brainer" from a financial standpoint, if you can write off the interest, now you know why.

The numbers also make a great argument for why Equity Harvesting is close to a no brainer even if you can't write off the interest.

**Example 2:** The next example is for a more "affluent" client. Let's assume you are 45 years old and have been living in your current home for 10 years. You and your wife bought the home when your combined income was $80,000 a year, and now your income is in excess of $125,000 a year.

Additionally, since you bought the house, you have added another child to the family and generally speaking need a bigger house to live in. Therefore, you are now ready to sell the current house and "upgrade" to a new house with four bedrooms instead of three and three-and-a-half baths instead of two.

You bought your current home for $200,000, and it is now worth $400,000. The current debt on your home is $75,000. Your current equity in the home is $325,000. For easy math, let's assume that after the sale of your home and realtor fees, you will have $300,000 of equity. Also assume that you found a new home, which you can purchase for $500,000.

You read this book on Home Equity Management and Equity Harvesting, and the light bulb went on. You have decided that having debt on your home is a good thing, especially when you can write off the interest. Therefore, assume that you put 20% down on the purchase of the new home which leaves you with $200,000 of equity left over from the sale of your current home to reposition into a low-expense, non-MEC cash building life insurance policy.

How will you be able to grow your wealth using Equity Harvesting using the $200,000? INTEREST DEDUCTION: When you sell your home, remove equity, and purchase a new home with more or significantly more debt, you can write off the interest on the new home's debt. How much could you remove "Tax-Free" from this Equity Harvesting life insurance policy in retirement?

Remember that in these examples, we are assuming a 7.5% rate of return inside your over-funded, non-MEC equity indexed life insurance policy, which pegs its growth to the S&P 500 index. We are also assuming that you will start taking tax-free retirement money from your insurance policy from ages 66-90.

We are also going to assume that the home loan on the new home is a 7% interest only loan. The amount you could borrow tax-free from your life insurance policy starting at age 66 is $61,000 each year for 25 years for a total amount of $1,520,000. Unlike Example 1 where you could not really live on the retirement proceeds from your life insurance policy, with this example, you can live very nicely on $61,000 a year TAX FREE in retirement. Question: So what will this cost you to create your retirement nest egg?

In this example, we assumed that you used an interest-only loan instead of a 30-year amortized loan. Why? Because you "get it" and understand that the best place for your money is not in your home. You understand that it is better to control your own money vs. giving it to a bank. Therefore, you opted for an interest-only loan where the debt on the home will remain constant.

Let's say that the new home loan amount is $400,000. With a 7% interest rate, there will be an annual mortgage payment of $28,000. However, keep in mind that the Equity Harvesting debt is only $200,000, and, therefore, when I talk about the cost of Equity Harvesting for this example, the costs we will be talking about relate to $200,000 worth of debt not $400,000.

What is the cost to borrow $200,000 for you? $14,000 a year is the cost. Question: If you could incur an expense that is $14,000 a year and where the "tax-free" retirement income is $61,000 a year for 25 years, would you incur the expense? Your answer should be yes all day long.

Remember, if the debt was nondeductible for you and the numbers were similar to Example 1, the plan should work out 20%-58% better than "doing nothing." With this Example, we will be showing you how well Equity Harvesting will work for you when the interest is deductible.

If you were to place $14,000 a year into a typical brokerage account with the same conservative assumptions from Example 1, you would be able to remove approximately $46,500 from the brokerage account from ages 66-90 vs. the $61,000 after-tax that could be removed from the life insurance policy.

With the most conservative life insurance illustration, you ended up doing approximately 31% better with Equity Harvesting vs. doing nothing. In this example though, we know that you CAN write off the interest because the debt is home acquisition debt. Let's see how that affects the financial viability of this example.

You are in the 25% federal income tax bracket and we are going to assume you live in a state with a 5% state income tax. If you were in the 30% income tax bracket, you would receive a $14,000 deduction on your taxes when they pay the interest expense on the $200,000 worth of debt allocated to the Equity Harvesting concept.

The "real" cost to you is not $14,000 but instead is $9,800. Therefore, when we create the financial comparison between Equity Harvesting using life insurance and doing nothing and investing money in the stock market, we will allow $9,800 to grow instead of $14,000. Let's see how much money you could take out of a brokerage account after tax from ages 66-90.

In the 30% income tax bracket you could remove $32,521 from ages 66-90 for a total of $813,025. Let's see how Equity Harvesting using life insurance compares to post-tax investing in the market with the money you would have had to allocate to the interest expense. The following chart is eye popping.

For the chart on the next page, we used the most conservative numbers when you access tax-free loans from your life insurance policy:

| Brokerage Acct. (30%) | |
|---|---|
| From ages 66-90 | $32,521 |
| Total for 25 years | $813,025 |
| Life policy from 66-90 | $1,525,000 |
| Improvement with EH | $711,975 |
| % Improvement with EH | 88% |

If you are curious, the numbers would be 118% better if you were in the 40% tax bracket. As we indicated previously, the prior numbers are with the conservative life insurance illustration where there is no spread in the interest rate when you borrow money from the policy. As we indicated previously, most experts believe that the long-term lending rates on life insurance policy loans will be 2% less than the average return inside the policy with growth pegged to the S&P 500.

If there is a 11% spread between the S&P 500 crediting rate and the loan interest rate on the tax-free policy loans, you could remove from your life insurance policy $69,800 each year from ages 66-90 for a total of $ 1,745,000.

| Brokerage Acct. (30%) | |
|---|---|
| From ages 66-90 | $32,521 |
| Total for 25 years | $813,025 |
| Life policy from 66-90 | $1,745,000 |
| Improvement with EH | $931,975 |
| % Improvement with EH | 115% |

If you are curious, the numbers would be 150% better if you were in the 40% tax bracket. If there is a 2% spread between the S&P 500 crediting rate and the loan interest rate on the tax-free policy loans, you could remove from his life insurance policy $80,000 each year from ages 66-90 for a total of $2,000,000.

| Brokerage Acct. (30%) | |
|---|---|
| From ages 66-90 | $32,521 |
| Total for 25 years | $813,025 |
| Life policy from 66-90 | $2,000,000 |
| Improvement with EH | $1,186,975 |
| % Improvement with EH | 146% |

**Real Life Example:** "Jim," a client, owns a small company, "A", which has substantial assets. He called in a panic. Fearing "A", or Jim personally, or both may be a target of a lawsuit, how can he protect his assets? Jim also is owner of another company, "B" with retained free cash, after operating expenses, of over $1,00,000. "B" is and will not be a target of the lawsuit. After tax, had Jim removed the money from "B", he would be left with $600,000. And there is no way to effectively shield "A" without potential "fraudulent conveyance".

Uninvolved in any legal battle "B", however, loans $1,000,000 in cash to Jim and Jim's spouse as Tenants by the Entirety. The parties will execute a note, and file a "UCC" (Uniform Credit Claim) that encumbers the TBE. The TBE eventually will owe the money back to "B". The TBE will have to pay interest to "B" at the "AFR" (Applicable Federal Rate for long-term loans, currently at little more than 2%).

TBE purchases an uncapped Fixed Indexed Annuity (FIA) with the tax-free loan of $1 million. The TBE only pays the interest for 20 years. At that time, the note may be extended or re-structured or paid in full. The income tax on the $1,000,000 may also be deferred depending on whether and how and when the note is paid. Over 20 years, it is likely that FIA will at least have doubled in value to

$2 million, while the $1 million principal balance has *not* increased due to ongoing interest payments. And the power of inflation is on Jim's side. In 20 years, the $1 million owed is likely to *feel like only $300,000.*

Jim now also has the capacity to strip out the cash revenues from "A", and to make loans for operating expenses to "A" from the TBE, as needed in the normal course of business. That loan would be another senior secured note with a UCC to TBE. The loans to "A" must be paid before any liquidation to settle any potential claims of the lawsuit creditors.

Jim has the liquidity.

The asset is protected.

Jim has harnessed the power of inflation.

The asset in the FIA grows tax-deferred.

**Summary:** Simply put, Equity Harvesting can be one of, if not the best way for many readers to build a tax-favorable retirement nest egg. While Equity Harvesting is not a cure-all topic to fix the shortfall of retirement wealth that nearly every reader has, the concept has many more pros than cons. Equity Harvesting can be postured as a low-risk concept if you choose to use a high cash value life insurance policy. Additionally, because you can use a life insurance policy that has guarantees on your cash value and locks in the investment gains, which can be pegged to the S&P 500 each year, you can have money positioned in a much safer and less expensive environment than investing money in stocks and mutual funds.

There are strategies to posture Equity Harvesting so the interest on your home loan is deductible. If you use one of those methods, using an Equity Harvesting plan to grow your wealth is probably one of the easiest wealth-building tools you'll ever find. Having said that and as you've seen by reading over the numbers in this chapter, Equity Harvesting can still work out much better for you than the typical "do-nothing" position we all take in life more often than we should.

Finally, we've done our best to give you real world numbers and examples in this chapter. In order to keep the chapter relatively short, we did not insert examples for every age and economic status for every reader. To do so would be interesting to some but boring to others. The way to determine if Equity Harvesting is "right" for you to use as a conservative, tax-favorable, wealth-building tool is to find an advisor who can help you.

If you'd like help to determine if Equity Harvesting is a good way to grow your wealth for retirement, please turn to our contact information and give us a call or drop us an e-mail. We'd be happy to help.

**Section 5:** *Investment Protection Strategy?*

**What is investing nirvana?** High upside potential, with little to no risk, and little to no cost or tax. It exists only in the land of unicorns. In the next few pages we will go into some myths, some truths, and the factors that make up successful investing, as excerpted from my book, *"The Science of Successful Investing Made Simple"*.

## HOW TO BUILD A BOMB-PROOF INVESTMENT PORTFOLIO: The 10 Myths That Cause Investors to Fail

Investing is a reality-based, evidence-based activity – or it should be. Unfortunately, for all too many investors, reality and evidence are circumvented by false ideas that prevent understanding and sound investment decision-making. Ten myths in particular hamper the investor and need to be recognized for the false ideas that they are. Avoid these ten fables and you will have a good start on the road to sound, scientific investment choices. Here are the myths:

1. **Investment is a Do-It-Yourself Project.** Most investors not only lack the expertise, they also lack the discipline and the

time necessary to properly develop, allocate and manage their investment portfolios. The DALBAR research organization shows that investors continue to <u>under-perform</u> by an astounding *3-7% annually* over any 20-year period of time.

2. **You Can Get Rich Through Investing.** This rarely happens. If you're already rich and have a lot of money both to invest and to hire the best advice and management, you can get rich*er* through investing, but for most people, whose capital for investment is limited, investment is a way of protecting assets and creating a fund for your goals, not a road to riches. Your gains will be a function of how much you have to invest, and a rate of return capable of turning modest means into great wealth is very unusual.

3. **Bond or Stock Picking Can "Beat the Markets."** There is risk inherent in all investments, roughly proportional to the returns, and it can't be avoided. It's true that at any time, some stocks or other investment vehicles outperform the market average, but relying on this to gain excess return is an unwise strategy. It's the nature of the beast that some investments will lose money.

4. **"Track Record Chasing" Can "Beat the Markets."** Just as some investors rely on stock-picking to achieve high returns, others similarly look for the best track record either of investment vehicles or of managers. While there is nothing wrong with judging an investment based on its track record (among other factors), and certainly you should carefully evaluate anyone you consider trusting with your money, the idea that you can achieve excess returns in this way is simply false. Risk is roughly proportional to the expected return, and although a good portfolio that is properly maintained will show a net gain over time, individual investments *will* lose money from time to time.

5. **Market-Timing Tactics Can "Beat the Markets."** Far too many investors sell out when the market is falling and buy back in when it's on the upswing. If you don't have capable investment advice and management by professionals, you may be doing this. Some investors believe that by choosing when to buy and sell investments based on their rise and fall, they can beat the market average and avoid risk. As with stock picking and track record chasing, avoiding risk is not possible. Risk is part of return. And market timing, by any name or means, is a fool's errand. Unfortunately, even many stockbrokers will still engage in this.

6. **Trading, Custodian, and Research Costs Don't Matter.** Many of these costs are not readily apparent. It's easy for unnecessary fees, taxes, and other expenses to eat up your returns if you don't keep a lid on them. Managing investment activity so as to contain these expenses is part of the package.

7. **Conspiracy Theories.** The belief that there is someone, somewhere manipulating prices, or that someone can employ "arbitrage" to outsmart the markets, or that people "in the know" can consistently take advantage of "mispricing" to get a leg up over other investors or managers leads to wild-goose chases, unrealistic pessimism, and poor decisions.

8. **Oversimplifying the Math.** The math of investment is more complex than a simple average, and it's possible to have an average return that looks like a gain but is really a loss. For example, suppose you invest $100 that has a 100% gain the first year and a 60% loss the second year. That averages to a 40% gain over two years, or 20% per year – except it's not, because the loss in the second year is based on double the volume of the first year's gain. That $100 investment becomes $200 at the end of the first year, and in the second year it loses 60% of its value, or $120, and you are left with only $80 – a $20 *loss*.

9. **The Wizard of Odds is Out There.** Some investors believe that there is someone with a special formula for consistent, low-risk

investment, and that enlisting that person's expertise (for a modest fee) will enable them to make a killing in the market. Expertise and knowledge about investing do vary, and sometimes people achieve surprising successes, but there is no magic formula, no way to consistently, reliably beat the market.

10. **Your Behavior as an Investor Doesn't Matter.** Peter Lynch, the famous investment-fund manager from the 1980s, once said, "Far more money has been lost by investors preparing for corrections or trying to anticipate corrections than has been lost in the corrections themselves." A lot of the value of stocks and other investment vehicles is created (or destroyed) by investor behavior, rather than by anything inherent in the stock itself. When the stock is doing well, money pours in, and when it does poorly, money pours out, in a pattern known as the "Greed-Fear Cycle." Risk tolerance changes from good to bad years, and investor panic or irrational zeal has ruined more than one otherwise sound portfolio.

A wise investor will see the investment market for what it is: a way to achieve a solid return on investment that arises because, overall, return outweighs risk. A wise investor won't see the market as a get-rich-quick scheme, or hold unrealistic expectations of never seeing an investment go sour, or suffer from equally-unrealistic fear of losing everything at once (virtually impossible with a diverse portfolio), or a morose conviction that ordinary investors can't succeed because some evil capitalist mastermind is fixing prices, or a lack of awareness of the way that their own behavior and that of other investors twists and shapes the market.

What should replace these misconceptions, these ten myths about investing?

Investors should treat investment rationally as a scientific enterprise that is statistically predictable even though the performance of any one investment may not be predictable. There are sound rules to investing and most of those are common-sense principles that are not at all hard to follow. These rules won't allow you to become wildly rich from your investments (see myth no. 2, above), but they will allow you to gain a steady and reliable return, to safeguard your assets from inflation and taxes, and to provide an income later in life when your investments mature.

## THE 16 TRUTHS ABOUT INVESTING FOR POWERFUL PERFORMANCE AND LONG-TERM SUCCESS

Many people hold false ideas or myths about investing. Some even believe in a "magic formula" that can avoid risk and provide a high return, or that a conspiracy drives the market and fudges prices, or that investing is a way to get rich. At the same time, there are a lot of true things about investing that many people don't know or don't believe. Here are the truths:

1. In the 230 years that equity markets have existed in 16 countries, there has never been a 20-year period of time when they have shown a negative rate of return.

2. There have been only two periods when stocks underperformed bonds on the average for 30 years. Those periods were the time ending in 1865 (and including the American Civil War), and today.

3. On the other hand, the markets have shown negative returns quite frequently for shorter periods of time. For that reason, you should be investing in the market with a long time frame in mind.

4. When you invest, know your risk tolerance precisely. This means expressing it as a number, not just a phrase like "I am conservative" or "I am aggressive." By what percentage can you accept your portfolio declining during a year? Although you can reasonably expect the value of your portfolio to increase over time, fluctuations downward will happen and there will be periods when it will lose value. How much of this fluctuation are you willing to accept?

5. When you invest, you should have a clear idea for what you are investing. Is it to pay for college in ten years? Are you on the

brink of retirement and concerned with having enough income for the next 30 years or more? Whatever it is, the purpose for which you invest will determine a lot of our decisions.

6. Inflation matters, even when it is low – as at present. It's never zero, and that means your income from investment needs to grow by at least enough to cover the loss in the value of money over the period you're investing to cover.

7. Investing is not a do-it-yourself, instinctive, by-the-gut endeavor. Our instincts evolved to avoid danger in a primitive environment, and many sound investment decisions go against that mindset. A good investment manager can help with this, as that manager is one step removed from the emotional impact of shifts in the value of your investments. But many managers can fall into the same trap. Even more than portfolio products and construction, therefore, you need an evidence-based, rules-based system that is sophisticated in its simplicity.

8. You will not get rich in the stock market. You already may be rich. If not, you should not place your savings at risk of the price fluctuations. Investing in the stock market is a good way to protect your assets from inflation and ensure long-term appreciation, but the prospect of turning modest means into great riches is a myth. It almost never happens.

9. It is impossible to predict exactly which company, manager, industry, geography, or asset class will outperform the market average. This is why it's important to diversify.

10. Shares in small companies outperform shares in large ones, over time. At the same time, they fluctuate more in value and so may present greater risk (which goes along with their higher average return). How much small company ownership depends on your risk tolerance, your time horizon, and the purpose for which you are investing.

11. Disciplined, strategic indexing will provide you with a solid portfolio—the core. This should be at least 50% of your portfolio. And it leads to the virtue of buying low, while selling high.

12. Fees, taxes, and expenses count, and they count a lot. Saving a mere one or two percent in these costs can have a huge impact on the value of your portfolio over 20 to 30 years (the average retirement expectancy). For this reason, we want low turnover in our portfolios. The less frequently you buy and sell company shares, the lower your transaction costs. If you are tempted to "micromanage" your portfolio so as to only hold shares in any particular company when they are increasing in value, keep this in mind. Every purchase or sale carries a cost, and those costs can easily outweigh any gains from time-hopping, particularly since that's unlikely to work well anyway.

13. Opportunity costs also matter a lot. Expenses, taxes, and other lost funds count for more than their face value, because they also cost you what they could have earned you if they had not been lost in the first place.

14. Government intervention affects the economy more than it does your long-term investment. The same is true of major economic events such as a recession, even on the scale of the Great Recession. Such things may affect your portfolio's short-term values, and the panic that sometimes sets in among investors can affect it even more (see Number 15 for how that can have a major negative impact), but remember that you should be investing over a long time scale. Watch the world, not the West, and concentrate on the companies, not the countries.

15. Sequence of returns is not important while your assets are accumulating value, but it becomes critical when you reach the distribution phase of your investments. When you are receiving distributions from your investments, a short-term dip in value can have a major negative effect because you may still have to take the distributions in order to maintain your lifestyle. This puts further downward pressure on your

account balances. Other strategies, in addition to investments, may be called for to offset this. While you are not actively taking distributions from the investment accounts, what the early or late returns are doesn't matter much. You are concerned mainly with the long-term trend and net investment return.

16. The best time to start investing is 20 years ago. The second-best time is now. Always keep your investments aligned with your long-term strategy, your risk tolerance, your time horizon, and your goals – not someone else's or some arbitrary figure that may have been supplied by an "expert" who doesn't know your situation.

There are other details to the science of investing, of course, but these 16 truths lie at the heart of an evidence-based, rules-based, disciplined system that can guide your investments. Those rules and that system are not intended to avoid risks or short-term losses (which inevitably will happen and are unavoidable), nor to let you turn modest amounts of capital into great wealth (which is virtually impossible and certainly can't be made to happen), but will help you to invest for the reasons investment is a good idea. It will help you to safeguard your assets against inflation, provide you with an income for whatever purpose you need it for, and let you achieve a measure of financial security in retirement.

## THE SEVEN FACTOR SYSTEM THAT SPELLS SUCCESS

Too many in the financial media suggest that investing is an "art." They encourage investors to seek help from "special" individuals who have unique talents in the "art" of "beating the markets."

In reality no individual and no method can reliably "beat the markets" over the duration of a long-term investment lifetime. But that isn't necessary. You won't get rich investing in stocks anyway, contrary to myth. You will enjoy solid growth, over the long run, without "beating the markets."

It is better to treat investing as a science rather than an art. It doesn't require any special talent or mystical insight. All that's necessary is an evidence-based system with sound rules and good discipline to follow it.

With that in mind, here is an outline of the Seven Factorä System: simple rules that drive powerful performance.

1. **Control costs and risks.** Each transaction (buying or selling) carries associated costs and fees. These can add up over time, and the more often you trade, the more fees you will incur. It's important to know these costs and to include them in your calculations. Also, it's important to know the risk of loss for any investment. Risk and return are two sides of the same coin. The higher the returns expected for an investment (on average), the higher the risk. Investments with very high return also run a high risk of losing money instead in any specific case, while relatively safe and secure investments are also low return. As discussed in Part 2, avoiding the losses is more powerful than picking the winners, and consistent excellence outperforms occasional brilliance.

   That doesn't mean there's anything "wrong" with either a low-risk, low-return investment or a high-risk, high-return one, but it does mean you need to be aware of the risk factor with any investment you consider.

2. **Own shares of the world's greatest companies.** Watch the world, not the West, and concentrate on the companies, not the countries. However glum the economic outlook may seem for the U.S. and some other advanced countries, the world is in growth mode, with millions of people exiting poverty every year and the global middle class growing quickly. The world's greatest corporations are seeing record profits, and owning a share of that business is simply good sense.

3. **Diversify broadly.** How can you tell which companies will do well and which will do poorly, so as to know where to invest?

You can't. It's that simple. No one can. You can make an educated guess, but unpredictable factors can undermine even the best companies and managers. Yogi Berra, the professional baseball star known for his malapropisms, said "predictions are difficult to make – especially about the future." The solution is to diversify your investments in a wide variety of companies, industries, countries, and management styles.

4. **Leverage inexpensive stocks.** "Inexpensive" here doesn't mean low-priced, but rather a low price-to-book-value ratio. There are many reasons why this can happen, and these are not the only stocks you should invest in, but they are an important part of any buy-low/sell-high strategy, as the price is low but the company has assets indicating it could generate more value.

5. **Utilize smaller companies.** Smaller companies have more growth potential and hence higher returns on investment. They also have higher risk to go along with that. This may not be obvious. It has to do with the way that growth works. Say you have a company that's worth two billion dollars compared to one that's worth 200 billion, and suppose that each grows by $500 million in a given year. For the smaller company, that represents 25% growth, but for the larger one only 0.25% growth. It's the percentage that affects the stock value rather than the aggregate growth, and smaller companies tend to grow faster in percentage terms because they start with a smaller base. At the same time, with a smaller base, the smaller company can also see heavier losses, not because it is likely to lose more total dollars than a big company, but because any such loss represents a greater percentage of its total assets.

Your portfolio should not consist only of smaller companies (diversify, once again), but these investments are the ones that can potentially grow the fastest and see the highest returns.

It's important to bear in mind that a risk of loss exists on every individual investment. The idea is not to avoid that risk (that's impossible), but rather to see a solid net return – gains minus losses – over time.

6. **Allocate strategically.** Know the reason why you are investing in the first place, and allocate your investment resources so as to achieve that goal. There are a number of models for doing this. One of the most effective is a "core and satellite" approach, in which you make a distinction between investments which provide a solid, steady return with lower risk (the "core") and those that can generate higher returns but carry greater risk (the "satellite" investments). Maintain a certain percentage of your portfolio in the core investments, and you may designate a portion of your investment funds as going to satellite investments. This goes beyond investing in stocks; bonds, commodities. And insurance products may form a part of a portfolio as well. The strategic allocation of resources into each asset class reduces risk, since factors that may impact one class negatively may have no effect or even a beneficial effect on others. This is called low correlations.

7. **Take a disciplined approach to managing your investments.** The investment research company DALBAR discovered that the average investor's portfolio underperforms the market average by three to seven percent per year. The biggest culprit, the firm found, is investor (and unfortunately, too many advisor's) behavior, specifically emotion-driven behavior such as track-record chasing, and the greed-fear cycle. Investment decisions driven by emotion and impulse can cause an investor to buy high and sell low, to make too many transactions and incur unnecessary fees and costs, to panic when an investment loses value and sell out when you shouldn't, or to jump on the bandwagon of a rising asset without considering whether the rise can continue or for how long, or that by the time an investor has noticed the growth the price is already high (and the price-to-value ratio may be higher still).

The use of objective rules; a recognition that all investments carry risk (albeit this is unavoidable); awareness of the costs and fees associated with transactions and how these add up and cut into the returns on the investments; and above all, maintaining discipline and avoiding impulsive actions based on emotion rather than reason -- is the key to making it all work for you. This may be the most important of the seven factors, as violating it is the main reason why so many investors see a poor return (in many years, actually lower than the rate of inflation).

There is a good deal more to the science of investment than these broad rules, of course, but keeping these seven factors in consideration at all times will allow you to invest and see, over time, a good return.

## GREAT EXPECTATIONS? OR RISK IS NOT VOLATILITY.

Have you heard the old joke that economists have predicted nine of the last two recessions[1]? And do you wonder why it seems like terrible events like a plane crash always make the news? It's because these are uncommon events, and events out of the ordinary are much more likely to make the news.

Risk has two major components; severity and probability. When you put those on the two axis, so many of us only focus on the severity of the risk and too many forget the probability of that.

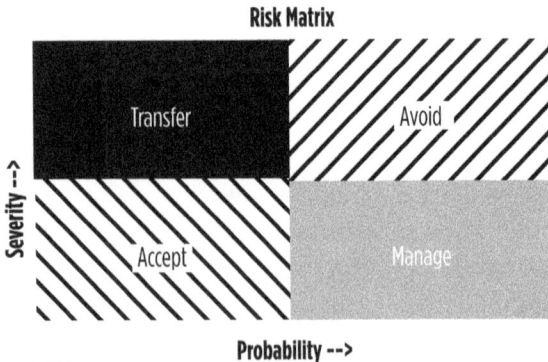

Risk Matrix

Transfer

Avoid

Severity -->

Accept

Manage

Probability -->

---

1 Could that be why economics is also known as the "dismal science"?

*For more on this topic, please see CHAPTER 1: Asset Protection Planning*

Severity of investment risk is that prices temporarily decline by about 50%. Probability of that risk of a large decline occurs every 30 years. Since 1926, the average time for a major market top through the subsequent bear market and back to full recovery is about 40 months (3.3 years). So if you begin retirement with three years' living expenses in cash equivalents, you have covered the great preponderance of possible historical outcomes, to safeguard that risk and to further enhance your returns within your tolerance for risk.

And when looking at risk, we must define whether this is a problem or a fact of life. If it is a problem then you can rest assured that there will be a solution. If there is no solution, it is a fact of life. Facts of life are not risks. Risks are problems. Many facts of life may or may not present risk. Is there such a thing as longevity risk? I don't think so. It is not a risk at all. It is a simple fact of life. We know there is a greater than 60% chance that for a couple aged 62 right now, at least one of you will live well into your 90s. That to me is not a risk. That is a fact of life. True risk is not planning that your assets and income carry you into your 90s and even beyond.

What about investment risk? Is there such a thing? It is a phenomenon, a fact that a properly constructed portfolio held for the long-term has no basis in reality. What about purchasing power risk? Well that is also an eternal fact of life[2].

A properly constructed investment portfolio will be able to withstand the risks over the long term. Charlie Munger of Berkshire Hathaway says, "if you're not willing to react with equanimity to a market decline of 50% two or three times a century, you are not fit to become a common shareholder and you deserve the mediocre results you're going to get compared to the people who do have the temperament to be more philosophical about

---

2 See my article, "The Third Sure Thing: Death, taxes and inflation."

market fluctuations." Of course, by this he assumes you are "over" invested in stocks. You are not. Very few are. Even fewer should be.

Our goal is to identify and maintain your comfort level of risk tolerance, so you never experience a 50% decline. We accomplish this through our diversified, allocated, rules-based portfolios. And thus it becomes axiomatic that the longer your time horizon, the more speculative bonds actually become. Yes, really—if you are "over" invested in bonds.

So if longevity is not a risk and purchasing power is not a risk, and investment portfolio value fluctuations are not a risk, what are the risks?

The primary risk could be investor behavior, and not having a comprehensive, collaborative plan.

We get distracted by too much (financial) news media noise. Let us be aware that this may encourage behavior that could result in a self-fulfilling prophecy worse than originally feared. For the next several decades, as more and more people come out of poverty across the world, more and more people will need more education, more transportation, more communication, more goods, and more services. Who best to provide them but the world's great companies?

According to Jeff Macke of Yahoo Finance, Warren Buffet became one of the world's richest men "by betting against doomsday," including through his wholly-owned insurance companies. Doomsday has been predicted for thousands of years. It's predicted almost monthly in the newspapers. It has not come yet and it is unlikely to come.

That is not to say that there aren't bad things happening in the world, in our country, and in our communities. It is to say that those bad things are not a risk but a fact of life. It is another fact of life that humanity will always seek out a solution to problems. We know that the average intra-year (by definition temporary) stock market decline has been 14%. It tells us that, however brief and evanescent it may be, somewhere along in here may come another correction. Is that very same volatility really risk? To some it could be, if their portfolio is not properly constructed and advised.

Clients want access to liquidity, generation of income for your cash flows, and management of volatility to reap future returns through a properly constructed, managed, and advised portfolio. No volatility occurs in cash only, which is the sure asset class to not keep up with inflation.

Volatility then only becomes risk if your portfolio is not properly constructed for your time horizon and your purposes for money. And don't we just love the upside of that volatility? Isn't that what makes our returns?

We might have to adjust our expectations. We might have to learn to love the volatility. Here is a word game that may be in our heads. Stocks are up = good. Stocks are down = volatile. What is missing? A market that's up a lot comes with volatility[3], the happy kind.

So let's consider this volatility. Average returns aren't normal at all. In fact, normal returns are extreme. They occur infrequently. Only when the high and low returns are blended do we get the average. Some investors may expect average but we rarely get it.

In all calendar years since 1926, US large company stocks (or "the market") have been down 27% of those years. So the market has been up 73% of the time[4]. And the market has risen by more than 20% in over half of those positive years (or 36% of all years)! That is, one out of every three years, the market has gone up by greater than 20%. Moreover, as an additional datum point, for the past 65 years, the market has reached a "new high" 1100 times, or once every 15 days. Hmmm....So when the market hits that next new high, should you sell?

---

3  Volatility is another word for temporary price fluctuations in the markets or in your portfolio.

4  In addition, the average year shows an intra-year decline of 14%.

In other words, if we don't get a down year, history favors large upside. Years with positive returns of around 5-10% (what most people usually expect as average) only happen one out of six years. More frequently and amazingly, years between 30% and 40% up are more common than years with around 5-10% positive returns.

So the "markets" tend to surprise in the extreme. Making volatility a dual-edged sword. Investors don't feel the up years as volatility because we enjoy them. Volatility it is nevertheless.

How much time does it take for the 20% upward run? Usually, three months or less. Moreover, the average intra-year decline since World War II has been 14%. That means that within a given year, you can expect a 14% decline in the short term pricing of the stock market. Yet a bear market is described as a decline of 20%. The so-called once-in-a-100-year storm of a 50% decline has actually happened over three times in the last 100 years.

And for those who were able to invest and stay fully invested for that 100-year period of time, you have been rewarded with an increase in the S&P 500 from approximately 15 to approximately 2,000. That's over 100-fold increase. Certainly we would take 100-fold increase with occasional short-term declines. Of course, few of us will get to enjoy 100 years of investing. Most of us will experience 20, 30 years, and more.

Attributed to Mark Twain, but with out evidence: "history may not repeat itself, but it rhymes."

Of course, we have much economic risk now: low employment participation, low interest rates, high debt, many new regulations, geopolitical instability, and more. If you have heard, "we have never been here before", I encourage you to recall another time we faced similar issues -- 1947. That's correct. Back then there was a prime interest rate of only 1.75% (now it is 3.25%, by the way), Communist China, newly returned GIs, a war to pay for, and the New Deal.

What ended up happening? A giant, long-term, bull market in stocks. That's what. I am not predicting another. I am not predicting anything. I am merely helping you put your point of view into perspective, as redundant as that may seem. Things are not "different this time". Things are never quite different.

We encourage you to make your decisions based on evidence, and rules. We do that for you, in our evidence-based, rules-based global, multi-asset class, properly allocated portfolio management, of dynamic strategic indexing, that is designed for solid growth, while safely managed, through our trusted advice. Working with our team of expert specialists, focusing on your plan, taking care of you through our service will empower you to succeed even in stressful times.

**Conclusion/Recommendations:** Like all the tools and strategies discussed in this book, not all are for everyone. If you worry about market fluctuations, and the economy, and inflation, and taxes, *and* you have a short (less than 10 years) time horizon, perhaps investing is not for you. See my article, "Watch the World, Not the West; Concentrate on the Companies, Not the Countries." *(By the way, most investors are in for at least a 20 year retirement, and then another few decades for their heirs to receive what is left over after we consume it in the distribution phase of our lives).*

We would encourage you, and we know how difficult this is, to NOT check your portfolio too frequently, avoid the financial media, and keep your eye on the big picture to help every investor sleep better at night. It is precisely this difficulty, and the "don't just do something, stand there" advice that you will get from a reputable Registered Investment Advisor. For more, check out the great investment advisor representatives at, **www.MySummitWealth.com** to see how they may help you.

**Section 6:** *Life Settlements*

For many clients, the idea of selling an existing life insurance policy is foreign. For what reasons would a person want to sell their life insurance policy? While readers of this book might not be the best candidates for a life settlement, chances are significant that the readers will have a parent or older friend or loved one who is a good candidate.

The reasoning behind Life Settlements (LS) is not complex. LS are for someone who has purchased insurance and no longer needs that particular policy and wants to sell the policy for cash so that they may use the proceeds for other uses. The typical seller is usually over the age of 65, and they must receive more from a life settlement company than the "cash surrender value" (CSV) of the policy.

The life-settlement industry is growing at an annual rate of just under 20%. This market is set to increase as more of the baby boomer generation reaches the age of 65. With the fact that our society is getting older, understanding and dealing with the topic of life settlements is vitally important for anyone who is trying to have the best long-term estate and financial plan for themselves or a loved one.

Why sell a life insurance policy? We think a better question is: Why should clients keep life insurance policies they have no need for? That question brings up why and when should someone buy a life insurance policy. The main reasons are: 1) To protect the family in case the "breadwinner" dies; 2) To pay for estate taxes; 3) To help offset expenses associated with replacing a key executive of a corporation. When determining if a life settlement is a good option for a client, the client needs to resolve whether the original need for the life insurance policy still exists.

So, what kinds of Life Insurance can be sold with a life settlement? All "individual" life insurance policies are able to be sold through a life settlement. This includes:
1. Term;
2. Whole life;
3. Universal life;
4. Variable; and,
5. Second-to-die.

To make the policy attractive to a purchasing company, the policy should have at least $100,000 of initial face for the death benefit. Additionally, the client should be over the age of 65 years old and in order to maximize the purchase price, the client should have had a change in health since the policy was issued.

In addition, the client is usually required to have a policy in force for at least two years, and be expected to live for at least two more years. Further, the purchaser would ideally like to see a client with a life expectancy of less than 12 years.

**When would clients consider selling a life insurance policy?**

1. When clients have insurance and/or estate planning needs that have changed, which makes their current policy inadequate or excessive for their current or future needs.

An example would be a client who purchased insurance to cover estate taxes, but no longer needs the policy because his estate is small enough to where estate taxes will not be an issue. Another example would be where the intended beneficiary dies before the client.

2. When premiums on the policy are no longer affordable.

Sometimes clients are no longer able to pay the premiums on their policy. The clients can choose to surrender the policy, decrease the benefit, or sell the policy.

3. When clients choose to realize the current value of their policy now instead of paying the policy from which they will not receive any benefit.

An example would be the client who still pays their premium for years even though they do not need the policy. They do this because they were used to paying the policy, and didn't realize that they had the option to stop. Once they realize that they no longer need to pay the premiums, and can instead sell the policy, many will decide to sell the premium for cash.

4. When clients wish to live out the remaining years of life without a change in lifestyle.

This is the classic situation where a client has been paying on a policy for 20+ years and is now in retirement. Because they live a lavish lifestyle, the client no longer has enough money to pay for all his costs. It is possible for the client to sell their policy and maintain their lifestyle.

5. When clients need cash in order to pay for a medical emergency.

This situation is happening more and more. Many clients are not even able to pay their insurance bills. If clients knew that they could sell their life policies for more than the cash surrender value, most would do so in order that they could pay their medical bills.

**Who is involved in Life Settlements?**

1. The Policyholder (our client);
2. A Life Settlement Broker (a person who helps find a purchaser;
3. The Provider (the purchaser). Usually a bank or lending organization

**Tax considerations:** Depending on a variety of factors, including cost basis, the cash surrender value, and the amount received from the Life Settlement, a life settlement payment could be taxable. There should be no tax liability if the settlement amount is less than the cost basis. An example:

TAXATION DIAGRAM: Assume a $1,000,000 Policy issued 10 years ago and a $400,000 Settlement Amount Paid to the Policy Owner. The policy owner paid $150,000 in premiums over 10 years. $225,000 Taxed as Long Term Capital Gain; $25,000 Taxed as Ordinary Income; $175,000 CSV (Tax Basis + Earnings); D $150,000 Tax Basis (i.e. past premiums paid).

Examples of Life Settlements:

1. Term Conversion
Dr. Smith is 79 years old and has lung cancer. His 20 year term policy is about to reach its conversion deadline. Dr. Smith cannot afford to convert the policy, and letting his $250,000 policy lapse would mean that Dr. Smith would lose everything. Dr. Smith applied to a Life Settlement company, and his policy was sold for $75,000.

Dr. Smith recovered all his premiums, and he walked away with a nice profit. Dr. Smith could then use the money to pay bills, go play golf on vacation, or put money away for later in retirement.

2. Unplanned Health Change
Roger was 76 and had just suffered a stroke, which left him permanently disabled was permanently disabled from a recent stroke. His family was not prepared for this possibility. After totaling all the medical costs related to the stroke, the family was unsure how they would be able to pay. Fortunately, his CWPPTM advisor suggested that Roger look into a Life Settlement when it was learned that he owned a $500,000 life insurance policy.

Roger sold the policy for $250,000, and was able to eliminate future premium payments. The money was used to care for Roger until he passed away three years later, and the remaining funds were given to his original beneficiaries.

3. Additional Insurance Needed
An elderly couple had a $2.2 million policy held in an insurance trust that covered the wife. Due to good investments, their estate had grown healthily and now the death benefit on the policy was inadequate to cover the couples' growing estate tax problems. Their CWPPTM suggested that the clients sell the life policy to help fund the purchase of a new $4 million joint survivorship policy.

A qualified Life Settlement broker was able to negotiate a $450,000 purchase price. The husband was in perfect health, and so the premiums on the policy were very affordable.

4. Key-Man
A company owns a $5 million policy on an older executive who had retired three years earlier. The surrender value was $600,000; and since the company no longer wanted to pay the $90,000 per year premium payments, the company was considering the option of surrendering the policy. Their CWPP™, when learning of the situation, suggested that the client consider a Life Settlement. The company was offered $1,000,000 for the sale of the policy and netted $950,000 after taxes, which netted the company a healthy profit. The tax calculations are omitted since the case is a fictitious case and for brevity purposes.

**Summary:** While the topic of Life Settlements is not in the mainstream, it is becoming much more prevalent as our society ages. Many clients have experienced sudden life changing events that would make a Life Settlement advisable. Now that you know what they are and how they work, hopefully, if you or a loved one can benefit from a Life Settlement, you'll be able to bring up the topic and provide assistance.

**Section 7:** *Private Placement Life Insurance (PPLI)*

PPLI is an intriguing concept to help those clients who have sizable brokerage accounts reduce the capital gains taxes and taxes on dividends that are paid annually with most brokerage accounts. PPLI can also pass wealth to the client's heirs in a tax favorable manner. What is PPLI?

PPLI is an individually negotiated life insurance policy that can be with a domestic insurance company or, more typically, with an offshore insurance company. We like to think of PPLI as a shell product that houses an investment. What are the potential benefits of PPLI?

- Tax free appreciation of investments;
- Investment flexibility, including the ability to appoint your own investment manager;
- Substantial liquidity in the investment account;
- Low-cost borrowing from the investment account;
- Low costs due to small or no sales loads and other administrative costs;
- Increased asset protection; and,
- Tax-free death benefits to heirs.

How does PPLI differ from traditional life insurance policies? The main difference with PPLI over traditional life policies is where the money can be invested. With a traditional policy, the consumer is limited typically to name brand mutual funds. With PPLI, the client can invest in almost anything that includes:
- Individual publicly traded stocks;
- Privately owned stock; and,
- Hard assets.

**Segregated account**: Almost all PPLI policies are held in separate "segregated" accounts at the life insurance company. That means the money in your policy is not subject to other creditors of the life insurance company. It is sort of like putting the money in your PPLI policy into a safety deposit box at the insurance company where no one, not even the insurance company itself, can access your funds for the benefit of another insured or creditor of the company.

**Investment options**: While previously we listed the types of investments money in a PPLI can be invested in; we need to more fully explain why this can be beneficial to clients with sizable brokerage accounts.

**Domestic PPLI** - Typically, with a domestic PPLI policy, the insurance company will have institutional mutual funds for the client to choose from. PPLI at first glance will sound like variable; but because PPLI is meant to house literally millions in investment dollars and because of the low insurance costs, PPLI is much different and more economically feasible than traditional variable life.

**Foreign PPLI** - With "offshore" PPLI policies, the insurance company typically will require you to choose your own fund manager where the qualification requirements for that fund manager are not nearly as stringent as a domestic PPLI policy would have. Additionally, with a foreign PPLI, you will have much more latitude in the investments you hold inside your PPLI policy.

**Expenses:** Because PPLI is an individually negotiated policy, there are set fees. However, typically with PPLI, there are no up-front loads that go to pay insurance agents. The insurance company is typically charging the lowest possible insurance rates for the life insurance to attract big money clients to the company.

**Annual Fee** - Because PPLI is really more of an investment rather than a traditional life insurance policy, the company charges typical money management fees between .5% and 1.65% annually on the cash value in the policy. Cost of Insurance - The cost of insurance is the cost the investor has to pay to cover the death benefit over and above the cash in the policy.

For more on Private Placement Life Insurance, please go to page 103.

# Chapter Five

# Reaching Critical Capital Mass (CCM)

Examples of what a Comprehensive Asset Protection, Estate Plan, and Income Tax Reduction Plan Should Look Like: In the following pages, we will cover what clients of different ages need to do in order to reach Critical Capital Mass (CCM). The following different types of clients will be covered: 1) a client just starting working, 2) a client who has been working for 5 years, 3) a client who has been working for 15 years, and 4) a client who is 60 years old.

We are going to assume that the examples below are clients who are married. While that is not always the case, most high income and/ or net worth clients are married and, even if they are not, most of the advice will be the same whether the client is married or not. We are further going to assume that the clients discussed below are professionals with "personal" liability.

1. **Client just getting started** - The typical client is one who just graduated from college, has a decent amount of student loans, very little in built-up wealth or assets, and his first job making a decent amount of money. Many times the client will be married with a spouse who is also making decent money from work.

Assets: Two used automobiles with no debt; a new house with a significant mortgage; a lot of personal property accumulated over the last ten years; one child, age 4. Assume this client makes $150,000 a year or has a combined income with the spouse of in excess of that amount.

**Recommended Plan:** Asset Protection - There is very little need for asset protection because there are no assets to protect. The client should make sure he has the maximum amount of disability insurance to protect the family in case of a disability. The younger you are when this insurance can be purchased, the better, so that the lowest possible premium can be obtained.

Income Tax Reduction - It is unlikely in this example that the client will have any disposable income to transfer to an income tax reduction plan. The client would typically start out as an employee and will not be vested in the new employer's pension plan for usually one year. Typically, the client would be allowed to make a voluntary 401(k) Plan contribution that would come out of his paycheck.

This client should fund the 401(k) plan up to the max and if he is lucky, the employer will also have a match of some kind. It would also be better if the employer had a Roth 401(k) instead of a traditional tax-deferred 401(k) plan.

Estate Plan - Chances are significant that this client only has a will and nothing else. He should immediately implement, in addition to a will, marital A&B Trusts and Durable Powers of Attorney as basic estate planning tools. The client probably only has $500,000 in term life insurance, which should immediately be increased to $2,000,000.

Financial Plan - It is unlikely the client has any significant brokerage accounts or balances in his bank accounts. Having said that, a terrific way to build wealth, for retirement, is the use of a low, expense over funded indexed universal life insurance policy. This client should fund X amount of dollars into an over funded indexed life insurance policy.

There are no maximum contributions to building tax favorable wealth through such a vehicle and doing so will allow the client to accumulate significant additional money for retirement. The client might also want to contribute to a Section 529 Plan to fund for the education of the only child.

Money in a 529 Plan is funded post-tax and is available if needed in a catastrophic situation to pay normal living expenses of the family. Assuming the money is not needed for family living expenses, the goal of funding for the child's education will be started. The client should not go out of his way to pay off the mortgage on the personal residence.

While there is no equity to build through Equity Harvesting, it would be wise to obtain an interest-only loan and to use the money that would normally be allocated to pay down the mortgage and allocate that to a new low expense indexed universal life insurance policy.

2. **Client who has been working for five years** - The typical client who has been working for five years is getting to the point where most of the debt is gone; and the client, if a professional, is now a partner in a medical, legal, accounting, or other professional practice. As a partner, the income of the client goes up as well.

Assets: Two new automobiles with minimal debt; House worth $500,000 with a $300,000 mortgage; $50,000 in a brokerage account; Two Wave Runners; Two children, ages 8 and 4. For this example, let's assume the client now makes $500,000 a year in W-2 income. Half-a-million dollars is too little for many clients and too much for many, but for the example, it should be a happy medium for applicability purposes for the reader.

**Recommended Plan:** Asset Protection - Like example Number I, this client is in the accumulation phase of assets. There are no large assets to protect besides the marital home and it would be a good idea from an asset protection and financial planning point of view to remove at least $100,000 of equity and change the mortgage to an interest-only mortgage.

This will allow him to start building maximum wealth with maximum security through an "Equity Harvesting" plan. If the client is worried about protecting his brokerage account, that account could be transferred to an LLC; but at this point, that is a judgment call for the client to determine if the cost of the LLC can be justified.

The client should seriously consider moving the Wave Runners to an LLC. Moving the Wave Runners to an LLC would not be done to protect the assets from loss but instead from the tremendous liability that goes along with being an owner of them. Once the Wave Runners are in the LLC, a potential creditor would have as his sole remedy the assets inside the LLC and not the rest of the assets of this client.

The client should make sure he/she has the maximum amount of disability insurance (DI). If this client were interested in getting the "maximum" amount of DI coverage, we would recommend pension plan protection DI and/or business overhead expense insurance.

Income Tax Reduction - In this example, the client is starting to get to the point where he can seriously look at an income tax reduction plan. If we assume the client is a small business owner, the client is now fully vested in the practice's 401(k) 1 Profit Sharing Plan and the client should be contributing between $30,000 and $45,500 to that pension plan.

How lavish the client and his family live will dictate how much disposable income he has to contribute to a supplemental benefit plan. Depending on the client's spending habits and if he has business partners or not, a captive insurance company should be looked at as a way to grow wealth in a tax favorable manner.

Estate Plan - Chances are significant that this client only has a will and nothing else. This client should immediately implement, in addition to a will, marital A&B trusts and durable powers of attorney as basic estate planning tools. The client probably only has $500,000 in term life insurance which should immediately be increased to $2,000,000.

Because this client will need "permanent" life insurance, he should do so in conjunction with a wealth building plan and do so through an indexed universal life policy. If the client chooses to create a CIC, buying life insurance in the CIC might be a prudent choice depending on how it is structured.

Financial Plan - This client has $50,000 in a brokerage account. We would suggest transferring some or all of that money to a Section 529 Plan to fund college tuition and expenses of the children. The money would be available to the family, if needed, but with the new income, that is not likely.

If funding for college education early is not a priority, then having a local stockbroker manage the money is fine. Some clients like to keep that money in a bank account in case of an emergency. Basically, the money could be invested just about anywhere except penny stocks; and it could be justified because of the very young age of the client.

If the client does not remove significant money from the business in a tax favorable manner, he should allocate X amount of the money available after paying income taxes on his take-home pay and fund a low-expense over-funded indexed universal life insurance policy.

3. **Client who has been in working for fifteen years** - The typical client who has been working for 15 years is getting to the point where most of the debt is gone, and the client is now starting to accumulate significant wealth and assets. Assets: Two new automobiles with minimal debt; New home worth $750,000 with a $300,000 mortgage; $500,000 in a brokerage account; 2 Wave Runners; $350,000 motor yacht; Two children, ages 18 and 14; Ownership in an office building with little equity; Vacation condo in Florida worth $200,000; Poorly designed ol,der universal life insurance policy with a $2,000,000 death benefit and $40,000 in cash surrender value; $700,000 in the business's pension plan.

For this example, let's assume the client now makes $750,000 a year in W-2 income. Half-a-million dollars is too little for many clients and too much for others; but, for the example, it should be a happy medium for applicability purposes for the reader.

**Recommended Plan:** Asset Protection - Unlike examples #1 and #2, this client has accumulated several assets that will continue to grow in size.

There are a few large assets to protect besides the marital home:

- Personal residence Tenants by the Entireties coupled with "Equity Harvesting." This will protect the house by placing a debt shield on it and equity harvesting is also a terrific investment due to the ability to write off the interest.
- Brokerage Account LLC#I - If the vacation condo were ever rented, the brokerage account would get its own LLC.
- Vacation Condo LLC#I
- Office Building
- 2 Wave Runners
- Motor Yacht
- 401 (k)/Profit Sharing
- LLC#2
- LLC#3
- LLC#4
- Qualified retirement money is federally protected.

The client's brokerage account is the most liquid asset in the entire estate and must be protected. A domestic LLC should suffice; but if the client wants to spend the money, an offshore LLC or trust could be warranted. The vacation condo has $100,000 in equity, and it will be appreciating in value.

The condo could go in the same LLC as the brokerage account as long as the condo is not rented. If the client rents the condo, then it should be in its own LLC. Lastly, if the client believes the vacation condo will stay in the family for years to come, then a family limited partnership (FLP) should be considered with a gifting program to transfer to the children 98% of the non-voting interest in the FLP.

The FLP will protect the condo and lessen the size of the client's estate without giving up control of the asset until death. The client should move the Wave Runners to an LLC. Moving the Wave Runners to an LLC would not be done to protect the assets from loss but instead from the tremendous liability that goes along with being an owner of them.

Once the Wave Runners are in the LLC, a potential creditor would have as their sole remedy the assets inside the LLC and not the rest of the assets of this client. The motor yacht should be owned by its own LLC due to the individual liability it poses to the owners as well as to asset protect the value of the asset.

The office building should be owned by an LLC. If not, it should be transferred immediately. The interest in the LLC can be owned by the client individually because of the asset protection features of the LLC.

Income Tax Reduction - In this example, the client should have already started a supplemental benefit plan that can reduce his income taxes. Depending on the type of business, this client could be a great candidate for a captive insurance company (CIC) to grow wealth in a tax favorable manner.

The client can afford to pay premiums of $300,000+ or more into a CIC. This is a great way to supercharge a tax favorable wealth building plan. If a CIC is not a good fit, the client could then look at a Defined Benefit Plan or 412(I) Plan if there were few employees.

Estate Plan - Chances are significant that this client only has a will and A&B marital trusts. This client should consider adding durable powers of attorney as a basic estate-planning tool. This client has an older and not well designed Universal Life (UL) insurance policy with a $2,000,000 death benefit and $40,000 in cash surrender value.

The client should 1035-exchange the policy for a new and well-designed indexed universal life insurance policy. The client should seriously consider transferring the vacation condo and possibly the personal residence into a Family Limited Partnership (FLP) where the client can start to give the value of the assets to the children when the client sees fit.

Financial Plan - This client has $500,000 in a brokerage account. Due to the age of the children, funding a 529 Plan at this point is not terribly beneficial. How the $500,000 is invested will depend on what advice is given. If the client likes his money actively traded, then a stockbroker should manage the money.

If the client does not want risky investments, then some of the money could be transferred to an indexed annuity with a minimum guarantee and growth pegged to a stock market index. If the client wants to get aggressive with protection he could use the Maximizer or if he wanted to have fun with some of the money, he could try a hedge fund as an investment.

Bottom line is that the client should diversify his post-tax investments and not keep them all in one pot. As the client gets older, moving money to a principal protected account will be very important. This client has the perfect financial makeup to use Equity Harvesting to build additional wealth for retirement.

The client should systematically remove $100,000-$300,000 of equity from his home over the next five years and use the money to fund a low expense indexed universal life insurance policy. Such a wealth building tool will be one of the most secure and tax favorable ways for this client to grow wealth in an effort to reach Critical Capital Mass.

4. **Client who is 65 years old** - A 65-year-old client is usually thinking about retirement and most of the time is close to Critical Capital Mass. Many clients simply enjoy working. The 60-year-old client has the greatest need for a proper asset protection plan, estate plan, and financial plan and is at a point in his life where charitable giving should be explored.

Assets: Two new automobiles with minimal debt; House that is worth $500,000 with almost no mortgage; $750,000 in a brokerage account; $350,000 motor yacht; Two children, ages 34 and 30; Ownership in commercial property with $500,000 equity; Vacation condo in Florida worth $400,000; Universal life insurance policy with a $2,000,000 death benefit and $300,000 in cash surrender value; $750,000 in the business's pension plan; $750,000 in an IRA.

For this example, let's assume the client makes $500,000 a year in W-2 income. Half-a-million dollars is too little for many clients and too much for others; but, for the example, it should be a happy medium for applicability purposes for the reader.

**Recommended Plan:** Asset Protection - Unlike examples #1, #2 and #3, this client has accumulated significant assets that will continue to grow in size:

1. Personal residence Tenants by The Entireties
2. Brokerage Account LLCI
3. Vacation Condo Family Limited Partnership
3. Commercial Property
4. Motor Yacht
5. 401 (k) Profit Sharing
6. LLC#2
7. LLC#3
8. Qualified retirement money is federally protected
9. Roll into the pension plan at work
10. Universal Life Policy Irrevocable Life Insurance Trust*

The client's brokerage account is the most liquid asset in the entire estate and must be protected. A domestic LLC should suffice; but, if the client wants to spend the money, an offshore LLC or offshore asset protection trust could be warranted. The vacation condo, unless rented, should probably be transferred to an FLP for asset protection and estate planning.

If the client believes the condo will be sold at some point, then an LLC might be used instead of an FLP. The FLP will protect the condo and lessen the size of the client's estate without giving up control of the asset until death. The motor yacht should be owned by its own LLC due to the individual liability it poses to the owners as well as to asset protect the value of the asset.

The commercial property should be owned by an LLC. If not, it should be transferred immediately. The interest in the LLC can be owned by the client individually because of the asset protection features of the LLC. The money in the client's 401 (k) Profit Sharing Plan is asset protected by federal law.

The client should roll the IRA into the business's pension plan or potentially into a new Profit Sharing Plan created inside the FLP. By moving the money in the IRA into a Profit Sharing Plan, the client then will completely asset protect the money. The Universal Life (ULI) policy is asset protected in some states.

While that's interesting, the life policy is in the client's estate and he has an estate tax problem. The client could gift the UL policy to an irrevocable life insurance trust so the cash value and death benefit will be asset protected and to assure that the death benefit will pass income and estate tax free to the heirs.

The problem is that there will be a gift tax upon transfer or he will have to use part of the onetime estate tax exemption to avoid the tax. A better option would be for the client to sell the policy to a life settlement company for approximately $450,000 and buy a new second to die policy inside an IUT.

The new policy will be less expensive than the current one and there will be less of a gift tax or no gift tax implication when funding the new policy. Plus the client pockets a significant amount of cash while still maintaining the insurance. Disability insurance is not that important a topic for this client.

Income Tax Reduction - In this example, the client already has significant money in qualified retirement plans and in a brokerage account. Income tax reduction is still important because the client needs his income less now than at any time in the past. Many of the income tax reduction solutions will not work for the older client because those solutions use life insurance as an investment.

He could create a captive insurance company that would be owned by his children or a trust for the benefit of the children. If structured properly, the tax deductible premium dollars could be available to the client in retirement in a tax free manner. If the client doesn't need the money in retirement, the money in the CIC will pass to his heirs estate-tax-free and in a tax favorable manner. This client should also strongly consider charitable giving as a way to reduce the size of his estate and as a way to receive a current income tax deduction. We would recommend the Charitable Gift Annuity (CGA).

Estate Plan - With a client who is 60 years old, we would hope that by now he would have a will and A&B marital trusts. If not, the client should implement both immediately. The client should consider adding durable powers of attorney as a basic estate-planning tool. This client should strongly consider using a Life Settlement to get out of his Universal Life insurance policy.

Using the money from a Life Settlement, the client could purchase a second-to-die life insurance policy owned by an ILIT. If a Life Settlement does not work, the client should consider gifting the policy to an Irrevocable Life Insurance Trust (ILIT) so the death benefit can pass income and estate tax free to the beneficiary.

The spouse could be one of the beneficiaries at the discretion of the trustee if needed. Future premiums (if needed) would be gifted to the ILIT, which would, in turn, pay the premiums. The client should seriously consider transferring the vacation condo and possibly the personal residence into a Family Limited Partnership (FLP) where the client can start to gift the value of the assets to the children when the client sees fit.

When using an FLP, the client can gift upwards of 99% of the value of the FLP to the children without giving up control of the assets inside the FLP. The key is to use the FLP to lower the size of the estate and to minimize the amount of estate taxes due at the client's death. The client should immediately start funding for long term care insurance

Financial Plan - This client has $750,000 in a brokerage account. If that brokerage account consisted of a handful of individual stocks, we would have the client consider the Stock Protection Strategy (SPS) to hedge the downside risk of those individual stocks. If the client's brokerage money is in mutual funds, the client should consider selling some of the mutual funds and moving his money to a principal protected wealth building tools.

This client could also consider gifting some of his appreciated stock to a Charitable Gift Annuity. By using a CGA, the client will receive an immediate income tax deduction and will fund his charitable planning goals. In addition, with wealth replacement life insurance, the client can pass to his children the same or greater amount of the gift.

In addition, the client will create guaranteed income down the road that will be paid by the charity. If the client does not have a charitable intent and has no need for some of the money in the brokerage account, that money could be moved to the FLP and gifted to the children at a discount.

The client also has significant money in an IRA and pension plan. That money is most likely in mutual funds. While we typically do not recommend annuities in qualified plans, however, for this client, the use of an Equity Indexed Annuity (EIA) would make sense to create a balanced portfolio.

The client could also use the Maximizer to protect this money and still give the client significant upside potential in the market. This client has many options, and the bottom line is that the client should diversify his post-tax investments and not keep them all in one pot; and at 60 years old, the client should seriously consider principal guaranteed investments.

The previous four examples are just that; every client has a different asset mix, different family situation, and different long-term goals. The previous examples illustrate typical situations we see around the country and the advice we might give to clients in similar circumstances.

Every client's ultimate goal should be to reach Critical Capital Mass, and this book outlines all the tools you have at your disposal to reach that goal. When you review or revise your asset protection, estate, and financial plan make sure you use consultants who give you individual advice instead of canned answers that they give to every client no matter what the circumstances.

The following examples illustrate complex case studies using advanced planning strategies. Some of these advanced asset protection planning strategies may *seem* to good to be true. And yet, *they are true.* The names, locations, amounts, and businesses have been changed to protect privacy, then we turned them into a composite, or avatar example. They are actual advanced planning concepts through a collaborative and comprehensive process with accountants, and tax and estate attorneys. It requires a tremendous amount of work and diligence to be certain we precisely follow the laws and regulations. Not all can take advantage of these concepts. Not all advisors understand how to implement these concepts. Not all are willing to do what you must to keep the clients "in the clear".

1. Coast Retailer—We implemented a **"Supercharged 401K"** including a "cash balance' overlay that led to an income tax reduction of $1.27MM in four years, and over $2.39MM extra into a tax deferred vehicle with over $100K to come out tax free, and the rest "stretched" over generations. The owner and his wife are putting in over $425,000 per year, and they receive 91% of the proceeds for their benefit. We created a buy/sell for his family to purchase installment sale of the business while he retains control and most of the income at long term capital gains rates instead of income tax rates, which saved another $68,400 per year for 20 years, which equals $1.368MM

2. A Sarasota marketing business "Wealth Extraction and Preservation" had $5.6MM equity in a building that was leased to their own family business. Business (with sales of $1.4MM, salary/income of $130K to Generation 1, owner, age 70; business has real net pre-tax profits of $200K) to be sold to next generation, age 45. Children could not

afford the purchase price. Installment sale of only 50% of net pre-tax profits reduced the pressure and the risk, while the building was refinanced through a new mortgage at $4MM. Business rent covered the mortgage and reduced the net taxable profit to each. The rent was applied to the purchase price installment sale for G2. G1 gets $4MM tax-free. G1 owns life insurance on G2 for the mortgage amount. G2 owes the mortgage; upon mortgage fulfillment G2 owns the building outright. Including their additional savings of $500K in their 401(k) and $500K in a brokerage account, they now have $5MM on which to support their $130K life style over the next 30 years. Taking more than the required minimum distributions (RMDs) from the 401(k) over 5 years pays funds life insurance policy on G2. $2.5MM Fixed Indexed Annuity (FIA) nets $125,000 annually, most of it tax advantaged, for the rest of their lives. $3MM invested conservatively should net an additional 5% growth for increased lifestyle or charitable gifting or legacy planning.

3. St. Pete—45 years old with a very high net pretax income of $3 million in a high risk, low value professional services business. Lives on $800,000. Has $7.5MM in cash only. Wants to retire in less than 7 years. Worried it cannot be done. Needs a risk transfer mechanism to protect against multiple business risks. We created a holding company (Captive Insurance Company or CIC) to deduct up to $1.2MM in risk premium from the business that grows within the CIC tax deferred, and comes out at worst at long term capital gains rates, to the extent there are no claims on the CIC. He saves $520K/y in tax for 5 years or $2.6MM. He nets $7MM in the holding company, assuming a conservative 5% return on investments. Funding a permanent life insurance policy (PLI) at $575,000 for 7 years will yield him $450K/y tax-free from 61-85. He uses $1.5 million for a FIA to net him an additional $225,000 per year, tax-advantaged from age 59 for rest of his life. The brokerage account of $6 million invested conservatively should yield 5% growth for the next 7 years or $8.4MM in an after tax account. From 52-59 we must fund his lifestyle expenses of $800,000 for 7 years from the remaining $15.4MM accumulated (CIC plus brokerage) or

5.5% of that accumulated amount, after tax. Therefore, we need to pull out 7% to cover the tax. Assuming a growth rate of 5% and 7% withdrawals, that is a net negative 2% for 7 years. This leaves him "only" $13.3MM. Then he gets $450K tax-free, plus $225,000 tax-advantaged or $675K/y, leaving another $200K/year to withdraw from the brokerage account or less than 2.2% of the principal amount.

4. Casselberry—62 year old owns a $20 million construction company with a fleet of 60 vehicles. The business has no profit, struggling even at that revenue run rate. The vehicles were leased at a cost of $300K/y. Lease factor only 4.2. "Imputed interest" over $130,000. Created and funded for 7 years Private capital Reserve Strategy™ (PRCS) to finance major capital expenditures (cap-ex in jargon) at $200,000 per year (1% of gross revenue, which we found by re-engineering the insurance premiums, and the retirement plans costs). That left him at year 7 with $1.6 million (with tax-free interest) in the PRCS to purchase for cash the 60 vehicles. However, he did not need to deplete his $1.6MM. In fact, it continued to earn tax-free interest at 3.2%. He used the PRCS as collateral and liened it with a non-recourse (meaning he does not personally guarantee the loan), non-structured loan against it. Non-structured means he can make the payments when he is able. If he had a bad quarter or bad year, and could not make payments, no harm no foul. He continued to make similar payments that he had been making to the leasing company. His $1.6 million continued to accumulate tax-free interest no matter what. We structured his note on the vehicles to coincide with their effective life of 6 years. We recommended he pay the lien down at a slightly greater rate than commercially available as it only increased his collateral capacity for the next time he needed to finance capital expenditures (cap ex). So his payments were $243,000. A savings of $57,000 per year for 6 years or $342,000 total. Plus his $1.6 million was now worth $1.93 million. So what we turned a $130,000 cost center into a $51,000 gain per year plus a $57,000 cash flow improvement per year. At no risk. He now has the ability to retire on the extra $1.93 million in his PRCS as well.

5. Minneapolis Printer—$8 million business, two owners, with very low margins. $400,000 salaries to the owners, plus $300,000 profit. Each saves $100,000 after tax per year. Worried about returns on the savings. If they could get 10%, that would be $10,000. We restructured their 401(k), and their Property & Casualty insurance, and their mortgages, without staff reductions. Business savings of only 1% added $80,000/y to the bottom line. Now it feels as if they are making a 90% return on their savings with no additional risk. This has increased their EBIDTA by 26%. Considering their industry carries multiples of 4x, this increased their net worth by over $320,000. They are preparing to sell the business and should net out $1,500,000. Process over product.

6. Investor with Phantom Income Tax (PIT)— client of an accountant with a $2 million portfolio suffered loss of $143,000 in 2011. He understood that markets go down. He was unhappy with the $85,000 taxable gain as a result of selling more winners than losers. Thus he had to pay $30,000 in tax for the insult of having lost money. We fixed that using True Market™ Models. The multi-asset class global structured ETF portfolio managed to Active Strategic Indexingä, due to offsets will not show PIT.

7. This couple, aged 60, owned a $5 million business, "donated" to charities $13,000/y as a form of marketing. They were not charitably inclined. The tax-exempt organization introduced them to us. They had $1+million in their IRA, intended for the benefit of their children. We found they also had substantial annual tax liability. We accelerated their IRA distributions (a Roth Rollout, not a rollover). This required substantial charitable gifting to reduce the increased taxability. Through advanced collaborative comprehensive planning, including the charitable gift planning, we eliminated their current and future annual income tax liability from their IRA, and left them with 50% more after-tax money, while increasing their charitable donations to over $80,000. Good for all.

8. Hedge fund manager (HFM) – This client had a very high net worth and income, yet was in poor physical health. We recommended and implemented our "Ultimate Gift™." The client contributed $10+ million to a charitable entity controlled by HFM. There was an immediate personal income tax deduction and estate tax deduction. The client the purchased a 10-year guaranteed annuity with that gift in the charitable entity, creating ~$1.1 million in income. He used that income to purchase high cash value, low death benefit permanent life insurance on his adult children. This created $44 million of death benefit that is all in the charitable entity. The entity will gift away 4% of that annually or more than $1.7 million annually, while the adult children can be compensated annually at $440,000 to run the charitable entity. Moreover, the cash value will exceed $12 million in ten years, and $20 million in 25 years, accessible to HFM or his designees, income tax free. To the extent HFM does access that cash value, he has further reduced his taxable estate. Charities win big. Current income taxes reduced dramatically. Children win big. Current and future estate taxes reduced.

9. NY Electrical Engineering Company Owner—Wanted to have income for life, principal protection, and purchasing power protection; he also was concerned about leaving a lump sum to his children. He was in a very low current income tax situation. Set up an Intergenerational Guaranteed Income Systemä, which works likes this: he deposits $5 million into a deferred annuity which after 25 years will pay his children and grandchildren $600,000 per year for 55 years, enough for two generations to live on. We also funded a permanent life insurance policy and a high equity exposure investment portfolio. He will maintain his current lifestyle for the rest of his life, leave a legacy for his wife and children, his grandchildren and charity with built-in spendthrift provisions, have significant asset protection and maintain low tax risk.

10. Global Software Manufacturer—had most of his investments in solid gold ingots held in Swiss banks. Set up an asset protection plan using trusts, and multi-member, manager managed, limited

liability companies. To strategically grow greater than the pace of inflation we developed an Investment Policy Statement that is evidence-based, and rules-based to achieve optimal risk adjusted liquid investments, through institutional style multi-asset class global ETFs that hold the worlds' great companies; and utilized high cash value, low death benefit life insurance as a component of the fixed income asset class because it has low correlations with both bonds and stocks. He is now positioned for a downturn in the economy, his business, or an increase in taxation and regulation. And he can access more capital to expand his business, while preserving and protecting his financial fortress.

11. Child was victim of personal injury in PA, and was about to receive a large settlement into his estate. This would have put him in the position of ineligibility for funding and rehab services previously available; and made the child vulnerable to asset dwindling. Comprehensive and collaborative planning coordinated by us with the accountants and estate attorneys helped the lawsuit attorney make sure the child's settlement did not disqualify government sponsored benefits, and protected income as well as assets for the child's entire life. A Settlement Protection Planä. This included utilizing some of the settlement amount to purchase life insurance on both the grandparents and the parents so that future large lump sum deposits will see their way into the child's trust.

12. Divorcee aged 62 from high earning spouse. She did not trust her ex-husband's advisers. We helped her find a new estate attorney, new CPA, and a new insurance agent. Planning helped her have a superior risk-adjusted investment portfolio to help fight future inflation, guaranteed income for life, with a doubling of her income up to five years for long-term care should she need it, tax free income to supplement, and helped her receive her social security payments in a lump sum, and tax-free, putting her in a superior tax position (since she was now as a single household subject to lower thresholds and higher brackets).

13. CEO of multi-state manufacturing company. Restructured 401(k) so that costs reduced by 1.3% of the $6 million plan, netting out more than $78,000 savings per year for the participants (after our fees), increased the amounts the highly compensated employees could contribute to the retirement plan, without additional cost to the company, provided a more efficient, effective qualified default investment alternative to all the participants. Employee retention increased, tax reduction for the company, and productivity improved. Used the cost savings to develop the Private Capital Reserve Strategy to fund capital expenditures in a tax advantaged way.

14. Young business owner with $5 million in sales. New family with two children. Tax and liquidity are at issue. Wants to sell business. Particularly concerned about concentration of customer risk, interest rate risk, competition, regulation, limited pool of available opportunity, and access to capital. In addition to a more balanced and properly constructed, and tax- and cost-efficient strategic investment plan, we helped him by developing non-qualified private retirement planning using high cash value, low death benefit life insurance (PLI). Placed $100,000 per year for seven years into the PLI. In 30 years upon retirement, this will likely have grown at ~5%, un-taxed, and un-interrupted to around $20 million. At that point, he will be able to withdraw $1 million tax-free, per year for the rest of his and his wife's lives.

15. California low-tech business with $35 million in sales. $5 million in profit. End of year tax bill was $2.3 million. Segregated the business into Operating Company (Op-Co), Equipment Company (Eq-Co), Capital Expenditure Company (Cap-Co), Real Estate Company (RE-Co), and Investment Company (Invest-Co). In addition he established several children's trust, and a family limited partnership. These increased his asset protection, provided greater clarity of the true costs and profits of each, led to significant efficiencies and cost reductions (after the increase in accounting and legal fees, which totaled an additional annual expense of $50,000 or 1% of the profit) of over $175,000. In addition, the owner realized substantial net tax

reductions of over $950,000 per year by using CICs to insure against his above mentioned business risks. After all legal, and accounting, and regulatory expenses, this will generate for him over $5 million in net tax income savings in just a few years, and keeps all that money away from probate and the inheritance tax. The CIC then may provide the capital for his children or other successors to take over Op-Co and Equip-Co. RE-Co can sell with a leaseback, freeing up more capital for expansion. Invest-Co funded his charitable foundation. The legacy is a now a multiple of what the family thought.

16. Four-generation family office with $185 million. Family dysfunctional due to substance abuse and excessive spending at all generations. Attorney/trustee brought us in to help to mitigate against the declining asset base that may dissipate completely after G-3. There was a $60 million death benefit life insurance policy on the one remaining founding-generation member (age 90) with $45 million cash value, and several $1.5 million past due premium payments. The policy was at risk. We stripped out the cash, paid the past due premiums. Used the remaining cash to purchase policies on several of the G-2 and G-3 members that will fund an additional $200 million for the benefit of the succeeding generations and charitable intents. In addition, the investments were expensive, complicated, heavily taxed, with much overlap, and significant long-term underperformance. Taking over the investments, using True Market™ Models, http://www.truemarketmodels.com/ creates much greater efficiencies, less overlap, lower taxes, lower costs, while being more transparent. Now the trustee and the family knew what they invested in and why.

17. Serial entrepreneur in high risk business, age 60. Segregated business into: a) operating company, b) finance company, c) marketing company, and d) equipment company, all with interrelated operating agreements, all owned by a Holding Company, a multi-member, manager-managed LLC. One of his equipment companies owns his vehicles. He purchases late model high-end vehicles for cash—no sales tax currently due—in this LLC. This LLC leases

the vehicle for a modest amount plus sales tax, to the equipment company as a deductible expense, who allows business usage to the owner. Equity harvesting of his properties (each in different LLCs) enables liquidity, use, and control of his own capital that is tax-deductible, through lease of properties to business. Changed his multiple-vendor Property and Casualty Insurer to one company, with higher deductibles, and lower amounts at massive savings, some of which is used to purchase large umbrella policy.

18. For this example, I want you to assume that a client is the owner of a three million dollar business. The business is the type that incurs more lawsuits than the typical business. The client currently has $700,000 of after-tax cash in the business bank account, and the business currently has between $500,000-$600,000 in accounts receivables. The client is currently experiencing some cash flow issues. He needs money to pay his vendors, and he would also like to guard against possible creditors that may arise as the result of a lawsuit. The client came to us, and we suggested that he consider Equity Harvesting. We told the client that he should take out the $700,000 of cash he had accumulated in the business account, and place it in a segregated, asset protected account that is completely unrelated to the business. If the business needs more cash, the client is able to loan directly to the business. So instead of adding more paid in capital, the business is incurring more debt (to the owner/client), and the client is basically borrowing from himself. After doing this, the client files a UCC. By doing all this, the client has positioned himself very well. He now has the money he needs to pay his vendors and cover any incidental expenses that may arise. He has also reduced the value of the business, which has made it a less attractive target for any potential lawsuits. Not only that, but also he is also a secured creditor, and is in line to receive his money back if the company were ever to enter into bankruptcy. This is how debt shields/equity harvesting works. Once you take the cash out, you can choose to forgive the debt or write-off the loan so that the debt can convert to equity. You can also choose to revert the equity back to debt if you want. This whole process does not really affect taxes either. This process is a great way to reduce risk.

It is not uncommon to find and help you keep tens, if not hundreds of thousands of dollars every year, you may not have been aware you were losing. The important thing is to protect, preserve, and prosper.

# Conclusion

Most of the topics discussed in this book are ones of which your local advisors are not familiar. The most common unfamiliar topics are Equity Harvesting, A/R Leveraging, Closely Held "Captive Insurance Companies", Section 79 Plans, SuperCharged 401(k)s, the New Fixed Index Annuity, High Cash Value/Low Death Benefit Permanent Life Insurance policies, Return of Premium Term Life Insurance, Leveraged Life, Charitable Gift Annuities, pension plan DI protection, Long Term Care Insurance, Life Settlements, Freeze Partnerships, 412(i) plans, the Stock Protection Strategy, ESOPs, ODOPs, Private Placement Life Insurance, PEDs, and Charging Orders.

Implementation is a key component of putting together an asset protection plan, and income or estate tax reduction plan, so it is important to work with an advisor who understands the topics discussed in this entire book and has what it takes to follow through until implementation is complete.

Unfortunately, for the vast majority of clients around the country, it will be nearly impossible to find an advisor who knows these topics. As stated earlier, the authors of this book are unique in many ways when it comes to being able to provide advice on "advanced" planning topics for high income and/or high net-worth clients.

The author is Certified Wealth Preservation Planner (CWPPä) and a Certified Asset Protection Planner (CAPP). In short, while is it possible to get help from a local advisor on some of the issues in this book, in order to have a complete, comprehensive and collaborative plan put in place, to help readers become completely asset protected, and help you reach, preserve and protect your Critical Capital Mass, it is always best to work with a "fiduciary" advisor who you know can get the job done right. A fiduciary morally, ethically, and legally places your interests ahead of his own. Always and everywhere.

If you do not believe your local advisors can put together that comprehensive plan to help you reach Critical Capital Mass, please give us a call 407-646-2252, and we would be happy to get you started and help your existing advisors.

Seminars and Speeches: We are also available to give educational seminars to CPAs and Attorneys and Financial Advisors on the topics covered in this book.

Review of Your Asset Protection, Income or Estate Tax Reduction Plan, or Estate or Financial Plan: If you purchased this book and want an analysis, you simply need to complete the following questionnaire and fax or send to one of the author's offices. Within three business days, you will receive a multi-page analysis detailing if your plan is in order and, if not, what changes you should consider making.

We hope you have seen how a good "quarterback" can help you to fly under the radar, and keep more of what you worked to achieve, and to protect your life's work from predators, creditors, and bad actors.

Feel free to contact us at (407) 656-2252 or MLevin@ MyAssetProtectionGroup.com. We look forward to your feedback. For a complimentary consultation, please complete the worksheet in the back of the book and mail it to Dr. Mitch Levin, One Orlando Centre, 800 N. Magnolia Avenue, Suite 105, Orlando, FL 32803 or fax it to Dr. Levin at (407) 656-8116, or you may send it to his email.

Make great decisions.

# Disclaimers

It is regrettable, and unavoidable in these times, in our country. But we must use these. It is a sign of the times we live in. Especially, in the book on asset protection. We would be violating a major asset protection rule if we did not write these. So here it goes. In plain English. No 'legalese:' Nothing in this book is implied nor should be construed as tax advice or legal advice or investment advice; nor is anything herein a form of advertising for or solicitation of any insurance or investment product. Past performance is no guaranty of future performance. What has worked for some, may not work for all. Moreover, since this is a plain English compendium, you may have seen or heard about many of these concepts elsewhere. We, however, compiled and organized and wrote this book ourselves, and took great pains using anti-plagiarism software to be sure no copyrights were violated. That is one reason, besides sincere and simple gratitude, that we acknowledge some of the names before.

## FINANCIAL LIFE SATISFACTION SURVEY

**DIRECTIONS:** The statements below will help you to think about and assess how satisfied you are with aspects of your financial life. Select and record your level of satisfaction for each statement.

| | | Not Satisfied | | Moderately Satisfied | | Very Satisfied |
|---|---|---|---|---|---|---|
| | I am satisfied... | 1 | 2 | 3 | 4 | 5 |
| 1 | With my ability to meet my financial obligations | | | | | |
| 2 | With the income my current job or career provides me | | | | | |
| 3 | With my spending habits | | | | | |
| 4 | With the level of debt I carry | | | | | |
| 5 | With the "extras" that I am able to buy for myself and/or loved ones | | | | | |
| 6 | With the level and quality of insurance protection I currently have | | | | | |
| 7 | With the amount of money that I save and invest on a regular basis | | | | | |
| 8 | With my current investment choices | | | | | |
| 9 | That I am on track to build a sufficient retirement nest egg | | | | | |

| FINANCIAL LIFE SATISFACTION SURVEY | | | | | | |
|---|---|---|---|---|---|---|
| 10 | With the level of employee benefits I receive | | | | | |
| 11 | With my style of personal bookkeeping and financial record management | | | | | |
| 12 | With my ability to provide financial help to family members | | | | | |
| 13 | With my estate plan | | | | | |
| 14 | With my level of charitable giving | | | | | |
| 15 | With the level of financial education I have attained | | | | | |
| 16 | With how I respond emotionally to my personal finance issues | | | | | |
| 17 | With my ability to communicate about my financial matters | | | | | |
| 18 | With the feelings I have about my money life | | | | | |
| 19 | That financial issues do not cause stress or strain in the relationships that are important to me | | | | | |
| 20 | With the working relationships I have with my financial service providers (i.e., insurance agent, banker, broker, financial planner, accountant | | | | | |

# About the Authors

Mitchell Levin, MD, CWPP, CAPP, is CEO and Managing Director of Summit Wealth Partners, Inc., a Registered Investment Advisory firm, and is the Managing Member of Summit Asset Protection Group, LLC, an independent insurance agency.

Author, speaker, trusted advisor, Dr. Mitch, The Financial Physician™, is the author of hundreds of articles, and several other books. He has appeared on ABC, NBC, CBS, and Fox affiliates, as well as in USA Today, Newsweek, The Wall Street Journal, Barron's, The Longboat Observer, Ophthalmology Business, Orlando Sentinel, and so many more.

His clients are nice, affluent people, who actually may be frustrated when they discover - too late - the poor outcomes, outrageous and hidden fees, the excessive risks they're taking, and unnecessary taxes they have to pay. They're bombarded with mixed, or negative messages by the "financial media complex".

As a small business owner, Mitch has built, grown, bought and sold several other business entities. In addition, he is a successful commercial real estate investor. Dr. Mitch is a major donor to charitable organizations, and has served as an officer on several Boards of Trustees. The knowledge he gained through these experiences contributed to his personal financial success and the ability to pursue his passion of educating and assisting others in their quest for financial freedom. Contact: **MLevin@MyAssetProtectionGroup.com**, or call the offices: 407-656-2252.

Kyle A Levin, JD is a graduate of Tulane University and The University of Virginia School of Law. He currently lives in Washington, D.C. His other contributions include the book, *How Elite Advisors GROW Using Trust Based Marketing*.

If you take nothing else from this book, we hope you take away enough motivation. The motivation and the tools to become pro-active: when trying to protect your assets; when trying to save on income, estate, and capital gains taxes; and when trying to more efficiently and effectively run your business, or your family enterprise; when you plan for transitioning your wealth.

It is our intention that you will have discovered for yourself the secrets to building and maintaining your financial fortress: That you find it useful to fulfill your purpose for your money, control, clarity, comfort, and confidence….for independence, and dignity through financial freedom.

Thank you for your kind attention. ENJOY THE BOOK! And feel free to share this with others.

For complimentary consultation with Dr. Mitch Levin, please send your completed Financial Life Satisfaction Survey to:

Mail: One Orlando Centre, 800 N. Magnolia Avenue, Suite 105 Orlando, FL 32803

Fax: (407) 656-8116

Email: **mlevin@myassetprotectiongroup.com**

www.ingramcontent.com/pod-product-compliance
Lightning Source LLC
Chambersburg PA
CBHW031501180326
41458CB00044B/6659/J